NOTES FROM LOWER VOLTA
Journals 1974-1986

William J. Duffy

Copyright © 2016 by William J. Duffy

ISBN-13: 978-1534945081
ISBN-10: 1534945083

Table of Contents

Author's Note
Between Past and Future (Detroit)
    1974   1
    1975   32
An Innocent Abroad (Washington, Korea)
    1975   41
    1976   54
    1977   87
Undiplomatic Memories (Korea)
    1977   107
    1978   121
    1979   129
The Road Less Traveled (Korea, Washington, Ghana)
    1979   161
    1980   180
    1981   238
Notes from Lower Volta (Ghana, Washington, Japan)
    1981   266
    1982   276
    1983   315
    1984   338
    1985   346
    1986   372

Author's Note

This book contains the journals I kept between 1974 and 1986. I have edited them for clarity, adding nothing which did not appear in them originally, except as noted in the text. The journals cover my assignment as a U.S. Foreign Service Officer to the U.S. Embassies in Korea and Ghana and to the U.S. Consulate in Fukuoka, Japan.

My five years in Korea coincided with the last years of the Park Chung-hee dictatorship and the beginning of the Korean economic miracle. I was in Ghana during a difficult period in that country's history, as it struggled politically and economically. Both countries have moved far beyond what I describe here. Park's daughter Park Geun-hye is now Korea's democratically elected President, and Ghana has also become a democracy, with one of the highest GDPs in Africa. My tour in Japan came at a time when some thought Japan would eclipse the United States economically.

Coups, assassinations, student riots, car crashes, soldiers in the streets, spying, divine visits, martial law, deaths, arrests, destitute Americans, naked festivals – they're all here.

To top it off, I was a gay man in the U.S. Foreign Service, a fact which – if known at the time – would have prevented or ended my Foreign Service career. In these pages, I lived as a closeted gay man. In these pages, I had a happy ending when I met Ken, my husband of thirty-three years, in 1983.

The book's first section (Between Past and Future), a mixture of diary and third-person narrative covering the year after my college graduation, sets the background for the rest of the story.

Except for historical and well-known figures, I have changed the names to protect the innocent and to spare the guilty.

William J. Duffy
Tucson, Arizona
July 2016

Between Past and Future (Detroit)
May 31, 1974 - June 13, 1975

1974

May 31, 1974 Friday.

Every time I buy one of these little books I wonder what will fill its pages. Somehow the pages get filled, although a conservative estimate says about eighty percent would have been better left unwritten. This book exists to allow me to write when I want to write.

I do not intend to keep a comprehensive diary, because nothing bores more than comprehensive coverage of a mediocre subject. Rather, my personal viewpoint leads me to believe that occasionally I think of something which is worth preserving on paper.

Today is a Friday night. Less than two weeks ago I graduated from Milwaukee's Marquette University. At that moment my four-year paid vacation ended. School may be difficult, but you can always skip classes or make sure that none are scheduled earlier than noon. When money runs low, a quick phone call home usually turns the trick, especially with a little wailing about the high cost of text books. Even without being nostalgic (can you be nostalgic only two weeks after something ends?), I can state that college was a wild party.

Now fifty years stretch ahead of me, fifty years in which I do not expect to find any four like the four at Marquette. Where will I meet the people I knew in Milwaukee? Such a fantastic collection cannot happen twice in one lifetime. And now I have said goodbye to them, almost certain that the occasions we will ever be together again can be counted on one hand's fingers.

Now at home I am alone. My high school friendships have withered through four years of neglect to the point where once-close friends now seem half-known strangers. I have no particular desire to reverse that course. That life lies far in the past. Already it is hard to imagine how big a jerk I could be in high school, and still managed to hold my head up. The immaturity, the narrowness, the selfishness, the ignorance of my senior year amaze me. Such a fool only four years ago, and I have learned so much since then – not just from books, but in life.

William J. Duffy

What scares me the most: in four years more the William J. Duffy of 1974 will probably impress (and depress) me the same way. I suppose it is better to see an evolutionary improvement through time. I mean, it is better to believe that one has grown into a better person than into a worse.

Enough of the past. How can I spend my time discussing the handful of years which are all the life I have yet known, when half a century lies ahead, fifty years which will carry me into the 21st century? This is the prospect that thrills me, that lifts me laughing with excitement out of my present depression. My life did not end May 19th when I ran out of the Milwaukee Arena with a degree in my hand to say goodbye to my school, my friends, my world of the last four years. My life has just begun.

Do I have plans? Do I have ambitions? The question is rather whether I have the energy and will to chase after them. I'm almost tempted to think the answer to that might be yes.

For the last ten years, more than anything else I have wanted to be a writer. Of course, nothing I have written during this decade is worth publishing. I can hardly picture myself with the patience or discipline to produce a whole book. So that somewhat dampens my chances for success in this direction. If I can't write well enough to be read in another five hundred years, then I don't want to write at all.

In the past year, I seriously considered pursuing a career as a professional student, somewhere winding up with a Ph.D. in history and teaching the German disintegration of 1929-1933 in a renowned university. Luckily for me (and equally for the academic world), I somewhat gracelessly backed out of history after being accepted at four graduate schools and being offered one tuition scholarship and one teaching assistantship.

The reason for this sudden reversal lay in the 717 I scored on the Law School Aptitude Test. After all, a person who scores in the 97th percentile in the LSAT must seriously consider applying to law school, mustn't he? My preparation before the exam hardly led me to expect such a high score. I never read the explanatory booklet with the sample questions, and stayed out until 2:00 a.m. the night before, imbibing a certain amount of fermented grain.

Do I want to be a lawyer? I don't know. But what better path to the Chief Justiceship of the United States than law school? Law is a profession I would be satisfied in, because it is a powerful tool to help others, to be important to others. (Which is basically my reason for considering college teaching: the ability to influence others, to be important in their lives.) The chance is better than even that in the fall of 1975 I will enter the hallowed halls of some prestigious Midwestern law school (the University of Michigan?). And in 1978 the Democratic presidential candidate of 1996 will receive his Juris Doctor.

What could keep me out of law school, aside from money? Only one thing: the Foreign Service. The Foreign Service has boosted my ego so much in the last year that I almost feel I owe it to them to accept any job they offer me. It was a thrill to pass the written exam. That was nothing compared to March 14th, 1974, when in Room 1608 of the Dirksen Federal Building in Chicago I impressed three Foreign Service Officers enough that they admitted me into that select group which passes the oral exam, even after my telling them that the primary motivation for taking the exam was that it was free. After all that, I expect the Foreign Service to disqualify me because, of all things, my 3,001 or so allergies.

Work in the State Department would offer me an immediate, prestigious career with good pay and benefits and a good chance at advancement. Most important of all, it offers a chance to make myself valuable to people. It would offer immediately the satisfaction which a law career could not bring for at least three years. Three years, though, out of fifty left to go seem like nothing. In the short run, I prefer the Foreign Service; in the long run, the law.

If every night I were to write as much as this, I'd have to go buy a few more of these books. Goodbye to May 1974.

William J. Duffy

The Student

The student opened his apartment door and stepped in, throwing the keys on the kitchen table. The air was stuffy and warm, more oppressive still because May was too early a month to endure summer heat more easily than winter snows. He walked to the windows and threw them open. He left the shades drawn to keep the sunlight out. Then he sat on the couch which faced the windows.

All day the apartment had stood empty, unaware that this day represented the culmination of sixteen years of schooling for the occupant, represented the end of childhood and the assertion of adulthood. Today the student had received his bachelor's degree. Today he was no longer even correctly called a student. Now he sat alone, disappointed that this day had brought more pain into his life than relief.

He compared what had happened today to what he had once dreamed graduation would be like. Once he had gotten to the Arena where the graduation had been held, he had not seen his family. He tried not to look too obvious as he unsuccessfully scanned ten thousand seats for four familiar faces. There had been no handshake from the university's president, no calling of individual names. Instead, each college stood as one, and he with a thousand other liberal arts students rose to be informed that their degrees would be conferred.

He had not even been able to sit with his closest friends. He should have known freshman year to make friends in his own college. Those friends who were not fellow graduates had been unable to stay for graduation.

After the ceremonies had ended, he found himself caught up in a rush of hurried good-byes with people he would never see again, with friends who disappeared with their families, with friends who were driving home that very afternoon. Only he had no idea where his family was.

He picked up the phone and dialed the hotel. When the operator answered, he asked to be connected to Room 417. He listened for a long time before the operator came back to say there was no answer.

He put the phone back on the desk, removed his suit coat and vest, and threw them carelessly onto a chair across the room. Then he sat on the couch again.

The room was quiet, quiet with the depressing calm of a hot summer afternoon. He heard disembodied voices walk by on the sidewalk outside of his window, shadow figures dancing across the shades, then two cars passed.

The afternoon sun spread its bright light through the shades. They glowed like a movie screen in a dimly-lit theater before the movie starts.

The tie around his neck pinched, and his collar rubbed uncomfortably.

He looked at his apartment. George McGovern and Mickey Mouse peered down at him from posters on the wall to the right, the White Rabbit from the left. The dismantled bookcases were stacked neatly in one corner, his textbooks packed into two boxes. Strange, he thought, that my college education can be crammed into a couple of cardboard boxes. A stack of records stood forlornly against an empty table which until last week had held a stereo.

This apartment was my home for two years, he thought, and this city home for four. Much as I hated both deeply and desperately, my memories of both are happy. Even the worst of times – a failed exam, a ruined romance – transform themselves into pleasant recollections now that the whole thing is over. Two years ago I rented this apartment and was on top of the world. I had escaped the dorm. I was independent. I had my junior and senior years ahead of me. At the time it seemed like the rest of my life. Funny that time in the future always seems so much longer than it turns out to have been once it's passed.

He pulled out his wallet and looked at the pictures it held, of dances, of parties, of outings to the lake. He thought of the pictures he had only in his mind: of quiet beers in the student union bar, of first snowfalls and snowball fights, and then the return of summer and the excitement of campus malls crowded with students; of social hours in the library the night before an exam; of late night runs to the Blue Deli or the Fatted Calf for a thick sandwich to finish what dinner had fallen short of.

It was over. It was all over.

Don't look back, he told himself. Don't bother looking back. Because you can never go back.

June 16, 1974 Sunday

Loneliness is only a symptom of my problem. The problem itself is homosexuality. All my life I have been completely homosexual. It's not something that suddenly popped out at me. It's not something I decided on. The decision was made before I knew there was a choice.

All these years I have led a straight existence, at least publicly, only occasionally slipping into the "dark depths of sin." Never have I had a gay friendship, although I have had friendships I wished were gay.

July 6, 1974 Saturday

I feel the need to justify my existence. Life in itself has no meaning: it is an accident of the universe. Life sees as its only purpose the creation of more life. For me this is not reason enough, perhaps because that way is closed to me. A man has not justified his existence in this world unless he makes the world a better and an easier place for those around him, from his immediate family to the population of the whole planet. And if I cannot do that, then I may as well end my life today. I do not believe in an existence after death. Consequently, it can only matter to me whether I die now or later if my life has meaning.

Most of all I am afraid that I will come to the end of my days in the 21st century and find myself unable to claim that my eighty years made any difference to anybody except myself. I want to leave this

Notes from Lower Volta

world with the knowledge that it has become what it is in part because I lived in it.

To reach for what we cannot grasp
is to reach for nothing at all.
And there is nothing so ungrasped
as Now, as the sands of our lives
sifting through our clumsy fingers.
Do we crave immortality
because it is the one thing which
we are certain we will not have?
O, that we could remain untouched
by time, like the earth beneath us
or the sky and stars overhead!
Such irony that only they
who cannot know eternity
possess it, while we must face death.
Time cannot be stopped nor escaped:
we are its slaves and its victims.
For us, even hope is hopeless.

***

I love you as I cannot another,
my love, you who I cannot tell,
cannot desire, who cannot be mine.
I love you, have loved you, will love you,
even as I know you are not mine.
If only once I could speak to you
as your lover without losing you!
If only once I could have reached you!
I am sorry, I am sorry, forgive me.
If only once I could have you
beyond my dreams.
But I lost you when I found you,
and now you have left, not knowing.
Hear, my love, and know.

William J. Duffy

July 7, 1974 Sunday

    Can long-distance friendships and long-distance love affairs survive? I think not. Both require the constant refreshment of shared memories. When memories are shared only second-hand, then the relationship fossilizes around the bones of "the good old days."

    Last night my dreams
    brought you to my side
    wrapped you in my arms
    made you mine completely.
    But last night's dreams
    ran before the sun
    woke me as they went
    and left me without you.
    Three hundred miles
    divide us, nothing
    next to what keeps us
    apart when together.
    You know nothing
    of this sin passion
    burning wild in me
    it aches most while thrills most.
    For you offer
    friendship as the end
    I ask your friendship
    as but a beginning.
    So read these lines
    Know I love you, friend,
    love but cannot speak
    the words which would lose you.
    Tonight perhaps
    when my dreams visit
    you will come with them
    I will win the love lost.

Notes from Lower Volta

***

To see that smile of joy
on the face of the one
who tempts me with friendship
when I want love is pain.
Would it not be almost
better to be hated
than to have to endure
this hurting happiness,
this ecstatic anguish?
Yet I still hesitate
between these hard choices:
hide love and hold friendship,
or speak truth and risk both.
Would not this intended lover who now holds out
a friend's hand clench that hand
in a fist, turn this smile
away in revulsion,
if told "You are my love"?
But no, safer to hide
this misery and truth
in obscure unread lines.

July 23, 1974 Tuesday

 I have been unhappier this summer than at any time since the fall of 1970, when I found myself incapable of forming friendships in my freshman year at Marquette. I was alone then, and I am alone now. It is no coincidence that I have begun to set down my feelings in writing now for the first time since that period. Writing lets me escape from my loneliness.

 I remain optimistic that in the future I can again find happiness, as my life turned around in February 1971, when I moved from Schroeder Hall into McCormick Hall. But I do not see how such a change can be effected; and I fear that if the initiative must come from me, then it will not come at all.

I do not want to pass my life in the world disguised as a heterosexual. I feel cheapened and deceptive when I must form relationships with men and women opposite to those I want to form with them. But I cannot yet commit myself to a gay life. That I can even put my homosexuality down on paper is an improvement from three years ago, but by how much? Perhaps my ignorance of gays and my own shyness increase my fear and cynicism of them.

I miss Marquette, terribly. I wish that college life could have gone on forever. And yet out of my handful of friends, there is only one whom I miss so much that it pains me. A year ago I eagerly anticipated the end of my four years at Marquette and thought that I could leave my friendships behind, settling for my memories.

But then Jack came into my life, and affected me as no one else has, only to have him leave it for good a few months later. In those few months, though, I was never happier. Perhaps life now would be easier if we two had never crossed paths, but I think that in the long run my life is better for having had him in it.

July 25, 1974 Thursday

Today the Bureau of Alcohol, Tobacco and Firearms interviewed me for a position as a Tax Inspector trainee. I enjoyed the interview, as I did the one with the Foreign Service in March. This surprised me both times, since I have always thought my shyness and self-consciousness would turn any interview (especially one with more than one interviewer) into a disaster.

Although the job starts at a lowly $7,200, it seems interesting enough and the salary quickly improves. Most important of all, it would provide me with a career now which doesn't require any extensive financial or mental investment on my part. I am afraid that five months into law school I would decide law was not for me. That would be a catastrophe.

July 28, 1974 Sunday

In passing, last night the House Committee on the Judiciary

voted 27-11 to recommend Nixon's impeachment on a charge of obstruction of justice.

August 5, 1974 Monday

I think I must be a worthless individual, unable to love and loved by others not for myself but for the screen I throw in front of myself. Everyone important in my life professes nothing but hate and contempt for gays. Even worse is their ridicule.

Would not, in fact, the very reasons that a friend likes me now be the very same reasons that he would hate me if he knew the truth? Would the wall separating us (which only I know of) become even more insurmountable if they learned of its existence? I cannot live with their rejection. What good can I do for others with my life if I can do nothing for myself with it?

By concealing my homosexuality, I have made it the overriding consideration in my life. I am two-faced, one straight and one gay, the straight fearful of losing the reassurance of past routine, the gay yearning for its free expression but equally fearful of entering an unknown world.

My whole life I have known no sexual orientation but homosexual. The only reason I would want to become heterosexual would be to escape the oppression of our anti-homosexual society. All the joking, all the derision about queers weigh like lead on my heart. I, too, to avoid arousing suspicion, have attacked gays as viciously and as disdainfully as anyone.

August 8, 1974 Thursday

I have just watched Nixon resign his office. That bastard wouldn't even admit that he had anything to do with "the Watergate matter." Such history I have seen in my short twenty-two years: political assassinations, space flights, nuclear confrontations, riots, Asian wars, Mideast crises, men on the moon, and now the first Presidential resignation in our history and the transformation of our electoral system into one in which the President is chosen by a majority of the hick voters in Grand Rapids.

August 11, 1974 Sunday
    Monday, August 26th, I start my new job as a Tax Inspector. I hope that the job puts some excitement back into my life. If it doesn't, I may kill myself sometime during the next year. I wish it was August of 1975, and I was about to enter law school.

    At this point I think law school is the only viable option. Even if the State Department offers me a consular career now, I think I would turn it down. In a few weeks I will make out cards for information and applications from (1) Northwestern, (2) University of Chicago, (3) University of Michigan, (4) Loyola (Chicago), (5) Wayne State, and (6) De Paul.

    One of the first three would be my first choice. Either of the last two would be an act of sheer desperation. I will probably apply to #1, #2, #3, and #4. I assume I can get into Loyola, if none of my first choices works out.

    From the fact that four of the six I want information from and three of the four I intend to apply to are in Chicago, it could be assumed that I want to be in Chicago in the fall of 1975. I want to get out of Detroit. I want a large city. And I want to be close to friends. Chicago fits the bill.

The Young Man

    The young man opened the refrigerator, its light flooding the darkened kitchen. He pulled a can of beer free from the six-pack and popped off its lid. With the beer in one hand and a magazine in the other, he walked into the living room to the stereo. After leafing through his record albums and choosing two, he put the headphones over his head and sat back to enjoy some high energy rock, oblivious to the world beyond.

    The young man hoped to lift his spirits with the beer and the music. He wanted to escape the depression and loneliness which had weighed on him since his return from school three months earlier.

Notes from Lower Volta

The records spinning out the old songs brought back other nights, of quiet parties and of loud parties, of the exhilaration of the first weeks of a semester and the exhausted relief when that semester drew to a close. Even now he realized only with difficulty that events which came to mind so clearly as if they lay only a week in the past stood removed by two or three years.

The young man had entered his senior year with no concept the course his life would take beyond graduation. As the swift rush of his last two semesters forced him to see that a day would come when he would no longer be in college, he went for job interviews, to find that the only use for a history degree in the business world was to sell insurance.

He took tests: Law School Aptitude, Civil Service, Graduate Record Exam. He did well on all of them, without knowing what to do with them and reluctant to commit his life.

He applied to graduate schools, momentarily deluding himself into thinking he could find happiness teaching modern German history on the college level. In the end he backed out of the opportunities offered him. He considered law school, but delayed until application for the coming year was impossible. Half thankful and half disappointed, he prepared for a year's wait.

In the end he found a job as Tax Inspector trainee, one day before President Ford froze further federal hiring. His position paid a bare living wage. But it offered ample and secure opportunities in future years, if he only waited.

August 19, 1974 Monday

And now I count twenty-two years. Already I am obsessed with the fear of growing old and missing life. I think a lot of my mood this summer (aside from the letdown of losing my friends at Marquette) can be attributed to the fact that my life seemed aimless, stuck as I was in my dead-end summer job and making no real move to escape from there. But now as I prepare to start my new job as a Tax Inspector and as I get involved in the process of applying to law school, this mood should lift.

September 3, 1974 Tuesday
   Last night I returned from three fun-filled days and nights in Milwaukee – a weekend in which I momentarily grasped my Marquette past, surrounded by the old faces, the old sights, the old bars.
   Today I got an invitation to my ex-girlfriend Roberta's wedding. The thought occurred to me that, if I were only a slightly different person, that might have been my wedding. I thought I loved Roberta in the fall of 1972. A month's vacation in England at Christmas convinced me that any heterosexual relationships I engaged in represented play-acting. If I were straight, I probably would have married Roberta.

September 5, 1974 Thursday
   This afternoon I rented Apartment #5 at 8650 Agnes in Detroit. The place makes two cracker jack boxes welded together look big. It has a living room, kitchen, bath, bedroom, and a sun room. The sun room is what makes the rest of the apartment worthwhile. It juts out from the bedroom and has windows on three sides.
   When I came home in May, my siblings Joan and John and Margaret all told me that no way would I last until the fall of 1975 at home. I didn't believe them. I thought myself better able to adjust to living with Mother than they, and I could see no way of saving money out on my own. But the three and a half months since then have shown me that I must go off by myself, and a few hundred dollars saved or not saved on rent will make little difference on an $18,000 law school bill.

September 10, 1974 Tuesday
   I spend a lot of time moping about all the good times I had in school, and yet today I thought of some of the bad times, some of the

nights spent sitting alone in the apartment with no one to call and no one to call me. I remembered especially, for the first time in a year, one weekend night last September (the first weekend after classes began) when for one reason or another nobody was around. I had nothing else to do except what little schoolwork had already turned up. Later I went out drinking by myself. It is because of times like those that I am glad Marquette lies in the past.

There was a time, a year and more ago, when I eagerly awaited graduation and independence and a job. I wanted to go out on my own and break my Marquette ties. Then, I thought, I could make my way into the gay world where I belonged and for the first time face people as I am.

I believe this past year has changed me and matured me more than any other year. Now instead of wanting to forget my Marquette friends, I seek to hold onto them.

I have been reading Oscar Wilde's *De Profundis*. It has lifted my spirits when they have been most depressed. My troubles are nothing compared to his. His two years in prison (for being guilty of what I am guilty of) make the coming year less heavy, less eternal.

September 15, 1974 Sunday

Yesterday I moved into my new apartment. I spent a good part of yesterday and today putting my stuff away and arranging the furniture and pictures to cover up the worst parts of the walls.

I intended to sleep late, but woke up at 8:30 a.m. I drifted around the apartment for a while, just happy it was mine. About noon I went out to buy some basics (food) but wound up instead on Belle Isle. I loved it, especially the western tip looking downstream to downtown Detroit and the Ambassador Bridge. I think I'll be spending a lot of time there.

At the moment I am caught in a cash flow crisis. I have the money, but in the bank. Being without a car, I can't get to it.

September 27, 1974 Friday
I used to think that loneliness came to me naturally – that it only minimally bothered me and ultimately pleased me more than companionship. Then my years at Marquette and this past summer made me think that I only accepted my loneliness because I had not really known friendship; and, having made personal close friendships, I could not easily live without them.

In the two weeks since I moved into my apartment, I have not felt lonely: I have missed my friends, but not desperately, and I have not craved for friends as I did this summer. Partly I suppose this is because I have been busy putting my place together. More important, I am basically a loner who, faced with a choice between solitude and constant company, would prefer solitude.

Living at home with my mother this summer prevented me from breaking the tie to Marquette which strangled me, kept me from full acceptance that the past was gone and not recoverable. Living at home left me in a state of quasi-independence. The fact of my adulthood was obscured by the retention of my apparent dependence on my mother. Now, instead of my memories depressing me, they remind me of the happy times with little pain and much satisfaction.

I consider my position in the world more seriously in such unhappy periods. I reflect this soul-searching in these pages, so I do not think such times are wasted moments in my life. Of course, I would prefer a bit more happiness to the alternative of self-examination.

The Office Worker

He lived by himself now, having taken a small, one-bedroom apartment on the edge of the inner city.

Five mornings of the week he arose at sunrise, dressed, ate a small bowl of cereal, and briskly walked the one block through the early morning chill to the bus stop. He found that the earlier he caught the bus, the fewer riders it would have; and therefore the better chance of a seat for him and a final few minutes of early morning rest.

The bus route carried him along the riverfront, past boarded-up buildings and iron-barred storefronts, past the once-grand parks of the city, past the dirty factories from whose open windows thundered the machinery of industries; until, after one last bend in the road, the soaring skyscrapers of the business district came into view.

Some mornings the morning sun blazed brilliantly off the sleek, modern glass towers and the massive bulks of the older buildings. Other mornings, misty mornings, the skyline loomed like some phantom in the shadows, its outlines uncertain, suggested only by the red beacons atop the highest structures.

He always felt a thrill of excitement when he reached the downtown. Suddenly buses were everywhere, indifferent to the surge of automobiles around them, daring individual motorists to oppose them as they moved between stops through traffic. Pedestrians swarmed the sidewalks, occasionally in small groups of businessmen or secretaries, but more often hurried individuals glancing left and right to avoid collision with others equally rushed. Over all the noise of the city rose and fell: the buses, the trucks, the blaring horns, the shrill police whistles. Suddenly, imperceptibly in the early daylight, the street lamps flickered out, unnoticed by the passersby except for a brief sensation unrecognized. The city had awakened for another day.

He enjoyed the scene, but he did not dwell upon it. His long strides quickly carried him the two remaining blocks to the building in which he worked. Once inside the cavernous lobby with its pre-Depression murals, silence descended. Usually at this hour the place was still half empty, exaggerating the click of his heels on the tiled floor into rolling reverberations.

The short elevator ride left him opposite his office. He let himself in with his key to find, as usual, two of his six fellow workers already present. They exchanged conversation, drank coffee, and waited for the rest of the staff to drift in. A little past eight, by which time the boss had arrived, each would shuffle off to a desk, open a drawer, and produce a pile of papers which might or might not have something to do with work.

He was no different from the others in this respect. Still unused to the ways of the business world, he remained amazed at how little work sufficed to earn the boss's compliments. He attributed his success to an ability to look busy while he doodled, to his readiness to flash a sheaf of fresh figures in his boss's face whenever he chanced to drift by his desk, and to the basic fact that, little as he did, the others did even less.

He disliked the boss, for no reason more specific than that the man was a "jerk." He believed the boss had no capability for either supervision or leadership. He attributed the man's easy-going attitude toward the work to suspected incompetence. National headquarters (he imagined) had found him such a detriment in the field that they could find nothing to do with him except put him in charge of a regional office.

His fellow workers did not seem to hold their supervisor in such low esteem. But then he thought only slightly more highly of his fellow workers. He limited his conversation with them to the broad topics of the weather, sports, and weekend plans. He preferred to lunch alone, to work alone, to be left alone. The others took no apparent offense at this.

Four of the men were ancient, each having been with the firm at least thirty years and each now waiting for retirement or death, whichever put them out of work first. They spent a good deal of the day recalling events which had happened before he was even born, or else figuring up their retirement benefits and discussing their retirement plans. The other two were only a few years older than he was, but their backgrounds differed so markedly from his own that little common ground remained.

In short, he disliked his job. A good deal of the time he daydreamed, or stared blankly out of the window, or both.

Across the street stood an old bank, detailed to resemble the

Parthenon and topped with two large attempted imitations of Greek sculptures. Next to it rose the bank's gleaming new skyscraper, presenting to his view a wall of white window-pierced rectangles reaching higher than he could easily see. The contrast between the old and the new fascinated him, between the gaudy ornamentation of a more confident period and the starkly unadorned facade of his own less certain time.

On the plaza in front of the new bank towered two intertwined sheets of metal which represented the bank's contribution to the culture of the city. They were called "Untitled," he knew, and he could easily imagine that the artist had called them that when he had finished hammering them into their interlocking arrangement and did not know what to make of them. If the artist understood what he had created, he for one did not. But he thought that such attempts, whether artful or artless, did not require his comprehension, if they indicated (as claimed) a rebirth of the city.

It seemed likely, though, that the rise or the fall of the city was more precisely indicated by the occupancy of the building behind the art. From where he sat, fully half the bank's floors stood in darkness, broken only here and there by short sequences of well-lit floors. Through their broad, tinted windows he could see much movement back and forth, office workers reduced by the distance to midget figures, moving among rows of desks which stretched beyond his sight.

It struck him as strange that modern buildings had abolished the idea of individual offices. Even his office with seven desks seemed large. He could not imagine himself comfortable in an office whose walls stood so far away from his desk that reading the clock would strain his eyes. He sympathized with the predicament of the office early bird who each morning had to find his desk among all the others. He supposed that one would get used to having two hundred spectators every time one entered the bathroom. No wonder so much of the building's space went unrented and unwanted.

When he had first started work, he bought his lunch in the

cafeteria downstairs. But even for little more than a dollar a day he thought he spent too much, and soon he began to brownbag it. Usually he sat by himself at one of the corner tables.

There was a time when being so publicly alone, eating by himself while others gathered in noisy social groups, disturbed him. He did not want others to think him friendless and unsociable. But now he no longer cared. He would sit, lost in his thoughts, oblivious to his surroundings.

On warm, sunny days he usually took his lunch outside to the small park built on the site of the old City Hall. To call it a park gives a false description, for it was principally a modernistic water fountain surrounded by paved walkways and stone benches with only a few patches of grass and a couple of city-sick saplings. Its critics called its design Mussolini modern. He had seen pictures of the old Gothic structure which had once stood on the site, and he saw no loss.

The park attracted a wide variety of people: other office workers out of the surrounding skyscrapers, little old ladies who had come downtown for a day of shopping, the bums and derelicts who only bothered others by their presence as they examined the contents of the litter baskets.

The highlight of each day came when the boss said it looked like it was time to call it quits. Even the aggravation of hearing the phrase spoken with the identical words every day did not suppress his enthusiasm at being released from bondage for another afternoon. He walked to the bus stop in a manner he hoped would make him look like a rising young executive whom business-wise people would watch. He always enjoyed the bus ride home, even though – because of the time of day – he usually had to stand.

His apartment, while on the edge of the slums, was only superficially part of them. It had the good fortune of a location, on the one side, only one block from the riverfront parks and luxury high-rise apartments and, on the other, one block east of a square mile section of grand old homes whose residents had successfully resisted the forces of decay by preserving their neighborhood in its early 20th century atmosphere. Thus on two sides he lived steps away from an escape from the desolation of the slums. On the other two, though, began some of the city's worst neighborhoods, dangerous by day and by night and stretching, for all he knew, to the city limits. His suburban background rendered him incapable of distinguishing the dingy bungalows of the lower working class from the boarded-up hulks of the ghetto.

He rarely ventured into the slums. The first time, on a Sunday afternoon walk, he had smiled at the flashily overdressed black families shepherded along to church by the mothers, sometimes with the fathers in tow and sometimes not. Other blacks sat on their shabby porches in loud conversation. As he passed they became deathly still, watching his every movement with hostile eyes. After he had walked down the block, their conversation resumed, punctuated by raucous laughter which he suspected was turned in his direction.

He came upon two empty blocks fenced off with dilapidated wood boards and marked by signs made illegible with graffiti. The earth was barren, except for a few gnarled trees and some patches of brown grass. He wondered if there had ever been anything there, and found his answer in the half-buried remains of broken driveways and an alleyway still partially bricked. Houses had once stood here. This, too, had been a neighborhood. It was no more, its buildings leveled and cleared and its families scattered without a trace.

He imagined what the place was like when the houses had been put up, what dreams the inhabitants had held. He thought of newlyweds in 1913 buying their brand-new home here, of the Southerners come north in the 1920s to work in the factories and their surprise at finding such comfortable homes and broad streets instead of the expected tenements.

He made his way homeward, distracted from his broodings only when he heard a female voice wail in the distance behind him about a white boy in a black neighborhood. He did not willingly venture into the area again.

His apartment, one of eight in an old building called the

Bennett, contained a living room, kitchen, bath, bedroom, and sun porch. It possessed the illusion of being larger than it actually was because the rooms strung out one after the other, with the doorways between them staggered.

In the living room he had piled his two bookcases and his books, three hundred of them, hardcovers and paperbacks, great literature and cheap science fiction. Faced with the choice of repairing the poorly painted walls or hiding them, he covered them with maps, with a reproduction of Monet's "Fields in Spring," and with approximately sixty old *Newsweek* covers which he had saved for no particular reason. The only other furnishings were two hard-backed chairs and his spare bed, which served as a couch.

The striking feature of the kitchen was the scarlet color of its walls, painted by some previous occupant; of the bathroom, its ancient, four-footed bathtub. The narrowness of the bedroom scarcely left room for both his bed and his chest of drawers. He wondered what sleeping arrangements the couple below him with the same floor plan had. Beyond the bedroom stood the sun porch, projecting out from the main building and enclosed on three sides by windows. He had rented the apartment for this one small room and, on the day he moved in, immediately positioned his desk so that it gave him a view down the street to the river, which would become visible as the leaves fell from the trees.

Of the other residents in the building he had seen little. He knew them best by the names listed on the mailboxes. Behind him lived the "Maharani," who originally he had surmised to be a student from India. One day the thought struck him, though, that Maharani was not a name but a title. Shortly afterward he saw the Maharani, who turned out to be a middle-aged woman at least as European as himself. She made a big show of dressing in long, billowy dresses. Across the hall lived a young married (or so he assumed) couple, one of whom appeared to be the Maharani's child. At least they both called her "Mother."

The couple below puzzled him. Both worked; both were in

their early thirties. Surely they could afford to live in a safer, cleaner neighborhood.

Whether the remaining apartments were occupied he did not know.

He spent his evenings reading, listening to records, and writing. Not quite broken from his college habits, he felt a necessity to read histories and biographies, underlining passages as he went along, studying the authors' ideas as if in anticipation of an examination.

When the reading bored him, he would set the books aside and put a few records on his temperamental player. Sometimes he would sit in his darkened living room and listen to a Beethoven symphony or a Tchaikovsky ballet. Other times he would listen to the grinding, precise jumble of Led Zeppelin, The Who, or Emerson, Lake, and Palmer.

When neither books nor music satisfied him, he retreated to his sun porch, lit only by the small high-intensity lamp on his desk. There he wrote in his diary, with no expectation of finding any reader other than himself. Some nights he wrote for hours, pouring onto the blank pages all the hopes and doubts and loneliness of his young years.

Writing provided him with an escape from his dreary present by allowing him to imagine some future, happier time when he would read what once he had written.

He walked frequently in all kinds of weather. In many ways he preferred the primeval power of a violent thunderstorm to the lulling soothing of the warm yellow sun. He especially liked the park down the street from him. It fronted on the river and there, on the old pier which the rising waters tended to wash over, he stood quietly for long periods.

His thoughts drifted over a broad range of topics, none of which commanded his attention for any great length of time. He thought of his friends, whom he had not seen for months, and he thought of the quiet, happy memories of his school years.

He stared into the murky depths of the water and considered the importance of water to life. He tried to imagine the early ages when living things first slithered out of the seas onto the dead rock of the mainland and thus began the long process of covering the world with grass and trees and insects and animals.

He thought of the Great Lakes which lay upstream from where he stood and of the cities which rimmed their shores. All this water gently washing past him had been there once. It had flowed past other factories and other skyscrapers as well as wooded shorelines. It would leave him to continue its slow course past other cities, until it lost itself in the ocean hundreds of miles away.

He loved to stand by the river and watch the sailboats drift by. When he turned to go home, he loved the sight of the luxury high-rise apartments rising in the distance on either side of him. Hoping to escape the miseries of the city, the rich and affluent had built their homes in the sky. But if their broad windows allowed them the vision of the shimmering river or the stark silhouette of the skyline at sunset, they did not hide the slums, which sometimes reached to within a block of the high rises.

October 18, 1974 Friday

Today I had an interview with Steve Jones of the State Department. Finally, they have begun my background investigation. For a brief time, the urgency in his voice over the phone made me think State was about to offer me a job. I had terrible visions of having to choose between my law school plans and my Foreign Service career, between the continued misery of Detroit for the next ten months and the relief of being whisked away to Washington immediately for a different type of life-long loneliness. Today, if I had been offered a career with the State Department, I would have taken it.

But Steve made me no offer. He only asked questions to get my investigation going. Any job offer lies months in the future. I do not think that I will take it. My interview with Steve and the realization that the State Department is not about to "take me away from all this" anytime soon strengthened my desire to go to law school. But fate, and people, will always be fickle.

Steve asked me a lot of personal questions which I found myself answering with almost no hesitancy. My openness surprised me, especially when I easily admitted I had occasionally used marijuana in college. I only became nervous when he threw out a few questions about my love life and my dating.

I think that if he had asked me about my sexual orientation, I would have told him the truth. But he didn't. Still, he must find out more details in an individual's life during that one-hour interview than a good many of that person's associates will ever know.

The office we sat in had on the walls pictures of Secretary of State Rogers and President Nixon, both of whom are now ex- as each.

October 19, 1974 Saturday

Autumn depresses me as does no other season. Perhaps it impresses me more forcefully than the other three with the on-going rush of time. Things die in the fall, the trees and bushes which only a few months before awoke from the winter.

Perhaps too a life of schooling has led me to regard September as the beginning of the new year rather than January. The break between summer and fall, between vacation and school, has always been sharp. The shouts of a group of kids playing football in the park echoing across the open make me think of fall afternoons in high school, and the excitement of high school football games. In four years at University of Detroit High School, I did not miss one varsity game. I used to think that was quite an achievement.

October 20, 1974 Sunday

"State your reasons for studying law," the application read. An excellent suggestion. Why do I want to go to law school? Basically, immediately, because I want to escape from this life of Tax Inspector. Ultimately, because I hope that a law degree will give my life a meaning and a justification which I doubt finding any other way. Money, surprisingly, is not a primary consideration. It is, of course, a recognized benefit (and welcomed), but not essential.

In the fall of 1973 I entered my senior year at Marquette with no conception of what to do with my degree in history and anthropology. I tried job interviews in the university placement center, but discovered that the prospect of selling insurance or installing computer systems (which were the two major opportunities open to someone with my credentials) as a life-long career lacked appeal. I applied to graduate schools with the notion of earning a history Ph.D. and teaching on the college level. I doubted that my interest in history was sufficient to carry me to that goal.

I did not consider law until I scored 717 on the Law School Aptitude Test. I held off even then, though, because I thought it absurd to determine the course of one's life on the basis of a single score. The test may indicate aptitude. I had to decide if I had the desire for law.

Now, in the fall of 1974, I have decided that I do want a law degree. My current employment as a Tax Inspector with ATF has convinced me that a paycheck alone will not satisfy me. I want to feel that what I do benefits others as well as myself.

I like the idea that legal training, rather than narrowly specializing the individual, gives him potential access to a wide variety of experiences, from government and business to individual practices.

In our complex society, I can imagine no profession better suited than the legal profession to enable the individual to cope with change. The technical sciences serve as the important vehicles for much of that change. It is law which allows us to study the effects of such change on ourselves, and which gives us the tools to control that change. Modern industrial society will not be of much use if we know more about our machines than about ourselves.

The financial rewards of a career in law are, of course, important. In the short run their greater importance rests in the assurance that I can fairly safely place myself in debt to earn my degree. It makes no sense to me to spend a fortune on post-graduate education if it leaves me in debt for years.

This, briefly stated, constitutes an explanation of my desire to study law.

The First Time

His initiation into homosexuality was a disappointment. Everything possibly sordid about a gay encounter happened that one night in September, his first month as a college freshman.

Free beer at the party had sent him spinning off on the first drunk of his inexperienced life. He sat, heavy with the beer in his stomach, on the couch with a few others. The student next to him (equally drunk?) slowly drew him into conversation until (suddenly, inexplicably) they began discussing the character in *Portnoy's Complaint* who whacked off into the dinner liver. He felt his heart pounding and the blood in his temples throbbing. His new-found acquaintance said how good a beat-off felt and then one of them (was it he?) suggested a walk. The full strength of the alcohol hit him as he rose to leave, but the lure of the adventure carried him.

Out on the street he allowed his partner to lead the way. The question of destination — neither felt secure in returning to their dorm rooms. They wound up on a basement ramp beside the ROTC unit, an empty place at midnight.

The bare concrete did not offer the most comfortable bedding, but he was impatient: impatient to drop his own pants, for his friend to drop his, to see and be seen, to touch and be touched. He wanted to fondle and caress. He wanted love.

His partner was aghast at the idea. Anything more than mechanical manipulation would be queer! Even with the aura of romance dispelled (his first love!), he came quickly and explosively under the stroking hand of his lover, who sighed in admiration at the discharge.

As soon as he consummated his half of the marriage, he felt sick and dirty. He wanted to be away from this spot. He felt ashamed standing exposed in the autumn chill. He hated his seducer. A strange sense of obligation to reciprocate held him until it was over, although he politely begged off when asked if he was interested in giving a blow job.

His partner wiped himself with a tissue with a brief word of thanks. The two strolled back to the main part of campus. The pointless conversation his friend insisted on carrying on only intensified the revulsion he felt growing in him. He escaped his company at the earliest possible moment and ran to his room. His head raced. He wanted to throw up. He wanted to die. He thought his world had ended. He was degraded to a nightmare existence.

He survived, of course, and the twenty minutes spent on a Saturday night behind the ROTC unit did not ruin him. Coincidentally, the following semester he moved onto the very floor where his partner lived. Neither ever mentioned the incident, or even indicated recognition of the other.

October 27, 1974 Sunday

No more than five percent of all the words written in this diary so far express anything except self-pity, despair, and depression. If I did one-tenth the whining around others that I do in these pages, nobody would have anything to do with me. This book is my safety valve, my crying towel. I have told it everything, even those matters I cannot bring myself to tell my friends. No matter how much I complain, it still waits silently for me to fill its pages with more of the same.

December 5, 1974 Thursday

I have been busy, believe it or not. My three weeks in Washington for Tax Inspector training were almost non-stop activity. The highlights included the whole day of November 4th. For eight hours of a beautiful fall day I wandered around downtown Washington by myself. Now I know the city better than I know either Detroit or Milwaukee. I glimpsed Haldeman and Ehrlichman as they left the U.S. Courthouse for lunch. I visited the Kennedy graves in Arlington, and saw at night the Eternal Flame flickering in the distance. I went to the Kennedy Center to hear the National Symphony on November 19th, exactly six months after my graduation from school. I felt that the future belonged to me.

Since my return home on the 24th, I have seen the Hudson's Thanksgiving Day Parade, I have been sick with the flu, the city has been hit with its worst snowstorm since 1886, and I have returned to the dull routine of the job I hate. Not even the fancy pocket credentials I now have (they are impressive) can help me like this job.

I count the months down until next fall. At this point almost any law school will do.

The State Department has told me that, even though I am now on their job roster, I should not sit around waiting for a job from them.

December 12, 1974 Thursday

This has been a good week. Sunday I went to see the Detroit Symphony at Ford Auditorium with a ticket my mother gave me. This coming Sunday I will go again, to see a performance of Handel's *Messiah*. Except for a few trips out to Meadowbrook in past summers, my only legitimate symphonic concerts have been a performance at Milwaukee's Performing Arts Center by the Milwaukee Symphony in January 1971, and my recent trip to the Kennedy Center.

The Kennedy Center got me interested in live performances and showed me that recordings are true-to-life only in their *sound* reproduction. But they miss the visual spectacle of the artists throwing their every effort into the music, of the conductor who uses his whole body to create the music, and even of the concert-goers themselves.

I also discovered this part Sunday that I enjoy the concert better if I am not familiar with the music. If I recognize the piece, such as Tchaikovsky's *Serenade for Strings* (which they played), I expect it to sound exactly like I have heard it previously.

I have finished the process of applying to law schools. Now I can only sit back and wait for their decisions. I applied to the University of Michigan, the University of Chicago, Northwestern University, Loyola University, and Marquette University. I applied to Marquette (much as I always thought I would never go back) because Dr. Hay, one of my mentors, suggested they might give a break to a Marquette alumnus. Although I now enjoy my job more since I do most of the work, I have no intention of being with ATF on September 1st, 1975.

Besides reading the Detroit *Free Press* five days a week, I subscribe to *Newsweek, Psychology Today, Stereo Review,* and *Rolling Stone*.

December 15, 1974 Sunday

Loyola has accepted me into its law school. What a surprise! My brother John, his girlfriend Chris, and I were driving out to our sister Joan's yesterday for a Christmas tree trimming party. Talking about law schools, I said I did not expect to hear anything until after the first of the year.

When we got to Joan's, Mother had brought over some mail for me. I sat there opening envelopes and we all kept right on talking, until I suddenly realized that I was reading an acceptance letter from Loyola. I was, in fact, starting the second paragraph before I realized the letter's meaning. The catch, of course: Loyola wants a $100 non-refundable deposit by the 23rd. I have decided to send the money, even though I still hope for good news from Northwestern and Chicago.

Even though Loyola is my least desired possibility, the acceptance now lets me look ahead – not just with hope, but with firm expectation. I see my future is taking shape, and becoming more than a vague possibility.

"All of us are a little mad in our thinking, and what we
call a philosopher is simply one who has systematized

his lunacy."
- Sydney Harris

***

I was in school once —
once? Eight months of every year
for sixteen years.
Still, I was in school but *once*
and that time of my life
stands behind me;
having run with me for so long
it now stands behind
to let me run alone
to let me discover
that all it taught me
helps me not, now.
Most painful of all,
the arrogant confidence of college
lies shattered like a childhood dream:
we who thought ourselves on top of the world
were released into the world to find it has no top.
Sometimes I wish those dreams had survived
unbroken.
Sometimes I wish those days had gone on forever.

1975

January 6, 1975 Monday

The New Year has arrived, the year which I hope will end my miseries. But can I ever be happy? As long as I conceal my homosexuality from my friends, am I not false to them?

Only twice have I known true happiness, and yet it was not true happiness. It was an illusion. In the fall of 1972 my relationship with Roberta brought me happiness, but the heterosexual nature of that relationship made it unreal. In the spring of 1974 I found a more satisfying relationship on my drinking weekends with Jack; but this, too, remained heterosexual. For me to represent it as anything more would falsify it. I have only the satisfaction that Jack considers me his friend, and the fear that he would no longer do so if he knew my true nature.

I fear that nothing I do in my life will satisfy me. I think that perhaps I expect too much from life. I hate my job as Tax Inspector because it appears so inconsequential, so unnecessary.

February 7, 1975 Friday

No, dear Diary, I have not died. I don't know of any sure reason to explain my failure to write. Most likely, the fact that I have worked the afternoon shift out at Heublein's Distillery would suffice.

The afternoon shift involves no work (even less than the day), so I have read about eight books in three weeks during "work." My boss thinks I am reading the Code of Federal Regulations. As if that is likely. Every morning I sleep in later and later, but I still go to bed when I get home (except for a big weekend night like tonight, when I enjoy the company of you and a beer). Consequently, my days have shrunk from sixteen hours to thirteen hours, so time goes faster.

I have bought a car, Joan's 1967 Opel, for $300. The car insurance costs as much. As far as saving money goes, buying it was a disaster. But I need a car for my job and, mass transit to the contrary, an auto is immensely satisfying psychologically.

I also received a grade promotion at work, which I figure will gross me $500 by the end of August. My federal income tax refund should come to $240, and my state refund will just about cover my city tax. If Congress enacts the tax cut it talks about, I'll get another $100.

Enough of trivial details. What theme dominates these pages? What appears to be my obsession? Yes, you guessed it, my homosexuality!

Rather than break precedent and write exclusively about non-homosexual aspects of my life, I will now inject my favorite topic. (Two beers when one has become an abstainer, as I have, and a happy mood do wonders to loosen the tongue and the pen.) Putting down on paper in this book my thoughts about my "condition" and particularly about my (supposed) love for Jack has provided immense therapy.

This fifteen-month gap between college and law school has hung on me like a jail sentence. Now that it has half gone, I feel like a person who has struggled up one side of a hill and who can now coast down the other.

I have considered that perhaps the driving force which leaves me unsatisfied with everything I do, which makes me burn for fame and popularity and achievement, is my homosexuality. I will never father any children.

Such irony that I, who recognize that all the shit and all the pain of having children is worth it, will never have the opportunity. I understand so well why people have no more ambition than to marry, settle down, and have a family. I cannot go that route.

Socrates somewhere (here's where my classical background comes into view) said something to the effect that we can achieve immortality either through our children or our ideas, which are our intellectual children. Well, with two choices, one of which is closed to me, no wonder that I feel I only have fifty more years to achieve, achieve, achieve! If I were heterosexual, I could drift on in my present job with no problem. But I am not.

Speaking of my ambition, my visit to Chicago over New Year's has made me desperate for acceptance to Northwestern or the University of Chicago.

February 13, 1975 Thursday

>From the radio drifts a song
it touches the memory
touches like a finger on a wound
brings to mind a forgotten night
when once before that same song spoke
carried its lyric away
on the hot night breeze
left me alone
then
now
now becomes then
weeks become months
half years become years
Lonely nights of restless summers
come back now with the winter winds
the same song
the same radio
the same... I?
soon becomes now
now becomes then
half years become years
and I become....

February 27, 1975 Thursday

Sometimes I think this year is good for me, by leaving me plenty of time to examine myself: my beliefs, my goals, my personality. Sometimes I think only a person who has lost his mind could live like this.

Notes from Lower Volta

The months roll past and stretch behind me in my memories as a vast featureless plain. Few events in the last nine months fix themselves in my mind to break that plain. I only exist, each day no different from the one before or the one after. Each week is indistinguishable from any other. Am I alive or dead?

March 8, 1975 Saturday

A week ago I received a rejection letter from the University of Chicago. So much for my #2 choice. I expect to hear from Northwestern between the 12th and the 26th. I also know *what* to expect to hear, with Chicago's decision as a guide. Still nothing from Marquette or Michigan.

For the first time since I applied to law schools last fall, I face the possibility that perhaps this fall will *not* find me in law school. I want so badly for Northwestern to say yes, for me to arrange it financially. I want to be in Chicago, and at Northwestern. But already it looks like a lost hope.

Where will I be in September? Is there any point in going to law school if it isn't one of the very best in the country? What would I do with a degree from Loyola or Marquette? I suppose Marquette grads have no trouble finding jobs in Wisconsin. I have given Michigan serious consideration. It would be the cheapest and perhaps the best of my five choices. I would be a fool not to accept admission.

April 20, 1975 Sunday

Such news that I have! Still no word from Northwestern. I even wrote them a letter to ask politely "What the hell have you done with my application?" However, on March 26th I got a letter from Michigan. Acting upon the contents of that letter, I stopped payment on the check I had sent to Loyola in December, dug out an Ann Arbor guidebook, and found myself walking around humming "Hail to the victors valiant...." Chicago may not recognize a future U.S. Supreme Court Justice, but Michigan does. I expect to be in Ann Arbor in the fall.

At long last it appears that Southeast Asia is finally going communist. I wonder if the loss of China in 1949 was as traumatic and crushing as the current disaster, both to those who supported the war and to those who wanted us out. President Ford is running around the country saying this is no time for recriminations and rancor, while all the time he points the finger at Congress.

Tonight I went to a service of the Metropolitan Community Church of Detroit, a church for gays. I will not go through life pretending to be straight.

June 6, 1975 Friday

Let me see if I can finish this book tonight. It only makes sense that the diary of my life between college graduation and my future should finish now.

My life has changed beyond recognition since Tuesday. My plans for law school are dead. On June 19th I begin training in Washington, D.C. with the Foreign Service. In six months I should be overseas. The job offer came unexpectedly, with a phone call Tuesday from Mr. Kelly of the State Department Board of Examiners. He asked me if I was interested in an appointment. I thought he meant another interview when he was offering me a job. I told him I would call him back later in the week, and proceeded to call Bill, Margaret, Joe, Don, Mary, and Val, all of whom said more or less "Go!"

I didn't intend to give my answer until Friday, at least not originally. But by Wednesday afternoon, I was so anxious that I left work early to call. With the words, "Mr. Kelly, this is William Duffy. I want the job," my life changed.

Yesterday I had to tell Alcohol, Tobacco and Firearms about my plans. I hate quitting jobs. But since ATF hardly compares to State, Detroit to Washington, and my current $8,500 salary to State's $10,520, it wasn't too difficult.

What about law school? Well, it will still be there in a few years, if I want to go back. I know that I have made the right decision. Only a fool could pass up such an opportunity.

Besides, law school costs money, about $4,500 for nine months, of which I expected to have only $1,600 saved by September 1st. I was also fortunate enough to have my bank accounts at the only Detroit banks not giving student loans. And all the other banks require an applicant to have been a bank customer for a year.

June 13, 1975 Friday

Today was the day for which I have waited months. Today I quit Alcohol, Tobacco and Firearms. And yet, as I said goodbye to everyone, to people I do not expect to see ever again, I felt an unexpected sadness. The others seemed genuinely sorry to have me go. The office chipped in and bought me a beautiful pen and pencil set inscribed with "ATF 1975." I almost thought I would cry.

But I have no regrets. At the moment my mental state borders on hysteria as I desperately attempt to get everything packed to go. The movers come on Monday (hopefully) and Tuesday I drive off into the sunrise to my new life, with an overnight stopover at Breezewood, Pennsylvania. (I don't want to tax my poor old '67 Opel too heavily – or myself – by making the trip all in one day.)

It is a strange feeling knowing that years may pass before I again look in these pages. What kind of a person will I have become?

All my books which I have loved so well all these years are packed away. Who will read them?

Suddenly it is very easy to throw out many items which I expected would remain with me through all my life.

I want to travel through my life as unencumbered with baggage as possible. Books are my weakness. Even those I have limited to Shakespeare's plays and sonnets, a collection of Revolutionary writing printed by The People's Bicentennial Committee, and a book (still unread) called *The Lives of a Cell*.

I want a happy life. I want friends. I know I approach my life with a handicap which threatens to preclude both.

An Innocent Abroad
(Washington, Korea)
June 8, 1975 - June 3, 1977

Notes from Lower Volta

June 8, 1975

> "I shall be telling this with a sigh
> Somewhere ages and ages hence;
> Two roads diverged in a wood, and I –
> I took the one less traveled by
> And that has made all the difference."
> - Robert Frost

July 16, 1975 Wednesday

One month after arriving in Washington I finally find time to write something. If I write at this rate, my life will end before the book finishes. Detroit seems light years away, the events of my first days in Washington seem like something out of another person's life.

At the moment I expect to go to Seoul around September 1st. I'll believe it when I arrive. Seoul was my third choice. Nairobi and Tokyo were my first and second. Nairobi was quickly snatched up. The more I considered the matter, the less I wanted to go to Tokyo. The threat of a new war in Korea scared me off at first, but I think the chances of one become less each day.

I think now is a good time to enter the Foreign Service, after the final end of the Indochina involvement. We no longer think we rule the world and we have learned that we, too, have limits. I doubt that I will ever go back to law school. What use is a law degree in a job market clogged with lawyers? The only moment of regret I felt about law school was when Northwestern University, after first putting me on its waiting list, turned around and accepted me, and then offered me $5,000 in scholarship and loans. Oh well.

August 17, 1975 Sunday

My weeks have been busy, but I can hardly remember what I have done. I feel almost that I have so little time that I should never do nothing, that I should not rest. I leave Washington on August 29th, spend the weekend in Milwaukee, fly to San Francisco on Labor Day to see my brother John and his girlfriend Chris, fly to Tokyo on

September 2nd, and arrive in Seoul on September 4th.

Right now I am in the consular course at the Foreign Service Institute, bored to tears with visas and passports (and hoping that I won't find the job itself equally boring). The highlight of the course so far was a trip out to Dulles Airport on Friday to watch a few international flights come in.

The whole four-week course allots a grand total of only two hours to take care of "administrative matters," namely getting out of the country. At first I was overwhelmed with the number of people I have to talk to and the list of things I must do. But somehow I have managed to get my shots and to apply for my passport. I have discovered that most of those whom I "must see" are basically useless and uninformative. The only exception was Dean Wellman, a Consular Officer just back from Seoul who told me more in two hours than I had learned in four weeks of hoofing around the Department. I have suspended all my purchases of things great and small, since everything (I am assured) is available either in the Army Commissary or on the economy.

Bill McKenny came to Washington the last weekend in June, and I went down to see him in Virginia Beach the 4th of July and last weekend. The Burtons were also down there, midway in their grand motor trip along the East Coast. Since their first anniversary had just passed, we took them out to dinner at the Officers' Club, complete with cheap champagne. Joe Wishforth, a former NROTC colleague of Bill, also turned up over the weekend. Since Wishforth enjoys talking about what a success he is, I gladly clobbered him with the details of my job.

Jack was supposed to have come down this weekend, but (typically) that fell through.

The muffler on the Opel fell off spectacularly in the middle of M Street in Georgetown. It cost me $71 to have a whole new exhaust system installed. If that car had fewer than 89,000 miles it currently registers, I would consider taking it to Korea with me.

Notes from Lower Volta

August 22, 1975 Friday

I sold the Opel for $180, ironically to a Korean (who probably is here illegally). It hurt to lose that car. It really gave me no trouble (except for the mufflers!).

As I consider the jobs and careers available to people, I see few that I think are terribly worthwhile or interesting. Have I settled into a Foreign Service career? Apparently so, unless the job is so bad that I become desperate to escape it as I did ATF.

I regret somewhat not going to law school. Undoubtedly sometime this winter I would have been sitting in my cramped little room in Abbott Hall studying for some impossible exam while outside the brown snows whipped past Chicago's gray skyscrapers, and I would wonder how I could have passed up the Foreign Service. I want both law school and the State Department, but both at the same time. And yet I want neither.

Basically I am a lazy person: I want the results and rewards of hard work without all the hard work. But then few things are more satisfying than seeing the results of one's own work.

The first few weeks in Washington I got something of an inferiority complex. Consular Officers are looked down upon by the Political Officers who think they do the "real" business of the Foreign Service. I was also afraid that consular work would be quite boring, that I would become a glorified paper-shuffler

Right now I don't expect that to happen. Consular Officers seem to acquire responsibility much faster and actually exercise greater influence on the lives of people than the hordes of would-be ambassadors cultivating their contacts on the cocktail party circuit in the hope they will anticipate the next coup by five minutes.

August 24, 1975 Sunday

I feel drained, indifferent to everything which passes. People ask whether I'm excited to go to Korea. Honestly I think myself completely passive to it. It seems no different than packing up for school in Milwaukee. In some respects, I don't see that Korea is any more exotic or East Asian than that fair city on the Neapolitan shores of Lake Michigan. I never seem to get as excited about things the way others do. I drift along, neither ecstatic nor despondent.

It's a strange feeling to know that I may never spend more than a small part of my future years inside the United States, that the friends that I have now may not always be my closest friends (perhaps become "friends" with whom the only communication is a yearly Christmas card), that I will never have a truly stable life.

September 2, 1975 Tuesday

My God! I am on a flight to Tokyo! I sit here under my $2.50 headphones on this Pan American 747 and listen to a mishmash of classical and modern music. Soon I shall be drunk on screwdrivers. A song just came on which was a "big" hit from last winter. I feel a twinge for the life which lies behind me. I never thought I would feel nostalgic for my past year in Detroit.

I am all cried out. I have done nothing these last few days except say goodbye to everyone I ever cared for. On Friday in Washington it was Mother, Joan, Claire, and assorted aunts and an uncle; on Sunday it was Val, Jane, and Mary; on Monday it was Joe, Lorraine, Bill, Jack, and Don; today it was John and Chris. I can cry no more. What have I gotten myself into?

Unlike other Foreign Service Officers, I am not completely sure that this is the life I want. I think I could have easily spent the rest of my life in Milwaukee or Chicago and been contented. Once the State Department offered this job, that became impossible. I had no choice but to take this job. Maybe sometime in the future I will leave the Department and go back there, picking up where I left off. But not now.

I almost wish this job had never come my way. Even now I would be starting law school at Northwestern. And yet (my atheism notwithstanding) I feel some fate pushing me through life. I do what I was meant to do.

I practically have the music channels memorized, and can

switch back and forth between Tchaikovsky, Glenn Miller, and some hard rock. I have heard *String of Pearls* about six times. It reminds me of the Ardmore bar.

Airplanes amaze me. They seem to represent what is right with technology. These huge machines which defy all common sense lift hundreds of people miles into the air and fly them thousands of miles without stopping. They do all this while providing maximum comfort.

September 5, 1975 Friday

I am in the Republic of Korea. By plane I am thirteen hours from Detroit. It is 5:30 in the afternoon here; 4:30 this morning on the East Coast; 3:30 this morning in Chicago and Milwaukee.

Tokyo was as I expected it, except that English was even more common in speech and signs than I had imagined. Culture shock! *Bewitched* and *The Flintstones* on TV dubbed in Japanese! Pan American put me up at the Tokyo Hilton overnight. (The airline was responsible for my accommodations because Northwest only has a flight out in the morning to Seoul.) The Hilton reeked of Americanism. I'm not even sure that the Japanese staff could speak Japanese. Tokyo, what a madhouse!

I didn't know what to feel on the flight into Seoul. I flew with Jay Bookman and his wife Jo, so my available moments for introspection were limited. But as the plane descended through the cloud cover and the green, cultivated fields and scattered villages appeared, I felt thrilled to have arrived. From the air, the Korean landscape looked like it had emerged straight from a JRR Tolkien fantasy.

September 6, 1975 Saturday

As I continued my grand excursion across the North American mainland (namely, my visits to Milwaukee and San Francisco), I had serious doubts about my desire to spend the next two years away from the United States and (even more) about my willingness to spend most of the rest of my life away. But in the forty-eight hours since my arrival here, those thoughts have not troubled me. I am more excited about my work as a Consular Officer now than at any point previously. I will start work in immigrant visas next week, because they are the simplest.

Last night I had my first excursion into Seoul (the five-minute walks from here to the Embassy hardly count). I went out with three other guys, two of whom speak Korean and are fairly familiar with the bars.

As we passed through the gate of the compound, I surprised myself with the fear I felt to leave the security of the American environment. The people pushing in all directions on the narrow streets and the smells and noise only made things worse. But the people we spoke with (well, so I sat there like a deaf mute) were so friendly and eager to please us that my fear disappeared. We ran into three girls just out of high school who were on their way home from their women's club meeting. We took them to dinner.

We were home by midnight. The 12:00 a.m. curfew puts a stop to Seoul's nightlife. It's an eerie feeling as an American to see the police setting up barricades in the street and the few stragglers rushing past in cars with the accelerator to the floor in a desperate attempt to get home on time.

I wonder what the Koreans think of the Americans, especially the Koreans who work for the Americans. I almost think they are pro-American because they have no other option and because they still remember the war. But I know how I would feel about a nation (any nation, no matter how good an ally) if it came to Washington, D.C. and walled off its diplomats behind barbed wire in a compound where they pursued almost exclusively their foreign life style with a standard of living enviably higher than any in our poor experience.

I think I have conquered my jet lag. It is 6:30 p.m. here; 5:30 a.m. in Washington and Detroit. When I first arrived, my tendency was to zonk out by 9:00 p.m. and wake up irreversibly by 5:00 a.m. Today I did not even wake up until 8:00 a.m., partly due to staying out to midnight. Hopefully my metabolism has adjusted. Now I can only sit back and wait for the full effect of culture shock and the ravages of disease which supposedly attend every foreign relocation. Seoul may be its own case. Why it was classified as hardship post until two years ago is inconceivable.

September 26, 1975 Friday

Anyong hashimnikka! Greetings from the Land of the Morning Calm! I could see the mountains out my front windows if it weren't for the trees in the way. The Embassy housing compound is amazingly well-landscaped. It used to be a Japanese compound pre-1945, and still includes some original Japanese houses. It's not at all what I expected (namely, typical American apartments with parking lots in front). It's more like a park. My building stands next to the year-round swimming pool and the tennis court, and my back door looks out on a Seoul street (with a brick wall and barbed wire to insulate us from the Koreans). I have a two-bedroom furnished apartment with wall-to-wall carpeting.

I arrived on Thursday, September 4th. On Monday, September 8th, I started issuing (and refusing) immigrant visas, fifty to sixty a day. Everyone's idea of heaven is to get to the United States, even if it means living in Detroit. (I had one applicant heading for an address on East Grand Blvd.) Since Korea's quota of immigrant visas is snapped up by relatives of U.S. citizens and of Koreans already legally in the United States, people will do almost anything to fit one of those categories. So far I've had tears, flattery, faked wedding photos, fabricated Family Registers – but NO BRIBES! The Family Register is all important. It records birth, death, parentage, adoption, marriage, divorce. But from our point of view it can be fairly easily changed.

I like Korean food. Even the infamous *kimchi* (supposed death to foreigners and described as pickled garbage) has not bothered me. Koreans eat the same stuff for breakfast, lunch, and dinner, typically, soup, rice, *kimchi*, various vegetables such as cucumbers or seaweed, and a meat or fish dish. I have become fairly proficient in the use of chopsticks.

I have a full-time maid, Mrs. Yi, six days a week, who makes breakfast and dinner, cleans, and does the laundry. (Lee – or Yi – is a more common name here than Smith or Jones in the United States.) I think she's about sixty. I pay her the generous (some say excessive) sum of 20,000 *won* a month, which works out to about $40. (And I pay no rent.)

Tomorrow we will go out to Panmunjom to watch the North and South Koreans yell at one another. On the 15th the Koreans had their monthly air raid drill. When the sirens went off, traffic stopped dead and in the space of a few minutes, everyone disappeared from the streets. That was eerie. So is the curfew between midnight and 4:00 a.m., when the police drag roadblocks into the streets. We've also been on security alert these last few days, because of Japanese Emperor Hirohito's visit to the United States. Security thinks the Japanese Red Army might try to attack the American or Japanese Embassy, which is two blocks away.

I started my Korean language lessons Monday the 22nd at 7:30 a.m., one hour every morning five days a week.

October 3, 1975 Friday

I arrived in Korea with no language training, and no background in the country except what I had picked up on my own. The Department prefers to send officers slightly more qualified, but the Consular Section here has been short-handed for months. My general lack of qualifications for anyplace else qualified me by default for Korea.

This place is exciting. Seoul has six and a half million people. While involved in a massive construction boom, it still has plenty of narrow streets and alleyways with strange smells and sights to remind the visitor that, in spite of the skyscrapers, he is not in America. Unfortunately, my study of Western European history in school is irrelevant here. My anthropology on the other hand has, I think, prepared me to adjust to the vastly different culture and to avoid (at least so far) terminal culture shock.

Everything I meet here – the customs, the food, the architecture, the language – is completely new: a situation which I haven't faced since childhood and which I think far preferable to an assignment in London or Paris.

Do I make sense?

October 25, 1975 Saturday

Last Sunday I went to Suwon with some friends (Molly Newman and her brother). Suwon is Korea's answer to Greenfield Village and Williamsburg, a folk village in which people still live using the old arts and crafts. It represents an attempt by the Korean government to preserve and exalt the national heritage. But unlike Williamsburg or Greenfield Village, Suwon is not a recreation of some long-past way of life. It reflects the way Koreans live even today in the villages in the countryside. The people flock out there, engage the village inhabitants in animated discussions about the old ways, a marked change from the attitude only a few years ago when Koreans wanted to forget their past and junked their beautiful furniture for the glories of formica and plastic.

The immigrant visa process works out as a game. Almost everybody gets a visa eventually. We presume that every document handed us could be fake. It might in fact be less trouble to produce a fake than to get the real thing. Sometimes I feel that our function is to make sure the applicants' stories are not too fantastic. If they are, I'll thunder in an imperial third person, "You dare to present this to the American Consul?" (meaning *me*). If they outsmart us, they get the visas. If we outsmart them, they don't, at least until they come back with a new story. The Korean War remains the endless cause of almost anything, from why a birth went unreported in 1933 to why a 40-year old woman suddenly appears on a Family Register in 1973 (a long-lost sister).

Sometimes I feel I have no right to decide whether these

people should go to the States. I doubt we would be Americans today if our grandparents had had to qualify under the Immigration and Nationality Act. The desire of many of these people to become American overwhelms me, and makes me feel inadequately nationalistic. The Korean word for American, *Miguk,* means "Beautiful Country," and the illusion is only encouraged by the glowing reports Koreans in the United States send back (even when they only pump gas and wait on tables) and by the way Americans live here.

I have made my first major capital investment. The travel people decided (I don't know how) that the government still owed me $640 for *per diem* this summer. So I have bought a Korean piano, a Horugel. On the economy a piano runs $1,000, but I got it (untaxed) on base for $757, one of the good points about having the American military around. I hope to have it by Thanksgiving. It's tailor-made!

November 1, 1975 Saturday
      Ancient Air of a Long Autumn Night:
            "The moon
      shining near the paulownia tree
         brings the autumn chill.
   An old plum tree with its sparse branches
         shadows the paper window.
            As flocks fly over,
               the first frost
               covers the sky.
         The sound of the grass insects
                in the night
              brings deep calm.
              From somewhere
       broken notes of a bamboo flute
              chill my heart.
            As the wind lingers
          in the bamboo sprouts,

Notes from Lower Volta

> even the burning candle
> sheds tears
> in this long, long night.
> Unfolding a poem from Tang
> I call for the sleep
> that is far, far away."
>   - Shin Seok Jeong

December 9, 1975 Tuesday

    I have not written. Why not? My life is not so markedly more exciting than it has been in the past. Some days I have fun; some days I don't; some days I am lonely. Again and again my years in college assume the dimensions of some fabled Golden Age, when I know quite certainly that they did not always appear so. I think that what sets those days off from these is that then my future held hopes. Now I have no hopes, no expectation that my life will be anything but an unending masquerade, only a desire that my time will be *occupied*: that I will be *busy*.

    Why do I write such depressing thoughts, so different from what have filled these pages previously? Tonight my records and books have finally arrived from America, neither of which I have seen (or heard) for six months, and tonight I have a bad cold (my only illness this past year except for my reaction to the typhoid shot last summer). I have attempted to treat it with a bottle of wine.

    Two problems bother me: I have yet to feel more than the slightest twinge of homesickness, and I have yet to miss even those closest to me more than perfunctorily. This is in marked contrast to some other Americans here, who seem to pine away for the States. Even more seriously, I feel only minimal interest in becoming friends with most people I have met here. I have actually received the most favorable impressions from Koreans, but there seems to exist some unspoken division between Americans and Koreans which I do not know how to break.

    My problem in fact is that I am lonely, and have met few

people valuable enough that I would escape this loneliness.

December 21, 1975 Sunday

Having a wife is such a tremendous social convenience that I can scarcely imagine how I have survived to my present ripe old age without one. A wife is an ever-ready partner for public functions, a made-to-order organizer for dinner parties, and a man's *alter ego* who can spend the day widening his social contacts for him while he is trapped in the office. In the Foreign Service a person is not complete without a spouse. I feel such pressure to marry that perhaps I should advertise in the papers and get it over with.

I don't think I will last long with this outfit. I don't have the ambition, the yearning for power needed to help me claw my way to the top. I feel alienated from the other Americans here both by age and interests. I'm fairly indifferent to meeting other people. I have a hard time carrying on conversations with people I don't like, a fatal flaw for a Foreign Service Officer.

December 26, 1975 Friday

Christmas, at least, is over. Here I am, completely indifferent to the greatest holiday Western commercialism could devise, hating the very sound of Christmas carols (whether in English or Korean), and refusing to put out more Christmas decorations than two red candles. It occurred to me that this Christmas did not make me lonely even though for the first time I have spent Christmas away from the family. After the disastrous family Christmases of 1973 and 1974, eight thousand miles is a good distance. Christmas is a children's holiday. It lost its magic by the time I was fifteen.

I called home today, to Joan's place in Virginia, to be exact. It was 10:30 a.m. here, 8:30 p.m. Christmas Day night there. What do you talk about when your conversation costs $5.00 a minute? At times like that talk is not cheap.

Christmas Eve I went to the Open House at Ambassador Sneider's. I felt like I was in a 1943 movie, a group of Americans far away from home gathered around a fire place and a piano (played by Mrs. Sneider) to sing the old carols. The Sneiders put on a brave show of Christmas cheer, considering their Jewish background. I guess that's just one more example of diplomats subordinating their personal beliefs to political necessity. For Christmas dinner I went to the Markmans'. It was very good, but ever since I was sick earlier this month, I've had no real appetite.

On the 14th the Wiltons and Molly sponsored a reading of Dickens' *Christmas Carol*, a very pleasant idea.

I got so into the Christmas spirit that I even went to Midnight Mass. I've heard of people who, although previously lapsed, found religion so comfortably familiar in the weird world of Korea that eventually they returned to the Church. I'd rather go back to science fiction.

William J. Duffy

1976

January 1, 1976 Thursday

A New Year's Message, a message as we enter the last quarter of this miserable century: Help! What am I doing with my life? I am reasonably content with it now, fairly excited to live in Korea, adequately satisfied with my job. But, my God, is this my life for the next forty years?

A year ago I dreamt of going to law school, of a legal career which in thirty years would culminate in my appointment to the Supreme Court. What do I dream of now? Appointment as Consul General to Paris? No, I no longer dream that far ahead. I still consider the notion of going back to school, of a law degree, of a masters in history or anthropology.

My life has become much more oriented to the present now than when I lived in Detroit, because my present life has become much more acceptable to me than my life in Detroit was.

"I slept and dreamt
That life was joy
I awoke and saw
That life was duty
I acted and behold
Duty was joy."
- Rabindranath Tagore

January 18, 1976 Sunday

I certainly am not making much of a dent in the way of keeping track of my activities in Korea. Basically either I do nothing, and then have nothing to write about; or I do a lot, and have no time to write.

I've taken up ice-skating, at the instigation of the Bookmans. I went to Mitopa Department Store and bought Size 96 skates, the largest size they had. A couple of Sundays ago we drove south to

Yongin and found a rice paddy iced over for the local kids. Since I had not skated since 1964, my style lacked finesse. Luckily for American prestige I stayed on my feet. Today we went just over to the Kyungbok palace and skated on the pond (more like a lake) there.

My English students are temporarily coming three times a week, Sunday, Tuesday, and Thursday. Have I mentioned them previously? They're female students from Ewha University whom I met through Joyce Overman, an American friend who teaches there. We meet once or twice a week. They are currently on their winter break and have no other studying to do. Right now I have six students: Misses Kim, Choi, Park, Chung, So, and Oh. Miss Lee dropped and Miss So and Miss Oh are new. Unlike the others, they are only college freshmen, and therefore not as comfortable speaking English. Miss Choi is in Inchon for the vacation and has not come.

We finished the textbook we had used since we started (in October?) and which I had never really enjoyed. The last couple of times we have just prepared (more or less) to discuss a general topic: "the most memorable trip I have taken" and "wedding customs of our home countries." I think this approach works better than reading through textbook drills, because both I and the students actually speak more English and we engage in a real conversation. All the students are loosening up, and seem to make more of an effort to speak English.

My own study of the Korean language continues. I find myself understanding surprisingly large segments of simple conversations (especially when connected with food or school).

January 25, 1976 Sunday

I returned this afternoon from an overnight trip to Suanbo, in the central part of the Republic. I went with the Bookmans, Beckers, Markmans, Ebert, and Joyce, ostensibly to take in Suanbo's hot springs but really to get away from Seoul. We rented a Chevy van (and driver, Mr. Kim) from the Embassy and drove the four hours down there.

William J. Duffy

I have yet to see an area of Korea which has no mountains, and Suanbo is no exception. After checking into the Savoy Hotel (built in tacky Swiss chalet style with the typically Korean touches of waterless toilets and unheated *ondol* floors), we set out climbing. Apparently the local *hankuk saram* (Koreans) see few *mikuk saram* (Americans, especially Jay, Tony, and Jay with their beards and me with my mustache). Our every movement was watched. One suspicious fellow even got a few of his friends and followed us out of the village (at a respectful distance).

The shoes I wore were not hiking boots, as I discovered when I could not stand up on the hillside. Eventually I fell behind the others (except Joyce, who had fallen behind all of us), and sat down on the hillside, looking back into the valley below and the mountains beyond, and the valleys beyond them.

The air was cool like an April day, not cold like a January, and only a light breeze blew. Except for the scattered patches of snow, it could have been a spring day. The quiet compared to Seoul's noise was impressive, so quiet that it was broken by such little things as a dog barking down in the village, some unseen door slamming far away, or a dirty bus passing on the gravel road.

This was the Korea I had imagined: hills rising from the narrow plains at dizzying angles, little clusters of villages whose houses had thatched or corrugated roofs, ancient buses careening down the twisted roads in a cloud of dust, and the whole landscape held together by the maze of curved and terraced rice paddies. I almost wished that someday I could quit my job and become a Peace Corps Volunteer there.

Seoul is almost too Westernized. In Seoul it's difficult to remember that I stand on the edge of Asia. But in the countryside there is no doubt: this is a way of life which has no connection to my own, which has gone on as it is for centuries and will go on long after this.

My hillside reverie was broken by a thundering herd crashing through the bushes nearby. Joyce had caught up. Behind her four boys five or six years old were in hot pursuit. She sat next to me. Our adversaries halted their advance when they saw that Joyce had acquired a mysterious companion. To break the impasse, we decided to descend the mountain and return to Suanbo.

At first the kids circled around to remain behind us, but once they realized I was no mountain god they became emboldened and caught up to us. They apparently understood no more English than "How are you?" and studiously ignored my attempts at Korean. Nevertheless, they stayed with us until we reached the first village, where we would have bought each a Coke, except that we were then besieged by an additional twenty kids.

The four's companionship on our descent was rather fun, especially when they tried to lure us to their hillside fort. Since both Joyce and I rode our rear ends down part way (including one spectacular back flip I did when I stepped on a patch of ice covered by snow), they undoubtedly acquired a dim view of Americans' physical coordination.

Back at the hotel (we arrived only ten minutes ahead of the others), we took our hot baths, which was the trip's rationale. (The waters of Suanbo have a wide reputation for curative powers. Mr. Kim picked up a bottle of water to take home to his family.) We then proceeded to get drunk, and also had a little food. All eight of us crowded into one room, a typical room about ten feet square with only quilts for furniture. Apparently we put on quite a show, because the staff used every conceivable pretext to pop in and see what was going on. (We did not have any monopoly on bizarre activities, because Joyce had a *ménage a trois* of two guys and a girl on the other side of her paper-thin wall.) We all crashed by 11:00 p.m.

Today we got up and, after several false starts, picked out a road which Tony assured us would lead to a monolithic Buddha we *had* to see. We walked and Mr. Kim drove behind in the van. It felt like some British colonial official on a safari with his boy in tow to help him out. Eventually we determined we were on the wrong road, the Buddha was not really all that interesting, and the road was good to walk along anyway.

Today also had its moments of adventure. When we attempted to return to the main road (I use the modifier "main" only in its Korean sense, not in any recognizable American equivalent), we found we had to ford three streams, each with ice of uncertain thickness and water of uncertain depth, except to say that the second was both wider and less solid than the first, and the third in the same relation to the second. But we survived.

Mr. Kim decided that the trip home would be both more scenic and quicker if we struck out cross country rather than return to the freeway. He was right on both counts. The road surface was also indescribably bad.

January 28, 1976 Wednesday

Getting out of Seoul for a weekend makes me happy to be in Korea. The city air is so dirty, and in the winter very dry. When I first got here in September, the pollution was not as bad as I expected it would be. Now because of winter heating there is so much dirt in the air it's visible, and you feel it. I haven't worn my contacts because of it. Driving into Seoul, you can see the brown pall which lies over the city. It's disgusting. The air is so dry. I have a vaporizer working full-time, but the apartment is still like an electric chair.

I have issued (and refused) my last immigrant visa, at least for a while. Miss Knight, the Consul General, has switched everybody around. Starting today I am in American passports and citizenship. I'm happy to move to a new department, but unhappy that once again I have no idea of what to do. I think I was just beginning to grasp the workings of immigrant visas, all the angles on Family Registers, affidavits of support, and family relationships as established by our beautiful Immigration and Nationality Act of 1952 (as amended). But now I don't know enough about passports to bluff very convincingly.

Notes from Lower Volta

February 6, 1976 Friday

Now I don't see many Koreans during work, but lots of Americans. I enjoy passport work less than immigrant visas. Basically I stand at a counter all day checking new passports and the reports of birth of American citizens to see if the typist has made any mistakes before I put the American Consul's signature on them. The biggest excitement so far resulted from an American's death. The hospital was ready to cremate him; we weren't sure his daughter in America would agree.

I also have to interview civilian Americans marrying Koreans, because in Korea the word *marriage* when used in reference to an American is often connected with the word *fraud*. Koreans marry Americans solely because that's the easiest way to get to America. Sometimes the American is used; sometimes he is paid.

The classic pattern involves an American arriving in Korea for the first time using a brand new passport to see the girl he has had a pen pal relationship with for two years, and when they see each other at the airport they fall so madly in love that they have to rush right down to the Embassy to get marriage papers. I've already heard the story twice.

My most bizarre experience so far occurred when an old Korean man showed up, asking to speak to the Consul. He presented two letters, one dated 1955 and one 1962, from an American indicating that at those times this old man had served as the caretaker of Inchon Foreigners' Cemetery for many years. Apparently he still does, because his purpose in coming was to request the esteemed American Consul's intercession with the Mayor of Inchon to get his salary!

At one time the cemetery was controlled by the foreign consuls, who assumed responsibility for its upkeep. Unfortunately, though, that is no longer so. I could do nothing for him. I went by the consular maxim: "Never help foreigners; and, if you can help it, never help Americans." To top it off the old man claimed he had asked the American consul for help in 1969, and got it.

William J. Duffy

February 14, 1976 Saturday

While routine citizenship work is a bore, my new job does offer more varied opportunities to make my mark. The Department does not care all that much whether immigrant visas are granted or refused. It does care when American citizens have problems.

This past week a report cropped up that an American being held in prison in Pusan on drug charges had been beaten by prison guards. The Department in the past has gotten a lot of flak for ignoring the abuse of American prisoners, so everybody fell over each other on this one. The immediate necessity was to send a consul to see the prisoner. He had written both his parents and us that he had been beaten. In his letter to us that line was crossed out, although it was crossed out in such fashion as to make it the most legible part of the letter.

Miss Knight decided to send me by myself. This floored me, since I had not visited any prisons previously and had expected to accompany another consul on a trial run. I didn't know whether to be pleased, that she was willing to put so much responsibility on my inexperienced shoulders, or disturbed, that she thought the visit so unimportant that she could leave it to me.

Thursday morning I woke up nervous, more nervous than I have been since the morning of my State Department oral in March 1974. The ride to the airport restored my confidence somewhat. Being chauffeured in a big black Chevrolet is certainly a dazzling display of American power. I worried that I would miss the plane, that I would throw up, that no one would meet me at Pusan Airport and I would be helpless, that I would fall on my face walking into the prison. As it was, none of these dire fears materialized. Korean Air Lines makes all its announcements in both Korean and English. I was met at the airport by the local USIS Representative. I was sure-footed all day long.

Although I knew it would not be allowed, I tried to carry my briefcase onto the plane. I hoped to bluff through on a complete ignorance of the language. I had not expected the agent would say in quite comprehensible English, "Please check that in, sir."

Airport security is unbelievable. Every traveler fills out a travel card so the government can keep track of who is going where. There are *two* body searches: one at the gate and one right before you board the plane.

Although the flight was smooth, domestic Korean airplanes (it was a prop!) are not designed for American bodies. If I had gotten my briefcase on board, there would have been no place to put it.

I was accompanied to the prison by Mr. Chung Yon-soo, the top Korean in the Pusan USIS office. Here I was, a punk Vice Consul, using a man twice my age as interpreter and all-around door-opening lackey because I was the American and he was the Korean; dressed in my most conservative dark suit; carrying my black briefcase partly because it had some official papers in it and partly because it made me look more official myself; representing all by my lonesome the Ambassador of the United States, the Government of the United States; and empowered, in effect, to bring down the wrath of them all upon the Pusan Correctional Institution and the Government of the Republic of Korea, if necessary. ("How do I react," I asked Miss Knight, "if they bring the American in and he's a bloody mass of scar tissue?")

I talked with the American in the warden's office for three and a half hours, partly because it is difficult to shut a man up who has had no one to speak English to for two months and partly because it made the warden (who I did not care for) miss his lunch hour.

The warden had the gall, first of all, to expect me to talk to the American in *his* presence. When I said that wouldn't do, he wanted me to tell him afterward what we had discussed!

Although there was little physical evidence that the American had received mistreatment (and quite a lot of evidence that he was treated much better than Korean prisoners), there was actually an indication in his prison record that some of his charges were true. He said he had been handcuffed for forty-eight hours for breaking a prison rule until he signed a statement which read, "I'm sorry for what I did and I will not break the rules again." His record had his statement, and a notation that he was in fact handcuffed for a day.

February 24, 1976 Tuesday

So yesterday Miss Knight and I paid a visit on the Ministry of Foreign Affairs to Mr. Lee who handles consular affairs. Although the Capitol Building is only a five-minute walk from the Embassy, it would be unthinkable not to drive. So we drove, pulled up in front of the Capitol, doormen ran up, and we were escorted into the VIP elevator and into Mr. Lee's office.

After a twenty-minute chat which opened with small talk (that's what you need to become Consul General), we hit the subject matter, and closed with a luncheon invitation for Thursday. We went back to the Embassy.

If people could only have seen me then, a green Vice Consul treading in the sacred precincts of Park's dictatorship. My inclination was to laugh. While Miss Knight praised the Capitol Building's beauty to our escort, I refrained from pointing out that the hideous structure had been built by the Japanese as the headquarters of their colonial administration.

If nothing else, the visit showed quite clearly what a tremendous advantage it is to speak English as a native language. We struggled through our conversation because we knew English too well and they did not know it well enough. As French was once the diplomatic language, now English is. What will it be at the end of the century?

Speaking of Park's dictatorship, I had the occasion to be detained by the Korean Army not once but twice this past weekend (only twenty-four hours before entering the Capitol).

I went to Daech'on with my Ewha students. I assumed they knew what they were doing. I was wrong on several counts. First, they put us on the third class local train, which took an unbelievable (and grueling) six hours to get the 150 miles to Daech'on. I thought I was in a movie about war refugees, with hard backed seats, people sitting in the aisle, bundles of goods piled everywhere. Too bad, I thought, that Korean transportation is no better than this. But it is. The girls later said for an extra dollar each we could have taken an express train which would have arrived in two and a half hours. But there are compensations. Few things equal the sensational reaction one causes by pulling a *can* of Coke out of a bag in a third class train.

We arrived at the beach after dark. Naturally our first inclination was to run down on the beach, waving a flashlight all the way. Within five minutes a soldier with a particularly menacing gun led us off to a blockhouse, where the local fascist-in-residence lectured us (or rather the girls: he knew better than to give an American diplomat trouble) for half an hour about security, army operations, and the Northern threat.

I tried to appear indifferent. Even though I knew I had no problems, it was not clear that the girls would be let go. Finally, he dismissed us, and told them to explain to the *waykuk saram* (foreigner) why we could not go on the beach at night.

So that was fine. We had a pleasant evening, a good dinner, a bilingual conversation, and some cards. I went to bed while the girls stayed up, apparently all night. Outside of the fact that the *ondol* floor was so hot my rear-end almost burned off and that a "virgin ghost" (nee Park Young Chu) visited me at three to kill me, I woke invigorated.

We explored the beach, all the way to the end where a pile of rocks rose up. Without hesitation we started to climb, because a little thatched hut stood at the top.

"What's that?" I asked.

"Maybe a toilet," replied Kim Mi-su.

The toilet turned out to be a gun emplacement, and we turned out to be prisoners once again. This time, though, we just laughed. The humor of the situation was compounded because no one else on the beach had climbed on the rocks until we did. Then about ten people followed us.

After a few questions in some hidden underground lair (if we had been spies, we could have drawn a map of the whole position) and the checking of ID cards, they let us go because (as Miss Kim related afterwards) the soldiers did not want to give a bad impression of Korea to the *waykuk saram*. Too late for that.

March 28, 1976 Sunday

Any doubts I had concerning the Park dictatorship have been dispelled since the March 1st Myongdong Cathedral incident. A joint Catholic-Protestant service called on President Park to step down. He responded by calling it a plot to overthrow the government and arrested dozens of Christian leaders. He appears determined to follow in the footsteps of Chiang Kai-Shek, Diem, and Thieu, and lose the country by default to the communists.

His argument that Western liberal democracy is not suited to Korea insults the people whose interests he claims to serve. Park, once a Japanese Officer, once convicted of a communist conspiracy, now a fascist nationalist (quite a versatile character), serves no one's interests but his own. To those who claim Park is popular, so was Hitler. Popularity does not excuse the destruction of a nation's freedom. The argument that dictatorship is the price the Korean people must pay to avoid communism is Orwellian.

Having lived in America all my life, Korea comes as a shock. People are afraid to speak openly. After all, isn't it unconstitutional to criticize the government? There is no peaceful, legal way to change the government. Park has allowed only a choice between himself and violence.

My English students were afraid to talk about the government with me, or to discuss the Myongdong incident, apparently because they thought all Americans support the government. I had to tell them bluntly, "I do not like the South Korean government," before they would talk.

One of them mentioned that occasionally *Time* and *Newsweek* show up with some of the pages cut out. I produced *Time*'s article on the recent crackdown and said, "You mean *this* page, for instance?" I read the article to them, pausing after every sentence to explain the general ideas and the particular words. They learned more English from that article than they have in the last few months. What would the police think if they found their notebooks full of words like *regime, dissent, repression, decree, crack down*, and *authoritarian*?

March 29, 1976 Monday

If a Korean had written what I wrote yesterday about the Park regime, he could spend the rest of his life in jail, or die. The American system looks better all the time. When Nixon indulged in his excesses, he was clearly outside of the law (clearly, that is, to everyone except Nixon). Park's repression, on the other hand, is within Korean law. Park's repression *is* the law.

Last weekend (March 19-21) I went to Soraksan with the same assortment of characters that went to Suanbo. We took Friday off from work. I needed it: I was ready to crack up. It was my first trip out to the East Coast.

Soraksan is incredibly beautiful. Although most popular in the fall when the leaves change color, the stark beauty of the bare mountainsides covered with patches of snow and ice, the frozen waterfalls, and the grey rock cliffs looming in the sky like some Martian landscape were fascinating. To top it off, there were very few people there besides ourselves, in marked contrast to the fall when the place looks like downtown Seoul.

Each of the three days we climbed, and each day the path was more sheer and more impossible than the day before.

On March 4th I went to Pusan to see the trial of the American there. By now I was an old hand at domestic air travel and Pusan traffic patterns. Mr. Chung who had helped me the first time was out of town, so Mr. Yun Sun-won acted as my right-hand man. When it appeared that the trial would again be delayed (it had already been delayed twice) for lack of an interpreter, I intervened with Miss Knight's assistance and supplied Mr. Yun as interpreter. We had opposed the idea of the Embassy providing an interpreter, but since I had come to Pusan for the sole purpose of witnessing a trial I was not about to let anything stop it.

As my previous Pusan excursion had been my first trip to prison, so this was my first time to court, a dingy room with a hundred seedy-looking defendants in padded blue prison clothes sitting in front of the three judges, who were flanked by the prosecutor and defense attorneys. The spectators stood along the walls, divided from the prisoners by wooden blockades and seedy-looking policemen, and looking only slightly less seedy than everybody else.

The fact that I stood in the back of the room and consequently heard little of what was said (and it was usually in Korean anyway) left me with only a vague grasp of what was going on. I still heard enough to know that if the court bought the American's story, then the judges were crazier than the American claimed to be. The trial was inconclusive, because the American's attorney wanted to call another witness. So ended my day in court. And the trial has not yet finished.

Afterwards I visited the American in prison again for forty minutes (brief by my previous standards). Then, since I still had time until my flight to Seoul, Mr. Yun took me on a drive around Pusan to see the sights.

April 5, 1976 Monday

Currently I am in a very good mood, perhaps as an aftermath of April Fool's Day. Miss Knight and Joe Oldman put together my Officer Evaluation Report which described my work in the Consular Section in dazzling terms and which included a recommendation from the Consul General that I be promoted to FSO-7 at the earliest opportunity.

This was another one of those three-day weekends, with the Koreans celebrating Arbor Day as a national holiday so everybody can go out and plant trees. On Sunday and Monday, I went to Makoksa with three of my students. We took the train and bus down, and the bus back. In many ways, this was the most satisfying of all my excursions so far, for much the same reason that I enjoyed Suanbo so much.

Makoksa is a fairly large Buddhist temple complex off the beaten path. In fact, the road leading up to it was such an ordeal that I expected to be sick from the bus ride. Rather than a *yogwan* or hotel, we stayed at a small temple up in the hills.

The *sunim* who ran the place (a *sunim* being a Buddhist monk or nun) was very friendly and quite human, in spite of her drab grey clothes and her shaved head. Some *sunim* I have run across previously have not felt kindly toward foreigners. Besides this resident *sunim*, the cast of characters in this Inn of the Seventh Happiness also included a few other *sunim* (whose heads were also shaved) who drifted through, a little nine-year-old orphan girl living there who expects to grow up and become a *sunim* while remaining the cutest child I have seen in the meantime, and several college students studying there.

Apparently it is common for college students (particularly law students) who have trouble passing their graduation exams to go off to the middle of nowhere for a year to study. One student, a twenty-eight-year-old law student, had failed his exam to become a judge. (As I found out from my trips to Pusan, the legal hierarchy in Korea runs from defense attorney through prosecutor down to judge, just the opposite of our system.) Another student there who was a third year student at Hongik University explained that he had come for the clean air because of his health problem, whereupon he gave me a coughing demonstration to indicate tuberculosis – and this after I had had twenty-four hours of contact with him.

Although the guys expressed every interest in meeting us, my students held back and wanted nothing to do with them. Both groups used the Korean analogy of wolves to rabbits to explain the relations between men and women in this situation, so I guess that explains why the girls backed off. It seemed that their reticence would prevent me from having any contact with the guys. We were at first blatantly rude when they tried to start a conversation.

Eventually, I dumped my students and wandered off late Sunday night with these guys to a campfire on the bank of a stream. We sat there for a couple of hours, eating pork (I pray to God it was cooked well enough) and singing John Denver songs (my TB friend played the guitar). They also interrogated me on American foreign policy.

Overhead every star in the sky which struggles for only the barest visibility in Seoul or Detroit glowed fiercely, a multitude which I had not seen for many years.

At last, we adjourned to one of the student's rooms where, in the intimacy of a shared blanket on the *ondol* floor, we continued the conversation until 5:00 a.m.

I got up at 7:30 a.m. And again at 9:30 a.m. Oh did my head hurt. And my stomach. And my body.

May 10, 1976 Monday

Happy belated Buddha's Birthday, which fell on the 6th. Buddha's Birthday has only become a holiday in the last couple of years. The Buddhists complained that Christmas has been a holiday for years. It's one of the two Korean holidays the Embassy does *not* take off, the other being Children's Day, which falls on May 5th. Senator Proxmire thinks we take too many days off. Since everyone in Korea assumed the Embassy was closed (just like every place else) nobody came in to bother us. Buddha was so offended that we worked that half the Americans in the office came down with the flu and three Americans living in Korea have dropped dead since May 1st. Keeps me busy.

The night of the Birthday, I went to see the big Buddhist parade, as Seoul's main temple is near my house. It looked like a Nazi rally, with hundreds of monks and nuns in their grey robes and shaved heads carrying candle lanterns decorated with Buddhist swastikas. It's also one of only three days in the year (Christmas and New Year's too) without curfew.

Notes from Lower Volta

This past weekend I took a trip by myself. (It's always wise to be out of town on weekends, as Americans rarely die during working hours, preferring instead Saturday morning at 2:00 a.m. or Sunday morning at 3:00 a.m.)

Anyway, I wanted to go by myself first to build up my confidence in my ability to get around and second to have a chance to meet people. If I travel with other Americans or my students, no one else comes near me, and I have no need to use my Korean. By myself I have to speak Korean or give up, and people figure I'm fair game for their attention.

To make things simple I went back to Makoksa, because I knew the way there already.

I'm proud to say that my Korean has reached a level to get me on buses, get me food, and show me the john. I also know enough of the language to cover all the topics which Koreans think important:

"Where are you going?"

"When did you come to Korea?"

"When will you go to America?"

"Are you married?"

"Do you have a girlfriend?"

"How old are you?"

"What is your job?"

"Do you think American women are more beautiful than Korean women?" (Actually, I know too much Korean when it comes to that last question.)

I also discovered that no one is more helpful to a foreign traveler than the frumpy vendor women in the bus stations who sell Coke, eggs, and cookies on the buses before they pull out of the station. I was sitting on one bus bound for Kongju when a vendor asked me where I was going. She declared the bus people were crazy to route me that way, dragged me bodily off the bus, changed my ticket, and put me on a direct bus to Makoksa.

The students I had met on my previous trip were not at the temple, and I was never able to determine if they were gone permanently or only temporarily. But the place had students coming out of the woodwork. For some reason they did not seem as interested in getting to know the fabled American (apparently my exploits had been often told) as my previous friends. I think that their very limited English probably caused that.

I met one guy, Chong Chin-ho, who was so enthusiastic that he sealed our friendship with a traditional sharing of a drink of *makgeolli*, a milky rice wine, and even suggested we sleep together. He dropped that idea before I discovered what it entailed.

The two Buddhist nuns, one middle-aged who ran the place and one very old and toothless, remembered me, and told me I must come again. The old one was amazed at how little food I ate, but the standard temple fare of rice, rice, and more rice did not suit me.

May 16, 1976 Sunday

Oh my God! I've gone to Makoksa a third time! This time I didn't even know it was my destination. We were on an overnight Royal Asiatic Society tour to Kyeryongsan, which is the site of the original planned Yi Dynasty capital and the site of several bizarre religious sects, including some which have mixed Christianity and Buddhism.

In all my months in Korea, I had avoided the monthly air raid drill. No more. Yesterday we were tooling down the Seoul-Pusan freeway when at 11:30 everybody pulled off. No sirens or anything, it's just that the North always attacks at 11:30 on the 15th of the month. I didn't even know the drill was held in the countryside, or that it is ever held on the weekend (generally they delay it until the following week).

Later in the day I almost started a real war. We were walking up a temple pathway which, like every other temple pathway in Korea, is lined with souvenir shops selling a ridiculous assortment of tacky knickknacks. When someone suggested buying one of their gaudy towels, I quickly replied, "Only if it has swastikas on it," without realizing that the German Ambassador was next to me. (The swastika is a common, well-meaning Buddhist symbol.)

We spent the night in Kongju, not one of your most exciting metropolises, as indicated by the fact we could find only one *makgeolli* house, and even they sold it to drink at home.

Today it was back to Makoksa, where I have spent more time than any other place in Korea except Seoul. I quickly dumped the RAS group and headed up to my own temple, whose route I could now find blindfolded. Chin-ho was there, and the other students who had been there last weekend, and also Yi Yong-kwan, who was one of those I met the first time but who had gone to Kongju last weekend. While RAS toured the temple, we had some songs and then some *makgeolli*.

May 21, 1976 Friday

This past week has kept me busy. On Tuesday night I went to a Korean production of *Godspell* at Ewha University. I had seen *Godspell* in English at the Fisher Theater in Detroit three years ago. At the time I was appalled by the religious fervor of it all. But this time, since I understood barely a word which was spoken, it was much more enjoyable.

On Wednesday night Joyce popped over with some of her male Yonsei University students (nine, to be exact) to visit with my seven students. My Ewha beauties had previously asked me to introduce them to some eligible bachelors (as if I know any). Everyone seemed to enjoy the evening (I certainly enjoyed it), including a round of charades. When we made suggestions for future get-togethers my students backed off. After they left, one of the guys commented that even if they were Ewha girls they were not pretty enough to be overly particular.

On Monday night I went to a dinner hosted by the Ministry of Foreign Affairs for Miss Knight, who is leaving the end of next week. There were five Americans, including Joe Oldman, Molly Newman, and Liz Ramsey; and five Koreans, including Mr. Lee, Mr. Yun, and *three* Mr. Parks.

I talked to one Mr. Park who is in charge of Korean passports. When he heard that I was in charge of American passports, he asked what our passport rejection rate was. When it finally dawned on me what he was talking about, I informed him (without overplaying such dangerous concepts as individual freedom and the right to travel) that anyone with $15 and proof of American citizenship could have a passport. The idea floored him, and that was the last mention of passports all evening.

June 4, 1976 Friday

One year ago yesterday as I sat in my slum apartment at 8650 Agnes in Detroit I got the call from the Department of State which resulted in my sitting today in my Compound 2 apartment in Seoul. What a strange year this has been.

The other night I stopped all conversation at a party the Beckers were holding in honor of their daughter Cathy's high school graduation. I casually commented that exactly six years earlier I myself had finished high school. That remark certainly aged some of the older officers, who have been out of high school longer than I've been out of the womb.

Last weekend I hit Ewha University's May Carnival. My students had indicated they would take me around, but they fizzled out. So instead Joyce got me into a lot of the events, since she is Ewha staff. The carnival showed a lot of interesting things about Korea, both old and new. The traditional costumes, dances, songs, and games always fascinate me. The modern Korean coed is a carbon-copy of the prim misses who graced American campuses about 1958, from the long flowery dresses to the obsolete hairdos to the white lace gloves.

I went to the carnival on three separate days: the first in jeans, then the second in a sport jacket, and finally the third in a suit and tie. The first two days, people ignored me. Once I showed up all dressed up I became the center of attention, with all the giggly Ewha girls vying for a chance to practice their English. Clothes make the man, as they say.

Last night I went out to a *makgeolli* house with Joyce's Yonsei guys, who speak English very well. They satisfactorily proved that point when they demonstrated their ability both to tell and to understand dirty jokes. The object of the evening was their request that I teach them English, which I shied away from both because the thought of taking on nine students appalls me and because I don't feel competent to teach English at their level.

My job goes on. My latest crisis involves an American citizen who was born Korean, married an American, went to the States, had her husband's four children, and then apparently developed mental problems. Her husband in his infinite wisdom shipped her off to Korea, because he thought that being with her own family would be beneficial. She has spent the last year largely destitute, only marginally supported by her Korean brothers (who certainly have little money and are unequipped to handle a woman with severe emotional problems) and not supported at all by her husband (who we occasionally cable with the suggestion that he remove his wife back to the States).

Yesterday she appeared in my office, abandoned by her husband, her brothers, and the local missionaries who have helped her somewhat. We spent most of the day desperately begging someone (anyone!) to take her for even one night and sending off another cable to her husband: "Korean authorities refuse to allow your wife to remain in Korea. Failure to depart may result in imprisonment."

At 5:00 p.m. she was settled for the night. At 6:00 p.m. I got a call from the Embassy Duty Officer. She had returned to the Embassy. I advised him to make one last contact with her brothers; if that failed, call the Korean police and have her removed from the Embassy. I also pointed out (truthfully) that I would not be home later. (Hint: Don't call me.) He did not call me again. But as late as 11:00 p.m. the lady was still drifting in and out of the Embassy. The Duty Officer was still busily calling every Consul he could think of and still getting the same advice I gave him hours later. The crisis passed when our unwanted visitor wandered off. We have not heard from her since.

Today we sent a cable to the Department asking them to intervene with the deadbeat husband. One colleague's suggestion was a cable to the husband every hour marked NIGHT ACTION IMMEDIATE (meaning, "take care of it now!") with the simple message: "Good God, man, this is the mother of your children!"

It may be a long weekend, and a long week.

July 3, 1976 Saturday

Life goes on, becoming increasingly busy, possibly because of the summer, possibly because I know more people now.

I've marked my first anniversary in the Foreign Service. Without overstatement, this past year has provided me with the most excitement, the most fun, and the most work of all my years. All things considered, I am satisfied with the job and confident that I perform as a consul at least on a par equal to my fellow officers.

Always there remains in the back of my mind the thought: Is this where I want to be ten years from now? Will I reach 1986 and regret that I've spent my time in the Foreign Service and thereby closed off all my other avenues? I hope not.

And I have drawn another Congressman's blast. So many have clobbered me that I have lost count, but I think this is Number Five (actually Number Five Blast, from Number Four Congressman, as Gary Brown of Michigan, my Michigan, has grilled me over two different matters).

I have been charged with refusing to see a woman who had her baby in her arms for a report of birth interview, an absurd accusation. The trouble with the passport office is not that people do not get to see the Consul, but that *anyone* gets to see the Consul. In this particular case the Congressman had previously expressed interest and the woman had been instructed to ask for me by name.

The cable I wrote (and which went out unchanged) stated: "It is unlikely, given the background of the case, that this happened." I was surprised that my boss did not tone the reply down, as he has in the past. He is fed up with the Embassy and will shortly return to Washington on a new assignment. He reached his breaking point the day after Francis Meloy, the U.S. Ambassador to Lebanon, was murdered. (The *smallness* of the Foreign Service becomes obvious in such circumstances. Any given officer whose name pops up is almost certainly known by someone at the Embassy.)

We had a routine deportation case. An American who twice previously the Koreans had deported got a new visa though a Korean consul's mistake in Hong Kong and returned to the country. Once the Koreans realized their mistake they took prompt steps to rectify it. They put him on a plane back to Hong Kong, even before he had time to talk to an American consul. (Would that American Immigration were so efficient!)

A routine deportation to be sure, except that rumor had it that the American worked for ABC. All of a sudden we were concerned, and quickly dispatched an IMMEDIATE cable to our consulate in Hong Kong. When Ambassador Sneider found out, he hit the roof and told my boss if this (namely, the delay in intervening in a deportation) ever happened again he would fire him. The question is, what did the Ambassador expect us to do? The answer is that the Ambassador, too, was a friend of Ambassador Meloy's.

The day was topped off when the grade school behind the Embassy burned down. All we needed was one spark to drift over to us.

We have a new Consul General, Stu Kennedy, who has come via Washington, Athens, and Saigon. Miss Knight has gone to Manila. Theoretically the Consular Section will soon expand to fill the entire second floor of the Embassy. The current Consular Section has been a temporary design for several years.

The Korean government acts in two ways: stupidly, and viciously. The paper-pushing stereotype of the American bureaucracy is a puff of smoke next to the jagged bulk of its Korean counterpart.

The worst excesses of the Nixon administration are farcical charades next to the appalling willingness of this government to flaunt its own laws to keep its citizens in line.

I will give one example of the Korean government's stupidity and one example of its viciousness. From personal experience these are not isolated incidents. Nothing in all my life has caused me to appreciate the American system of government, the principles of America, the American constitution, more than living in the Republic of Korea.

Stupid: An American divorcing his Korean wife here in Korea comes to the Embassy at the direction of the Ministry of Justice to obtain a Certificate of Non-American Citizenship and a Certificate of Non-American Residence for his wife. How should I know whether she's an American citizen, or whether she's ever been to the States? I sent him back to the Ministry with the suggestion that they check with their own Immigration Bureau to see if the woman has ever left Korea, much less gone to the States.

Vicious: The Korean government wants to control the ability of Korean nationals to leave the country. Therefore, the government is uneasy when confronted with a wealthy businessman married to an American woman with two American citizen children. How can they control the businessman if they have no control over the family?

The solution is simple: Force the parents to renounce the American citizenship of the children on the flimsy ground that only Korean nationals can inherit property in Korea, and the children cannot obtain Korean documentation (namely, mention on the father's Family Register) as long as they are Americans. The argument is absurd. It recognizes the ability of children to derive nationality through the *mother*. Korean law states a legitimate child's nationality comes from the *father*.

When the American mother came to the Embassy to renounce the children's citizenship, I quickly took the matter up with my boss.

When we asked if she would return the following week to meet with the Consul General, she said the matter had to be taken care of immediately, that her husband was waiting for her to return with the matter finished, that the family had been brought back from the beach by the authorities for this specific purpose.

Renunciation cannot be accomplished in one day. It must go through the Department of State. There is also the question in this case both of coercion by a foreign government and of the parents' power to take oaths in place of these children, who are only ten and six.

We solved the problem by canceling the children's passports and giving the mother an incredibly verbose statement on Embassy letterhead saying nothing more than that we had received the renunciation applications.

August 14, 1976 Saturday

The rainy season which supposedly occurs in July finally materialized this week.

On Wednesday Joyce returned to the States to study at the University of Wisconsin. Last weekend I had a dinner Friday night for Joyce with the Bookmans and the Suhs from Ewha University. Saturday night a group of us went drinking, including Bok Sae-you, my swimming teacher. We drank *yakjoo*, a rice wine. I don't think I have ever been so drunk. I came home and threw up twice, and Sunday morning I was very unclear on quite a few of the previous evening's details.

July 23rd my Ewha students gave me a birthday party. I think they realized I'm in the mood to dump them so they couldn't wait until my actual birthday next week before taking some preventative action. It was kind of a fun party, with more Koreans than Americans present. We ended up playing bilingual charades.

Where have I gone traveling? We - Joyce, Erwin Lee (a Korean-American also teaching at Ewha) and I – hit Songnisan, which is halfway to the South Coast. We almost didn't make it out of Seoul: we arrived at the bus station at 10:00 a.m., but the tickets were sold out until 12:15. We proceeded to spend a small fortune (I spent more money in the following two hours than I spent the rest of that weekend) running around Seoul buying last minute items. And we almost missed the bus.

When we got to Cheongju, we faced the same problem of no bus available. So we hired a taxi to drive us the eighty kilometers to Songnisan for $10. You know you've been in Korea too long when you can ride in a Korean taxi and not flinch at the way they drive. We arrived at Songnisan in record time and proceeded to check out the restaurants, beer halls, and (oh yes) the temple. The following day we returned to Seoul aboard a bus whose conductress would not allow us to open the windows. That would imply that the air conditioning, which was pumping 88-degree F air onto us, was not working properly.

We also went to Kangwha Island, northwest of Seoul almost all the way to North Korea. Erwin's long hair and Korean appearance look suspicious to all the fascists on freedom's frontier. Every time the bus stopped at a roadblock, the police invariably asked for his ID card. They were suitably baffled when he presented an alien's residence certificate instead.

Once we got to Kangwha, Erwin was dragged into the police station for no very clear reason. Joyce and I marched in after him. We all threw our IDs on the table. Well, I dropped mine, but Joyce and Erwin thought I threw it down intentionally, so they followed suit. The police became indecisive once they realized we were all (in particular, Erwin) Americans. They satisfied themselves with copying down all the vital information in our IDs. (They examined the back pages of Joyce's passport as if it were some important state document, especially the part about not bringing fruits or vegetables back to the States with you.)

It has taken me almost all of the past year to build up a circle of friends here. Already some of the Americans have left and returned to the States. Next year I will also. Is this what I will spend the rest of my life doing, meeting friends and then losing them?

Notes from Lower Volta

September 8, 1976 Wednesday

On August 18th the North Koreans murdered two American officers in the Joint Security (?) Area of Panmunjom. Both the North and South and the American forces went on military alert. The Deputy Ambassador (the Ambassador was in the States) ordered all Embassy gatherings canceled for forty-eight hours. For the first time since I've been here armed guards were posted at the housing compound. No one could enter without presenting identification.

On Saturday the 21st the UN forces cut down the tree which the North Koreans had not allowed the Americans to trim on Wednesday. Rumor has it that if the North had interfered with the tree-cutting, we would have had a war. That would have interfered with my birthday party planned for that night.

The major casualty of the whole thing was a reading of *The Devil and Daniel Webster*, which some of us had planned for the evening of the 19th. Since we had invited one hundred guests, we were stuck with fifteen ice cream pies, a case of cheap champagne, and a birthday cake for me large enough for a hundred people which read "Hapy Birtday, Bill Dufy." We've rescheduled the play for September 16th.

I invited twenty-four people to my birthday party, one for each year. It's amazing how simple a dinner for twenty-four people becomes when you can hire an extra maid and a bartender.

Lim Soong-jae, a former student of Joyce's and a zealot of the English language, took me to Myongdong Cathedral for Mass. Catholicism in Korea is both a religion and a political statement. It plays a somewhat similar role in Korea as Catholicism in Ireland did in opposition to the English. I was impressed by the complete participation of the congregation in the service.

Labor Day weekend I went to Cheju Island with Erwin and his brother Dennis, who is visiting from the States.

Cheju-city on the north side of the island was an absolute tourist trap; Sogipo on the south side was great fun.

Theoretically Cheju is subtropical; the extent of its

subtropicality is indicated by the fact that when we ordered orange juice for breakfast they brought us Tang. Cheju is not Hawaii, but it is quite a welcome relief from Seoul. The staff at the hotel we stayed at in Sogipo (the Honeymoon House) provided exceptional service, even to the point of accompanying us to the docks and negotiating our way onto a fishing boat for sightseeing. The view of Mt. Halla, the highest point in South Korea, was spectacular.

Saturday and Sunday we traveled around the island by taxi. Although we had been specifically warned against the taxis, the drivers' persistence wore down our resistance. We talked them down to driving us for W2,000 apiece each day with a Japanese tourist we picked up on the way paying W4,000 each day.

Saturday was fine. We covered the west end of the island, saw spectacular beaches, caves, and waterfalls, and arrived in Sogipo.

Sunday's tour provided no satisfaction. The driver obviously wanted to dump us as soon as possible. When asked if we would see the famed women divers of Cheju, he said there they were – and pointed to some women sitting on the beach. We forswore further taxi service and resorted to buses.

I think that one of my fondest memories of Korea will be bouncing down narrow country roads aboard a bus, the wind blowing in my hair and twangy Korean pop music playing over the loudspeaker.

I have dumped my Ewha students, who haven't learned a word of English in the past year. I told them I just did not have enough time, which was quite true. If I'm going to spend my time teaching English, I intend to have students who seriously want to learn the language.

Somehow my attempt to disengage from English has backfired. I now have more students than ever: Park Mi-ju and Chin Mi-kyung visit me as many as three times a week; Kim Mi (who I thought was *my* Korean teacher), Kim Sang-sik, and Choe Wuan harass me once in a while (their English is at best underdeveloped); and now Lim Soong-jae has talked me into another group of five students (including him) who are all fairly proficient at the world's most popular language. At least from Soong-jae I extracted the concession that once a month they must take me on a weekend trip into the countryside.

October 21, 1976 Thursday
    I have been to Kyongju (twice), to Haeinsa, to Inchon, to Namisam near Chuncheon. I have been around.

    My mother left today after a two-and-a-half week visit. Her airfare cost only $300 round-trip, because she went back as an orphan escort. The adoption agencies need responsible adults to accompany the infants and children going to the United States for adoption by Americans. Each flight may have up to a hundred orphans and a handful of escorts. So the agencies give people a cut-rate roundtrip fare to Korea to pay them.

    I went to Kyongju in September with Erwin and his brother Dennis in a car put at our disposal for the weekend by the President of Ewha. Kyongju is noted for cheap hotels and hotel rooms which all look alike and Western-style toilets which don't flush. It's also the repository of most of Korean history.

    For some reason we got up to catch the sunrise at Sokkuram over the East Sea (along with 30,000 chattering middle school students). According to Koreans, it is the most beautiful sunrise in the world. It's a sunrise like any other sunrise.

    The second time (last weekend) I went with my mother, the Bookmans, and Jay's boss, the Mitchums. This time we stayed in the best tourist hotel in downtown Kyongju, whose service improved because the hotel staff labored under the mistaken notion that Mitchum was the American Ambassador.

    We asked the manager for the best *kalbi* house in town (*kalbi* being one of the two best Korean dishes). We wound up in a shack in an alley off the main street with billows of smoke pouring out of the barbecue buckets sitting in the middle of the rickety tables. The place was filled with hard-drinking (*soju*) working men who looked like extras out of a movie about the Rape of China. But the food was excellent.

The diplomatic incident of the trip came when we inadvertently walked all over Historic Landmark #1, the abalone-shaped Posok-chang through which the ancient Silla kings floated glasses of wine to their courtiers 1,500 years ago. The guard quickly chased us off after we had undoubtedly confirmed his worst impressions of Americans' insensitivity.

Kyongju has historic sites scattered over a fairly large area, as indicated by Mitchum's remark when we were making our 38th stop of the day: "If this is 4:00 o'clock, this must be National Treasure #18."

My mother's visit almost turned into a disaster. Three consecutive trips I tried to put us on fell through either because they were canceled or because we couldn't get hotel rooms.

To round out her perfect visit, the trigger-happy soldiers around the Blue House (where President Park lives) decided to fire on a Northwest cargo plane the evening of October 14th. For all we knew, the war had finally come or Park was on the same way out as he had come in, in 1961.

We were treated to two separate displays of fireworks overhead in the space of half an hour and shrapnel falling into the housing compound. About thirty people were hurt in Seoul and one died. I can hardly wait for the day when the idiots actually hit a plane and it crashes in downtown Seoul in a blaze of glory and kills hundreds of people.

The Embassy informed the Korean government that we don't care to be bombarded for no good reason. To top it off, the plane under attack was so far out of range that it didn't even know what had happened until it arrived in Tokyo.

October 25, 1976 Monday

I think my mother came looking for a rest. I practically killed her dragging her from one palace to another, from royal tombs to

Buddhist temples, from Historic Landmark #33 to National Treasure #441½. I doubt she'll be back.

I made a bargain with Lim Soong-jae and his friends that, in exchange for allowing them to visit me once a week to speak English (no big deal, since I generally speak English anyway, although my command of the language has started to crumble under the pressure of prolonged absence from the United States), they would take me on a trip once a month.

They almost killed me on the first try on October 1st, Armed Forces Day, with a bicycle trip "up towards the Demilitarized Zone." Well, the trip was not quite towards the Demilitarized Zone. It was all the way *to* the Demilitarized Zone, as I found out thirty miles and three hours later when we reached Freedom Bridge. I really must drill them on prepositions.

But my achievement was only half finished. We then pedaled our rented two speeds (SLOW and STOP) back to Seoul. I prayed, I begged, I cried for death. Worst of all, I could not act exhausted, because the girls kept on trucking without a care in the world. I hesitate to ask what they have planned next.

I had the honor this past weekend to be invited to the One Hundred Day's Celebration of Kim Sang-sik's daughter. Although I now know a rather wide circle of Koreans, this was the first time one invited me to his house. Kim Sang-sik's house, in spite of all its black lacquerware, was quite Westernized.

Since the One Hundred Day's Celebration after the birth is very important, I was very happy to be included. My anthropological instincts were not completely satisfied, as I (together with the other non-family guests) was kept in a separate room. The highlight of the evening occurred when Kim Sang-sik, quite drunk and exceptionally sentimental, persisted in holding my hand all the way to the taxi stop, while I counted to 258 and reminisced about all the bizarre food (especially the raw fish and octopus) I had eaten.

William J. Duffy

November 14, 1976 Sunday

I spent an interesting weekend boozing to excess with Kim Sang-sik and his friends. We started Friday night at 8:00 p.m. Sang-sik insisted that I spend the night at his house, even though it was a twenty-minute taxi ride from where we were and we were only ten minutes by foot from my place.

Apparently having a guest spend the night in one's house is both an honor for him (to invite me) and for me (to be invited). I suppose I may have committed some *faux pas* the last time I visited Sang-sik's house and refused the offer to stay over. I assumed it was related only to the problem of midnight curfew.

We resumed drinking at 4:00 p.m. Saturday afternoon, if only to warm ourselves from the freezing rain which fell all day. We eventually wound up in a sleazy place called the Young Il Motel (I won't mention why) for the night.

Somewhere in the course of the night 30,000 won ($60) disappeared from my wallet. God only knows how. I would have doubted I even had the money with me except I remembered distinctly checking it at our last beer stop. I finally arrived home at noontime and promptly slept for three hours. It was a drunk unequaled since college days.

The Hancocks hosted a big Halloween party October 30th. I didn't have the vaguest idea what costume to wear, but finally decided to build an outfit around the tacky Levi jacket I got for my birthday which has a map of Korea embroidered on the back. To that I added beat-up blue jeans, sunglasses, and my hair slicked straight back with Crisco vegetable shortening. To achieve complete authenticity, I shaved off my twenty-three-month old mustache. No one in Korea had ever seen me without a mustache, so that plus the shades kept them guessing my identity.

November 25, 1976 Thursday

Another American Thanksgiving, shared as are all holidays with people I scarcely know and occasionally scarcely wish to know.

Notes from Lower Volta

It sometimes wearies me to have to meet new people daily, to guess whether I will ever see them again and therefore whether I should bother to remember their names. On the other hand, it saddens me to think of my friends, of the people I truly want to be with and from whom I will part within another year.

Making friends is a difficult enough process, especially for someone such as myself, without having to start all over every two years. Many Foreign Service Officers seem to keep their long-distance friendships intact over a long period of time. I doubt that I can. I have never managed it in the past and am unlikely to do it in the future.

I am now working in non-immigrant visas, which, in a country such as Korea, is an exquisite pain. Since so many Koreans wish to emigrate to the United States and since only so many can emigrate under the quota, many think a non-immigrant visa is the next best way to go (and stay). In American passports, decisions were usually black and white. There was no question about the right answer. But in non-immigrant visas, everything depends on the Consul's judgment. Flipping a coin might be a more productive method.

Two weekends ago I went to Naksansa on the East Coast near Soraksan with Lim Soong-jae, Kim Young-bok, Park Mi-ju, Hong Chee-hee, and Song Chin-o. This trip left me only slightly less exhausted than our previous expedition to the Demilitarized Zone in October. Naksansa is on the sea. I only seem to visit the beach in the depths of winter.

The only other people around were fishermen and soldiers. Access to the beach is restricted because a strip of sand about twenty feet wide was swept clean to prevent North Korean saboteurs from slipping in during the night without leaving a trace. There were only a few narrow paths through the strip. Who knows, maybe the strip was mined?

We met one soldier whom I democratically ignored on account of his presumed fascist tendencies. My political conceits and my supposed ability with the Korean language received humbling shocks when my compatriots informed me at the end of the conversation (which passed my ears undeciphered) that he, too, was a Yonsei student drafted into the army two years earlier and sent to this bleak outpost because of his participation in an anti-government demonstration.

We stayed at the beach resort of Mr. Kim, a respected elder of the local community. He showed his affection for me (because I was an American) by plying me with Korean wine and various American-made black market items, and his affection for Miss Song (because of some undetermined quality) by referring to her with the endearing, if suggestive, term of *yobo*.

As with virtually all journeys, the visit to Naksansa almost ended in catastrophe. We arrived enroute back to Seoul in Kangneung at 5:00 p.m. Sunday. Kangneung is four hours by bus from Seoul, assuming of course that bus tickets are available. Sunday evening is an inopportune time to purchase express bus tickets. They frequently sell out, as they had on this occasion. The local bus would never reach Seoul before curfew. We had only one apparent alternative, catching the train at 7:00 p.m., which would arrive in Seoul at 5:00 a.m. And the train had no heat. A chilling prospect.

So we took a taxi. For a mere $40 we completed a trans-peninsular journey on the historic level of Lindbergh's transatlantic crossing or the first transcontinental railroad. Prying six of us and one driver into a Korean taxi was by itself an achievement I will not soon forget.

Or the moment when the taxi died on the highway in the mountains. Suddenly everything became quiet and the darkness of the night set in. Even with the seven of us, the highway was a lonely place. But fortunately the engine turned over and we took off.

Notes from Lower Volta

1977

January 1, 1977 Saturday

December exhausted me as have few months in memory. I welcome the end of the holidays. I scarcely concealed my glee when I put my sister Margaret on an airplane enroute to Hong Kong today on her way back to the States.

Frightening to think that another year has passed and all the events of my life have been contained within the covers of this book. This past year has left me with many happy memories of new friendships formed, of new places visited, of new things learned.

It's ironic that I am more worn out after two weeks of leave than after a regular work schedule. At least, though, I was in Japan for the week preceding Christmas and consequently missed most of the parties here.

Theoretically the Japan trip provided rest and recreation. In some places (such as Seoul) the U.S. Government thinks you deserve a vacation somewhere else with transportation at government expense. Curiously the government has designated Tokyo as our R&R center. Considering Tokyo's nature, that is a contradiction in terms.

I managed to mesh my R&R with Margaret's proposed grand excursion to the Far East. A week together in Japan, and then a week together in Korea. Perhaps one week too long together.

My trip to Japan was my first out of Korea since my arrival here sixteen months ago. I did not realize until I made it how necessary the trip was to my sanity.

January 3, 1977 Monday

We spent the weekend of December 18-19 in Tokyo, in the Ginza. To an American arriving from San Francisco, Tokyo may look like East Asia; to me arriving from Seoul, Tokyo looked like the United States: the bustling streets, the traffic jams of expensive cars, the fantastic displays of neon lights, the American fast food restaurant chains. There is no comparison between Tokyo and Seoul, except one which is unequivocally unfavorable to the latter.

At my insistence, Margaret and I spent most of the weekend consuming Big Mac hamburgers at MacDonald's, singing Dixieland music over a plausibly convincing pizza at Shakey's Pizza Parlor (where the walls contained such traditional Japanese thoughts as "The bank doesn't make pizza and we don't cash checks"), or toasting mugs of beer and wolfing down authentic frankfurters at a European beer hall. I loved it. For a taste of authentic Japan, we spent four days in Kyoto (getting there by bullet train).

The exceptional quality of the inn we stayed at in Kyoto justified the entire expense of the trip to Japan. The Bookmans had recommended the Three Sisters Inn because other Americans spoke highly of it. It is truly a hotel like no other, accommodating only thirty guests in Japanese style. That bare description falls short.

The inn is an old farmhouse in a setting reminiscent of Teahouse of the August Moon. The three sisters, with the assistance of some young people, run the place themselves, and that includes personally preparing the meals and flagging down taxis for departing guests. The Japanese lived up to their reputation for politeness; the staff of the Three Sisters carried it to an ecstatic extreme.

When we weren't basking in the services provided by the inn, we did sightsee. Margaret seemed more impressed by Buddhist temples and Shinto shrines than I. I've spent over a year looking at my share. There's not a great deal of difference between Japanese and Korean temples. Well, except that Korean Buddhists paint their temples in gaudy colors and Japanese Buddhists leave theirs plain wood. But the architecture is the same.

We became familiar with the Kyoto trolley system, which certainly helped when one conductor changed route number signs after we got on and turned down a track which we recognized as decidedly not in the direction of our hotel.

We also visited Nara, an even more ancient capital of Japan than Kyoto. We saw the sacred deer of Nara. All the travel brochures claim they have been tamed for a thousand years. The tour guide recommended buying little packages of crackers to feed them. (Since we had not yet stopped for lunch and they resembled graham crackers, I only refrained with difficulty from eating them.) The tour guide assured us that as December is a slow tourist season, the deer would give us their undivided attention. Slow tourist season seems also to mean less food. These crazed killer deer almost made mincemeat of Margaret when she wasn't quick enough in doling out the crumbs. Enough said.

We regretted leaving Japan. We would have stayed longer except the three sisters told us they had given our room away (an incredible lack of foresight on their part). So on Christmas Eve we flew to Korea.

After my weeklong exposure to the Japanese, I did not care to see the Koreans again. My newfound distaste for Korea and things Korean (never in fifteen months had I been down on Korea) only increased when we encountered the usual less-than-friendly welcome offered everyone (native and foreigner alike) at Kimpo Airport.

I waved my diplomatic passport and Korea diplomatic ID around as if I were the Ambassador. I did it successfully, slipping us past all the hurdles on our way into freedom's frontier. My efforts reached their climax when I haughtily informed the Customs Inspector that I refused to open *Margaret's* bags because *I* was a diplomat. He, flustered at nearly causing a diplomatic incident, waved us through without realizing the ground I stood on was quicksand.

My hatred for Korea crystallized when we reached the taxi stand in front of the airport and, for the first time in my experience, customers outnumbered taxis. I was crushed. Fighting for a Korean taxi takes a special kind of energy, a unique bloodlust which I rarely have and which I definitely lacked on Christmas Eve.

So I hated Korea. Worst of all, my last act before I began my vacation was to tell the Department of State how eager I was to study Korean in an intensive course and stay here an extra two years (i.e., the end of the decade). Although the odds of the Department saying yes are almost a hundred to one, it seemed at that moment that my chances of remaining imprisoned here were overwhelming.

Then a miracle happened. A taxi driver pulled up who insisted, over the protests of all the waiting Koreans, that he would take the Americans. Once we were safely ensconced in his cab, he put on an eight-track tape of junky Korean music, the kind which brings back memories of careening down narrow mountain roads on hot summer days in aged buses where everyone but yourself is bound to market. I knew I was home.

We had arranged our schedule to arrive back in Korea Christmas Eve so we could attend the Open House the Sneiders had at the residence. As it turned out, we spent only a little more than an hour at the residence before proceeding to Myongdong Cathedral for Midnight Mass.

As Christmas Eve is one of the few nights without curfew, the streets of the Myongdong district were overrun with drunks enjoying an unusual taste of freedom in an atmosphere most nearly resembling an American New Year's Eve.

We arrived too late for the start of Mass. All the seats in the cathedral had long since been taken. But since we were foreigners, the ushers insisted upon seating us, even if it meant (as it did) that we had to sit in the sanctuary.

The Mass, presided over by Cardinal Kim, was dazzling, fed by an unending flow of chanted singing from the large congregation. The exquisite beauty of the choir's Christmas carols made me wish that I could believe the idea behind the art. People of such faith deserve better than the Koreans have.

January 14, 1977 Friday

Our schedule of activities threatened to keep Margaret from ever getting outside the American compound: the Christmas Eve reception at the Ambassador's residence, Christmas Day dinner at Molly Newman's, a Boxing Day open house at Mary Alice McClelland's and dinner at the Bookmans, and a New Year's Dinner at Liz Ramsey's. If nothing else, Margaret had the opportunity to compare the different ways people managed to decorate the same apartment floor plan.

Christmas dinner at Molly's was the highlight of the holidays, a delicious meal shared with people to whom I feel closer than to my blood relatives.

We plunged into local Korean color, vigorously. Unfortunately, the Korean people (my own friends and complete strangers) chose to show their worst characteristics to us, with the result that Margaret left with a confirmed dislike for the country.

The centerpiece of it all was a trip to Soraksan. I thought it best to give my sister during her short visit exposure to the beauty of the countryside. In true Korean fashion everything went wrong. To mention that the trip to Soraksan, which is five hours under optimal conditions, took twenty-four hours gives a sense of the dimensions of the disaster. Nor was it a natural disaster. This disaster centered on Lim Soong-jae.

Soong-jae, I thought, would dazzle Margaret with his brilliance. Instead he confounded her with his stupidity. After telling Kim Jong-uk and Park Yong-ju to rendezvous at my house at 8:00 a.m. to begin the trip, he decided on his own it was too cold and assumed we had abandoned the trip. He did not bother to confirm this with anyone else. So at 11:00 a.m. he strolled in to give me a Christmas present and to meet my sister, totally unprepared for any trip more arduous than a cross-town bus ride.

When at last he collected his things and we arrived at the bus station (around noontime) the tickets were sold out until 3:30. If I were a Korean, I would know that custom dictates that everyone goes home to the country at New Year's and therefore the buses are busy. It never occurred to any of my friends. By then I was ready to abandon the trip, but Soong-jae looked so distraught at the thought of not using the $2.50 tickets he had bought that we had no choice but to persevere.

William J. Duffy

The bus ride was straight out of Dr. Zhivago: the coldest Korean winter in fifty years, the windows frosted to opaqueness, the bus reeking ever so obviously of kimchi and sweat. We arrived in Kangneung on the East Coast at 7:30 p.m., too late to push on the extra hour to Soraksan. So we spent the night in Kangneung and arrived (by taxi) at Soraksan at noon the next day.

Thus our planned two-night stay had been cut to one, leaving us with little more time than enough to take the cable car up the mountain and visit a nearby temple. We arrived back in Kangneung the next day in plenty of time to catch the return bus (two hours early). Both Margaret and I were ready to do bodily harm to Soong-jae, the final straw breaking the camel's back when it turned out he had put us on a bus leaving twenty minutes later than he said. (I could see the headlines in the *Korea Times*: "U.S. diplomat murders Korean national in Kangneung bus station assisted by crazed sister.")

As a good part of the trip involved discussions between Margaret and Soong-jae about human rights (or the lack thereof) in Korea, I eagerly anticipated Margaret's reaction to the military inspection of the bus when we entered Seoul. She did not disappoint me. When Soong-jae questioned the strange expression on her face, I explained, "She's just glad you live in a free country."

New Year's Eve we went to a Korean restaurant with the Bookmans, the Lapeers, the Millers, and Liz Ramsey. After dinner we went to hear them ring the old city bell, the Korean equivalent of New York's Times Square. I've read that this particular bell in the old days was rung when the city gates were opened in the morning and closed at night. Hard to believe. We finally heard a dull "plunk plunk" when our watches said midnight and decided that was it.

There was a large crowd waiting with us to hear the bell (this was, after all, East Asia's answer to Guy Lombardo) and we for some idiotic reason stationed ourselves near a group of candle lamp-carrying Buddhists chanting beautiful (though probably anti-Christian) verses. The longer we stood, the thicker the crowd got, the angrier the police got (maybe they resented the political implications of a night without curfew), and the tenser the atmosphere got.

When one brainless Buddhist held her lantern in such a fashion that the candle set the whole thing on fire, I quickly stamped it out ("quick thinking" Jo Bookman called it, but I think "self-preservation" is a better term) and we, having had enough, departed. Happy New Year.

January 17, 1977 Monday

I have received my first promotion in the Foreign Service. One down and six to go. Frankly I deserved it, if for no other reason than the eight months spent in the passport section. My satisfaction dimmed somewhat, however, when I saw from the whole promotion list that almost everyone who started with me in June 1975 got promotions also. Well, it means an extra $1,500 a year, $13,478 altogether.

January 19, 1977 Wednesday

January, the usual month of post-holiday listlessness, has this year already produced more than its share of surprises. First came my promotion. Then today I learned (although a friend let it slip unofficially last night) that incredibly the Department of State has agreed to my request for language training at Yonsei University. My initial reaction of excitement quickly gave way to dismay with the realization that this will keep me in Korea until 1980, eight months of language training followed by a second two-year tour.

The Department, I thought, could have at least argued the point a bit without giving in so enthusiastically and confining my future career to one Foreign Service post out of over a hundred. But then the alternative to remaining in Korea is *not* remaining in Korea. Given the choice, I prefer the former alternative.

American friends expectedly are dismayed by my stupidity, although they recognize my fondness for the country. Surprisingly Korean friends express surprise that I want to stay because I have left them with a strong impression that I dislike Korea (the government yes, the country no).

In order to begin studying at Yonsei in September, I will go on home leave this summer. (Paradoxically, by staying in Korea longer I get to go home sooner.)

Personnel also has decided to move me April 1st (April Fool's Day) to the Ambassador's office, where I will be general lackey in charge of nothing. It also means weekends shot to hell because of Saturday mornings wasted at the Embassy. I'm not looking forward to the assignment. It is one of those things which look good in a personnel folder. Since I'm going to the States in the summer, it will only last a few months.

March 19, 1977 Friday

The United States at last has a new President. President Carter's actions since his inauguration have provided a welcome contrast to the Nixon-Ford years. I feared that once he reached the White House the Georgia populist would quickly forget all the things he said on the campaign trail, but instead he has gone out of his way to repeat them.

The inauguration was magnificent, highlighted by the singing of *The Battle Hymn of the Republic*. Such a contrast to the pious patriotism of the Nixon spectacles in 1969 and 1973. From the comments of my Korean friends (and I assume this is probably true in all countries with a democratic tradition slightly less developed than our own) the change of administration was beneficial – even necessary – to highlight the glory of the American system at its best. The Koreans marvel at the fact that, when the time to change power came, there were no bullets, no riots, no bombs, no murders – only a handshake between the two Presidents.

The Koreans have realized with a touch of panic that President Carter's talk about troop withdrawals is more than campaign rhetoric. It will be interesting to watch this country for the next three years, even if it includes a swing to anti-Americanism. The opposition party (which often appears more pro-government than Park) even staged a demonstration at the Embassy last Saturday against the proposed withdrawals, a kind of "Yankee, go home" in reverse.

Koreans have started making the argument that Americans caused the division of Korea, so America is responsible for Korea's defense. I point out that America is first responsible for the fact Korea is not still a Japanese colony and also for the fact South Korea is not communist.

The last few months have produced little excitement. We mounted one expedition to Haeinsa (which we visited last October and sought to return to under slightly less mob conditions). The trip was originally scheduled for George Washington's Birthday's weekend, until we realized in dismay it was also lunar New Year weekend, when everyone travels. We postponed Haeinsa a week, enjoyed it immensely, and almost conquered Mt. Gaya (except that time ran short and we had to head back to Seoul).

I attended Yonsei University's graduation in February. God only knows why Korean universities insist on holding such affairs in the middle of winter on what is invariably the windiest day of the year. Some schools (such as Yonsei) hold these things outside, which is unbearable. Others (such as Ewha) hold them inside. Inasmuch as large buildings such as auditoriums are not commonly heated, the difference between inside and outside is imperceptible.

With graduation the Yonsei guys have disappeared either into the army or into business. The soldiers are out in the country being trained; Korean businessmen work until 8:00 or 9:00 p.m. Consequently, I rarely see any of them. Least of all I see Lim Soong-jae.

On top of the Soraksan debacle in December, he orchestrated an outing to see the new version of *King Kong* (which the Korean censors managed to cut). He told one person to arrive at my house at 9:00 a.m. and a second at 10:00 a.m. He didn't bother to inform me of either appointment, so the first arrival turned me out of bed. Soong-jae himself appeared at 11:00 a.m., by which time my temper had simmered for two hours. In my most precise English I informed him that he either gets to my house on time or not bother coming. He has not been back.

March 20, 1977 Sunday

John sent me a newspaper article on the KCIA. When you live surrounded by secret police your awareness of them sinks to a subconscious level. The KCIA is everywhere, each agent dressed in a dark blue suit, tieless, in white shirt with the collar hanging over the suitcoat lapel. No one ever hears of the KCIA doing anything against the North. I suspect that they deal exclusively with terrorizing the South and Korean-Americans.

My friends joke about the KCIA in my home (even though we assume they listen in). In public their willingness to discuss controversial political subjects diminishes. Criticism of the government to a foreigner is illegal. Under Emergency Measure #9 introduced in the spring of 1975 (shortly after the fall of Vietnam), the law at any given moment reads the way the President wants it to read.

The hand of the KCIA lies heaviest on the college campuses. Park well remembers that the students alone brought down the previous government in 1960. A common estimate says every classroom contains at least one KCIA informer to keep tabs on both students and teachers.

Occasionally the faculties are purged of the more outspoken elements. In the last major purge in the fall of 1975, only President Kim of Ewha refused to fire the professors the government ordered her to. She successfully defied them on the strength of her own position. More usual are reports of students disciplined and expelled for "poor academic records." Perhaps. Whether or not they're drafted into the army and sent to the front, they can never get into another school and never find a job.

Strangest of all, most Koreans don't seem concerned. They argue that the threat from the North is too great, that in pursuit of the country's impressive economic development some freedoms must be sacrificed. In fact, though, the country is becoming less free. The press prints and the television reports what it is told, the movies are censored, every record album includes one *kunga* ("Soldier's Song") and the *Saemaul* movement (the "New Village" movement, which when most harmless resembled a rural development program straight out of the New Deal 1930s) has become transmogrified into the *Saemaum* movement, the "New Thought" movement.

I imagine this country today bears a great resemblance to Germany in the 1930s: a people willing to give up what little freedom they had so long as the regime produces an economy strong enough to provide them with cameras, televisions, and stereos. Only troublemakers have to worry about the KCIA. Only the Americans have time to worry about luxuries like human rights. South Korea looks good only in comparison to what lies thirty miles north.

April 24, 1977 Sunday
This month's report from the Ambassador's Staff Aide:
Dr. Loris, who serves as the State Department's Regional Language Officer based in Tokyo, visited Korea this past week. Personnel decided to have him test my Korean to give an indication of where I stood. So last Wednesday he and I went out to Yonsei University for the test. God forbid, I thought, that anyone I know should see me being chauffeured in an Embassy car! Loris supervised the oral exam given by Dr. Park of the Korean Language Institute.

Exceeding everyone's expectations (including my own), I scored a two in speaking on a scale of five. Now a two is not by itself all that dazzling, and in connection with a European language it has little significance. But a two in Korean represents a level rarely achieved by foreigners. It lets me end the language probation period which has hung over my head.

Suddenly I face the tantalizing prospect that, if I do well enough in my eight months at Yonsei, I will become one of the very few Korean language experts the Department has. I have taken an almost irreversible step toward becoming a Korea hand. The

Department would have neither the desire nor ability to leave me in the Consular Section. Much as I enjoy consular work, I have no ambition to spend the rest of my Korean career mired on the second floor.

Work moves along. The past few weeks have been busy, with the Ambassador recently returned from the United States conducting a series of meetings with the top Korean leadership and with a visit two weeks ago by a group of American congressmen. What I have seen of American congressmen in my brief career has not produced a favorable impression of either their capabilities or their ethics.

The major issues continue to focus on human rights and the troop withdrawal (drawdown, reduction, whatever). The United States insists that no connection exists between the phase-out of American ground forces and the lack of human rights in Korea, but no one (including us) believes our statements except President Park.

This spring the students and opposition are more active than they have been for a couple of years, apparently because of President Carter's emphasis on morality. For that matter, the police and KCIA are also more active, although they apparently are acting less heavy-handedly than they did previously. From the States the papers are talking about "mass arrests," with the clear implication that anyone who talked with the Congressional delegation while it was here has been rounded up. The opposition has attacked Ambassador Sneider as insensitive to human rights and several American papers have suggested he should be replaced.

Now that I work in the Ambassador's office and read virtually all incoming and outgoing cable traffic, I have seen all the Ambassador's reports on his recent meetings with the President, the Prime Minister, and the KCIA Director. I know that, whatever the past history, neither the Ambassador nor the American government is insensitive to the Korean opposition. The Ambassador has made the American position clear. It seems probable that if the Park regime fails to liberalize shortly, President Carter will attack it publicly.

Notes from Lower Volta

April 30, 1977 Saturday

When we don't receive immediate action cables concerning human rights, we do get them on the alleged illegal activities of the Korean government in the United States. The Koreans until now have been satisfied to block our every move. It has fallen to the Ambassador to point out to them that continued obstruction will only boomerang in the future to their discredit. We don't ask them to implicate Korean officials. We are only interested in catching the Americans involved.

Work in the front office, while it involves few activities on my part with practical results for the Embassy, has been an eye-opener for me. I have seen the summit and am appalled by the discovery that the future of the United States, Korea, and presumably all other countries rests in the hands of men possessing only a little more experience and not much more competence than myself.

Curious fringe benefits attach themselves to my job: the spy novel routines of driving out in a chauffeur-driven Embassy car with a sealed envelope marked "Eyes Only" for a general who happens to be out golfing, or riding shotgun in the Ambassador's Cadillac with flags flying as we speed to a helicopter pad after which I will safely return the classified cables he is reading in the back seat to the Embassy for destruction.

I have finally seen my first Korean masked dance. For some reason masked dances have a way of getting canceled by the government shortly before starting, so I was pleasantly surprised a few weekends ago when Kim Mi and Lee Kyu-sok took me to one at Yonsei. What a surprise! None of this stately, flowing court dancing I have grown accustomed to, or even the colorful farmer's dances. The grotesque costuming, the crouching movements, and the flurried exchange of opinions between dancers and spectators through the chants remind one more of African tribal rituals than any sedate East Asian spiritualism. No wonder the government fears so much that the excitement and frenzy of a masked dance might turn into an anti-government demonstration.

Paranoia pervades the nation, and it has even begun to affect me. A week ago I went to a *pansori* presentation with Erwin. *Pansori*, as far as I can make out, is a series of old songs sung a capella (with only a minor drum accompaniment), perhaps similar to the ancient telling of the Homeric epics. It lacks any interesting features.

I had my photograph taken three times. By the same photographer. This particular photographer exhibited an excessive interest in the audience, in contrast to his apparent indifference to the performance. In fact, on those few occasions when he did take picture of the stage, he did not bother to use his flash attachment. Now in the past I would have been flattered to be the object of so much attention, especially considering that he used a telephoto when shooting me. I have developed a nagging belief that his photos never made it into the papers but presumably adorn my undoubtedly thick KCIA file.

May 6, 1977 Friday

One might expect that two years' residence in a country would reduce the number of daily new discoveries and surprises. Perhaps Korea forms an exception to the rule. Perhaps all countries continue to surprise foreigners even after a prolonged residence.

Last Sunday I experienced one of the more unusual trips in my Korean adventures, an expedition to Kangwha Island. I have been to Kangwha twice previously. It lies only a one-hour bus ride northwest of Seoul.

Consequently, a day-long picnic with Park Mi-ju, Hong Jee-hee, Chin Mi-kyong, and Im Bong-jin seemed to present no insurmountable difficulties. We assembled at the Kangwha bus station together with the other six million Seoulites planning to spend the day on the island.

They packed them into the buses like sardines, so that a bystander on one side of the bus would be unable to see through the crowd to the other. It being Sunday, and Sunday being the only day I have off (completely), it was raining. For the third Sunday in a row after six weekdays of beautiful sunshine, and after I had made the rash comment to assorted Embassy personnel that one more sunless Sunday would produce my resignation from the Foreign Service on the Ambassador's desk on Monday.

We decided to try for a taxi. Bong-jin wandered off to make arrangements and quickly returned with the welcome news that he had found one for the incredible sum of only 2,000 won. So off into the rain we drove, bypassing the Kangwha road which I had previously traveled and instead getting on the Seoul-Inchon Expressway. Interesting, I thought, I've never gone this way before. "Is this the road to Kangwha?" I asked. The four knowledgeable natives quickly reassured the ignorant foreigner that of course the driver knew better than us.

As we pulled off the expressway at its end and the driver turned to us to ask, "Where are you going in Inchon?" I had reason to believe my suspicion that Koreans know less about their country than anyone. The price of that discovery, according to the driver, would run an extra 9,000 won to finish the trip. Our wallets decided on an afternoon in Inchon, a fairly cheerless city whose major redeeming feature is a quick train back to Seoul.

We repaired to Wolmido amusement park, which looked like a poorly planned and inadequately financed Coney Island abandoned since 1957 to the ravages of time and weather. As the tide was out, we hiked across a causeway to an island about half a mile offshore. There we picnicked as comfortably as possible in the ramshackle restaurant so typical of those found throughout Korea at the end of every hiking path.

The rain could not conceal the fact that the tide was coming in. Scarcely had we begun considering a return to the mainland when we discovered that, in fact, the tide *was* in and we were on an island. Panicked inquiries to the establishment's proprietor (her position has no English equivalent, as her duties range from head chef to scullery maid) brought the response that there was a boat available. When pressed, she pointed to a very insubstantial-looking twelve-foot motorboat tossing in the waves and quickly taking on water from the rain. A mere five hundred won from each of us purchased our passage back to *terra firma*. Five hundred won and all the water we could bail out. So ended another chapter in Duffy's Never-ending Adventures.

June 3, 1977 Friday

Under Secretary of State Philip Habib and Chairman of the Joint Chiefs of Staff General George Brown have come and gone to begin consultations with the Koreans on troop withdrawals. Nobody seems to understand the professed American reasons for withdrawal, including those who state them. The Koreans are unanimous in their disapproval with an attitude of "We'll play along but after the North overruns us just remember whose fault it is." Apparent disagreement between the Administration and the military (notably General Singlaub) only complicates the issue.

I know the reasons I wish we would give for the withdrawal, namely, human rights and the Park dictatorship. But from President Carter on down U.S. officials have bent over backwards to make clear that those issues have no connection to it.

The Ambassador gave a reception for Habib and Brown on Thursday, May 26th, with about two hundred guests. The Koreans criticized even that because the guest list included "convicted criminals," such as Yun Po-sun, Korea's only living ex-President, whose crime was to speak against Park. He escaped imprisonment only because the government felt that putting an eighty-year-old statesman in jail might not look good overseas.

The visit also brought about the first major demonstrations since my arrival, one by several hundred (thousand?) Christians against the withdrawals and one by members of the small Democratic Unification Party after their convention. Theirs followed the first by only an hour or so and quickly degenerated into an anti-government clash with police, resulting in two busloads of bloodied demonstrators getting carted off. My one desire was to be home in the United

States so I could catch the whole thing on the network news and understand what was going on.

Speaking of major events, Mary Alice McClelland, Roz Fisher, and I gave a farewell party billed as a South Pacific Happening May 21st for the Hancocks, who have returned to Washington. The idea was to have the season's first major outdoor affair with roast pigs, exotic sweet potatoes, and an unequaled punch made largely of rum, wine, and natural fruit juices cut only by ice which took three days to ferment.

Unfortunately, the weather on the occasion was extremely South Pacific, akin to a monsoon near Antarctica. We shivered though cocktails outside (although the punch had a miraculously warming effect) before retreating to the Embassy Theater for a sit-down dinner. We justly deserved recognition for our logistical feat of seating sixty guests in the theater without adding a second building. Somehow roast pigs don't look as good in the flesh as they do in the cookbooks. Frankly the plateful of heads was revolting (although I suggested they might have made unusual centerpieces) and we abandoned our plans for their public display.

At 4:00 p.m. the party teetered on collapse; at 6:00 p.m. when the guests began to arrive I thought it had collapsed; by 7:00 p.m. when the punch had begun to work its effect (the Deputy Ambassador asked for some to add to his car) the party was being hailed as the event of the season. And well it might: expenses ran a little higher than we had expected, eventually reaching a total of $500. Lucky I get overtime.

Undiplomatic Memories (Korea)
June 6, 1977 - September 14, 1979

Notes from Lower Volta

June 6, 1977 Monday

Am I fated forever to trips through the Korean countryside which teeter on the edge of disaster? We returned yesterday from an overnight trip to Chongpyong, which lies about two hours east of Seoul on the road to Chunchon: Park Mi-ju, Im Hee-ok, Song Jin-oh, Jim Mi-kyong, Chong Im-young, and Lee Yong-gun. Lee Yong-gun studies Chinese at Kyunghee University and was recently brought into our merry group by Hong Jee-hee. Im Bong-jin planned to come also but for some as yet unexplained reason backed out on the morning of departure. Yong-gun went ahead of us to rent a "bungalow" (which appears to be one of those words the Koreans have lifted out of our language and made curiously their own) since the rest of us could not depart Seoul until mid-afternoon.

It was a good day for a trip out of the city: sunshine, a cool breeze, and hordes of Koreans trying to take advantage of a three-day weekend. The bus roared along the two-lane highway at varying rates of excessive speed, slowing down to tailgate a truck spewing black smoke and carrying a load of lumber fastened none too securely and speeding up to pass another bus whose driver was determined not to be passed until we were well into a blind curve.

In short, the ride was uneventful, until our bus broke down. The engine had offered us subtle hints that its mechanical efficiency was in decline by various coughs and wheezes. Finally, at one stop where I could see nothing but rice fields and mountains (who would get off there?), the engine ignored the prodding of the bus driver and shut itself down.

The busgirl assured us that more buses would pass shortly. "Shortly" in the context of Korean history could involve the rise and fall of a dynasty. The location was quite scenic and it was, after all, a nice day. Only Yong-gun, who was expecting our arrival at any moment in Chongpyon, was likely to be concerned at our delay. I felt a certain amount of unease, however, when the next bus arrived with passengers already packed into it like sardines into a can. Our busgirl, somewhat frantic to get rid of her own passengers, managed to wedge a few more on.

With some relief Mi-ju and I entered into negotiations with a taxi driver headed toward Seoul who appeared shortly. He wanted 5,000 won to cart us the remaining distance. We pointed out that a driver back in Seoul had offered to drive us the whole distance for only 6,000 won, and we offered 4,000 won for the distance which remained. The negotiations collapsed. After equally fruitless bargaining with some other bus riders, the cabby drove on towards Seoul.

A while later a second bus arrived, sagging under the immense weight of its passengers who were (incredibly) even more tightly packed than their predecessors. Nevertheless, the busgirl began to push more on and we, feeling that it was a situation of now or never, joined the crush.

As I stood poised to get on, afraid of missing the bus and even more fearful of making it, I spotted an empty taxi approaching from the direction of Seoul. Rushing toward it with as great a show of nonchalance as our present straits allowed, I almost gagged to discover it to be the same driver we had spoken to only twenty minutes before. But now I was ready to pay his price, any price. He, on the other hand, apparently unsuccessful at any attempts in the meantime to locate a fare, came down to our price. So we reached agreement for 4,000 won and the six of us piled in.

The cabby, while no smarter perhaps than most, quickly changed his mind when he discovered four more passengers than he thought he had bargained for and, faced with the prospect of all sorts of dire legal consequences for carrying more than the legal number (five) of passengers, ordered us out. We persisted to no avail and were saved only by the miraculous intercession of our busgirl who, fairly ecstatic at the prospect of unloading six of us from her care at once, did not intend to let this golden opportunity slip past.

At last we got underway, keeping our eyes open at all times for policemen or soldiers. As we approached a military checkpoint on a bridge, we unloaded Jin-oh and Hee-ok before driving past the checkpoint and waited for them further down the road. Curiously, we waited within sight of the checkpoint, which seemed not to bother either our driver or, for that matter, the soldiers, who presumably could count all of us as we hopped back in.

The charade proved less than necessary, as Yong-gun awaited us at the bungalow he had found only a short distance further down the road.

We immediately began dinner, which meant (typically) that after many false starts and intermediate uncertainties we sat down several hours later to a meal of such simplicity that I am still unable to fathom why it took more than ten minutes. The food was quite spicy, perhaps the hottest I have tasted in Korea. In fact, each meal left such a sand-blasted feeling in my mouth that it did not occur to me to brush my teeth. In true Korean fashion I ate it without any accompanying liquid to douse the fire.

Dinner stretched into coffee; coffee into conversation; and the conversation into a singing performance by Yong-gun and me which concluded at four in the morning. Already the first dim indications of dawn were appearing.

We took a walk down a country road between the shadowed figures of dark green mountains whose peaks were wrapped in the morning fog. In the quiet we heard only the distant barking of a dog and the curious sound of a woodpecker hammering; in the pre-dawn dark we saw only the campfire in the valley below of others who had also passed the night without sleep. We returned to the bungalow and crashed.

June 26, 1977 Sunday

I am getting excited about home leave, so excited I hardly pay attention to my work and instead sit around planning itineraries and poring over atlases. Last week I even went home and left my safe open, with classified materials "up to and including Secret." The Ambassador was not pleased.

Work does have its interesting points, including the most

William J. Duffy

recent press report that the United States bugged the Blue House, President Park's residence, in 1975 either from the Embassy itself or perhaps from the Housing Compound (maybe my apartment).

I've had a reconciliation with Lim Soong-jae, who called up a week ago having finished his four months of military training in Chinhae. He came over, we got a few people together, and spent an impromptu afternoon in Inchon's Songdo Resort.

I have bought a 1974 Honda Civic from a departing U.S. Army Captain. It's the same model and silver color as Liz and Roz have, so we have to remember where we each park our cars. Now that I have a car, I've discovered a wonderful mobility which allows us to get out of the city on weekends, so far to Inchon and to Chunchon. Of course, I miss the bizarre local color of country buses and faded blue taxis.

Chris Dombrowski mentioned in a recent letter that she never knew whether I liked Korea or not. I love it. The culture fascinates me. Every day I encounter something new and different. On the other hand, I develop a different perspective on our own culture. Two years is not long enough to learn about this country properly, so I will stay. Also I have my friends. On the purely personal level, I have become too close to some of them to leave Korea *now* (and of course learning the language will keep me coming back).

This Foreign Service business of packing up every two years and moving to another continent bothers me. People need roots. The Foreign Service itself becomes an extended family. The Americans I have met here these last two years will continue to pop in and out of my life for a long time to come. Already I have friends scattering to Europe, Asia, Africa. The warmth of holidays shared only with friends and even with strangers exceeds by far that of some spent with blood family. But my Korean friends I will see only in Korea.

I have not, however, gone native. I appreciate Korean culture and even admire many of its aspects. But it is not my culture. Always being the outsider, though, does not bother me. I always felt something of an outsider even in America.

I'm afraid that my anthropological instincts are such that I don't hesitate to use my friends for cultural study. In the next few years, I will watch them in the process of finishing school, entering the military, getting married, beginning their careers, and starting their families.

July 9, 1977 Saturday

Two Saturdays ago I attended Lee Yong-gun's engagement ceremony, which made for an interesting afternoon. I probably would have understood better what was going on if I had arrived on time rather than fifteen minutes late, causing myself considerable embarrassment making a rather conspicuous entrance into the hushed room and confirming the forty assembled Koreans in their most recent anti-American prejudices.

There were some remarks, an exchange of rings, some more remarks, followed by a long and labored Chinese lunch during which the young man to my left attempted English conversation on the subject of Blue House bugging and ex-KCIA directors who had absconded to the United States, and finally some impromptu entertainment provided in the form of songs by the two fiancées, her younger sister, and his friends.

Afterwards we (namely Yong-gun and a few of his friends) returned to a club for a few beers to await his fiancée while she underwent the intricate process of removing *hanbok*, the Korean dress. Then we went to my house, where the whole day nearly ended in disaster. Yong-gun rashly suggested showing the slides from our Chongpyon trip. As each picture flashed on the wall with Yong-gun in assorted poses with strange girls, the fiancée's temperature rose visibly and her contributions to the conversation dropped off.

July 10, 1977 Sunday

My only previous experience with Korean wedding customs had been the marriage ceremony of Bok Sae-yul, the swimming pool life guard, in a wedding hall last December. His was an arranged marriage. Up until that very day he still referred to his bride as "Miss Cho."

The men sat on one side and the women on the other, continuing their less than whispered conversations right through the strained piano chords of the "Wedding March," the remarks of the presiding VIP, and the exchange of vows. The audience, in short, paid the proceedings less attention than they do their televisions.

July 17, 1977 Sunday

My long-standing acquaintance with Park Mi-ju and Song Jin-oh seems to have come to an end as the result of a trip to Sokumgang on the East Coast two weeks ago. Eight went: four guys and four girls. The four girls objected because the four guys wandered off Saturday night to drink *soju* (a vile Korean whiskey concocted from industrial waste apparently) without inviting them along. To this initial complaint they added a whole list of tribulations before packing up and heading back to Seoul at noontime Sunday by bus, leaving us to enjoy the scenic wonders of Sokumgang in silence.

I thought the matter had been smoothed over at our next Wednesday meeting when we apologized "unconditionally" (the lingering effects of the *soju* was proof enough that the gods were punishing me for my behavior). After a brief lull, the ladies opened fire on Lim Soong-jae in Korean (Im Bong-jin and Lee Yong-gun, cowards that they were, had failed to show) with the recapitulation of their lamentations.

Their continued complaints after accepting our apologies and their use of Korean which I could follow only with difficulty and to which I could not respond angered me, until I shouted that if they intended to continue discussion of the matter to get out of my house. Out they got and as of yet have not returned.

Sokumgang is one hour and seventeen miles by unpaved road from Kangneung on the coast. I thought that buying a car had freed me from the scourge of Korean taxis. Not so. I drove to the East

Coast with the four girls, where we met the three guys who came by bus.

They then negotiated with a taxi driver to guide us to Sokumgang. Everyone else assured us it took two hours over a bad road. He assured us it took one hour and the road was not particularly bad. I should have realized that an unpaved Korean road is inherently bad, but I scarcely had time for thought as I attempted to keep pace with the taxi's suicidal speed as it wound its way around curves, carts, and children.

The reason he drove so fast, as was later explained, was that he wanted to be far enough ahead of me so that I did not have to drive in his dust cloud. As darkness fell, the road began to climb and to twist and turn even more.

When we drove out the next afternoon, I was appalled to see the way the road barely clung to the mountainside. Since I could not drive the car down the middle of the road (there was a ridge of dirt which continually scraped the car bottom with ominous grinding sounds), I had frequently to come quite close to the cliff's edge and a quick exit from the Sokumgang "expressway." It was probably fortunate that I first drove the road in the dark, or else I would have been too upset to continue.

The girls rode with me to the coast and the guys took the bus; on the way home the girls took the bus and the guys took the Honda. It undoubtedly made for some interesting comments at Kyongpodae, the beach near Kangneung. I stopped there both Saturday and Sunday and walked along the boardwalk, each time with a different set of Koreans in tow.

August 2, 1977 Tuesday

This is Honolulu. The rhythmic sound of the surf rises from eleven floors below; the cool ocean breeze fills my room. I sit here sunburned, filling a dozen postcards with witty descriptions of my Hawaiian adventures – or rather, non-adventures, as so far I've managed only one walking tour of downtown Honolulu recommended for its historical value when in fact it only served to lure the unwary into the heart of the shopping district; and one hydrofoil boat ride to another island which had to be canceled when none of the boats worked.

And yet here I am for the first time in twenty-three months in the United States. So far no culture shock, but perhaps I must wait until I return to more familiar neighborhoods before I see the changes of the past years.

August 3, 1977 Wednesday

Today I rented a car to drive around the island of Oahu, which turned out to be much less green and lush than expected. Perhaps Hawaii is having a drought. At any rate, Korea in the summertime is a more attractive place.

I really haven't enjoyed my visit much, partly because I'm traveling alone but even more because I've failed to put my time here to good use.

I expected to spend hours getting this diary up to date or studying my Chinese characters. I have done little of either. One would expect that my first return to the United States in two years and probably my only trip home before 1980 would generate some introspection. Curiously I have none.

There was a time when these pages were filled with little else besides ruminations on my feelings and thoughts. But then those were days I was decidedly discontented with my life; perhaps my general satisfaction with my life the last two years has dulled both my ability and my willingness to self-analyze.

I've talked to Mother, Joan, John, and Chris Dombrowski on the phone. To me it doesn't seem so long since last we talked, but they sounded as if I were an unexpected ghost.

August 15, 1977 Monday

I have arrived in Detroit via San Francisco, Los Angeles, Phoenix, Flagstaff, the Grand Canyon, and Chicago.

Notes from Lower Volta

August 16, 1977 Tuesday

Of all my flights so far, the Chicago-Detroit segment turned out to be the worst. The flight was delayed two hours because of maintenance problems, followed by an exceptionally long wait at the baggage claim in Detroit.

Seeing old faces has been great, Chris Dombrowski, Joyce Ott, Jane O'Connor, and Don O'Shea. I've experienced only the most minor twinges of culture shock. Basically the United States seems to have remained pretty much as I remember it. Minor changes: the new cars, the skateboard craze, the television shows. But beyond that, it feels almost as if I were returning from only a brief trip overseas rather than two years in Korea.

September 14, 1977 Wednesday

I have hardly kept as careful a record of my home leave as desired. Now I am enroute once again from the United States, caught in that twilight zone of whether this is Tuesday afternoon (as in the United States) or Wednesday morning (as in East Asia). I have opted to switch back to Korean time with the hope that I will more easily overcome the jet lag. On my last trip out I remained on American time until reaching Tokyo and arrived exhausted. I am, in fact, on the same flight as two years ago: Pan American's #1 Around the World.

Here is a statistical tally of my trip.

Four countries passed through: Korea, Japan, Canada (8/17), and the United States.

Sixteen cities visited: Seoul, Tokyo, Honolulu (7/31-8/4), San Francisco (8/4-8/9, 9/9-9/13), Los Angeles (8/9), Phoenix (8/10), Flagstaff (8/10-8/12), with trip to Grand Canyon, Chicago (8/12-8/14), Detroit (8/14-8/18), Windsor (8/17), Philadelphia (8/18-8/21), Washington (8/21-8/30), Virginia Beach (8/30-9/2), Milwaukee (9/2-9/7), Seattle (9/7-9/9), and Annapolis.

Fifteen airports visited: Kimpo, Haneda, Honolulu, San Francisco, Los Angeles, Phoenix, Flagstaff, Chicago, Detroit, Philadelphia, Norfolk, Washington National, Milwaukee, Minneapolis-

William J. Duffy

St. Paul, Seattle.
 Eight airlines flown: Northwest Orient (Seoul-Honolulu, Chicago-Detroit, Washington-Seattle), United (Honolulu-San Francisco, Detroit-Philadelphia, Norfolk-Washington), Pacific Southwest (San Francisco-Los Angeles), American (Los Angeles-Phoenix), Frontier (Flagstaff-Phoenix), Trans World (Phoenix-Chicago), Western (Seattle-San Francisco), Pan American (San Francisco-Tokyo).
 I also took the bus from Phoenix to the Grand Canyon and back to Flagstaff; and from Washington to Virginia Beach, changing in Richmond; and traveled by car from Philadelphia to Washington.

September 30, 1977 Friday
 Unwittingly I chose a most appropriate day to arrive back in Seoul, the 15th, with its usual air raid drill. After fighting my way through Customs and Immigration to get out of Japan, I then had to fight my way past the same sort of people to get into Korea. My diplomatic passport and a determined glare helped immeasurably. I then spent some twenty minutes parked on the South Bank of the Han River waiting for the air raid drill to end (the first time in two years it caught me outside), got caught in a traffic jam caused by a fire at Namdaemun market, and had to detour around City Hall because of some sort of civil defense drill. Even as I returned, the Embassy staff continues to change: Molly Newman left the morning I arrived (so we missed each other) and Russ Siebold departed September 28th.
 Things have not all augured well. I arrived on Thursday and woke up the following Tuesday morning with a cold which I have not yet shaken. Chances to use my new $80 tennis racket (which Mother bought and Margaret strung) have been limited, since they are now tearing down our tennis court before building a new one.
 On Monday the 19th I started my Korean training at Yonsei University. (My cold kept me out of class two days the first week.) Classes run from 9:00 a.m. to 3:40 p.m. with an hour lunch break and a few other short breaks. I am the only student in my class, which I prefer because presumably it will force me to learn more. It certainly

allows no time for daydreaming. The instruction involves so much material that I fear less than four hours of study each night at home will end in disaster.

While in the United States I reached a decision that the time had arrived to begin investing in things Koreans. Consequently, in the last two weeks I have spent almost $600 on two small chests, a small *babsang* (dining table), and two bookcases. They, together with my American Express bill from my trip, have depleted my finances.

It has been good to see my Korean friends again. I am impatient with myself because of my inability to understand their language and sincerely hope that my current training will rectify the situation.

As to what I will do once I finish language training, I had a conversation with Mr. Clark, the Political Counselor. He expressed a strong interest in my coming into the Political Section next summer, as I am more familiar with the country than anyone the Department is likely to send out. He also appeared more sympathetic to (and even seemed strongly in favor of) extended language training.

October 10, 1977 Monday

A good deal of my trouble with Korean probably derives from the fact that the school assumes I actually learned everything I've studied the past two years. In fact, until about eight months ago, I worked on the theory that any vocabulary or grammatical constructions too difficult to learn in one cursory reading were unnecessary. Those, of course, are the precise matters the teachers at Yonsei want me to use all the time.

I met one of Lee Yong-gun's friends who happened in the course of conversation to mention that one of his uncles ranks high in the North Korean government. He quickly added that undoubtedly his uncle was not a true believer in communism but only "playing along." I started to make a remark about people who, by playing along for thirty years, maintain the very system they supposedly stand in secret opposition to. It was clear that Yong-gun's friend actually believed what he said.

I've seen this immense ability for self-delusion before, notably last February when I had dinner with Kim Chul, a Korean Foreign Service Officer. He propounded several geopolitical and genetic-sexual theories which seemed to me, at best, bizarre. He believes a man must control his wife and limit sexual activity to only a few times a week. Such a course will produce sons. Failure to control either one's wife or one's sexual appetite will only produce daughters.

After that scintillating bit of wisdom, Kim then informed me that Westerners right back to their Biblical roots and the Soviets back to their nomadic steppe origins are violent and warlike. Koreans, on the other hand, are exceptionally peaceful and gentle people – a rather clever dismissal of 5,000 years of history.

October 25, 1977 Tuesday

Today Yonsei students staged their largest demonstration since, I assume, the imposition of Emergency Measure #9 in May 1975. It began about 12:30 p.m., actively involving several hundred students and drawing many more as spectators. With shouts of "Away with the Yushin constitution" and "Destroy the KCIA" (*Yushin cholpae* and *Jungang jongbobu haechae*) and a few choruses of the Yonsei fight song, the students taunted the first contingent of riot police, who were content to remain by the main gate and hold the rock-throwing students at bay with a few canisters of tear gas.

When reinforcements arrived (namely, armored tear gas trucks and prisoner buses), the police then swept the campus until not even the language school (which is located off to one side) escaped the drifting gas. The sight of unarmed students blindly rushing armor-plated trucks in an attempt to put their gas guns out of commission suggests that the student population is not as quiescent as the government hopes.

Life has picked up. I returned from a weekend trip to Kwangju with Roz Fisher and Yong-gun (a last minute substitution when Liz Ramsey woke up sick Saturday morning) to visit Dave Morton, the local USIS man.

It was my first excursion to the southwestern part of Korea. Although we stayed only overnight and saw very little, I enjoyed the escape from Seoul. Yong-gun was in the curious position of being a Korean who knew less about the region than the foreigner showing him around.

We got ourselves lost in Kwangju twice. "We saw that fire station before," Roz commented at one point. We had been lost the previous time we had seen it, so we were lost again.

More than anything else, I remember the suicidal driving patterns in Chollado. Drivers thought nothing of using the oncoming lane to pass regardless of what was oncoming.

At one point I foolishly assumed it to be safe to follow a bus in passing, only to have the bus suddenly swing back into the right lane and leave me confronted with a semi barreling towards me.

December 2, 1977 Friday

My Korean improves daily. I can sense an immense difference between my capabilities now (especially in reading) and my capabilities three months ago. As always, my great worry remains that, much as I learn, I will reach next May still basically incompetent in the language. My assignment has been definitely set for the Political Section beginning in June, where I will replace Doug McCain. McCain is renowned in Korea as speaking this bizarre language like one of the natives, a tough act to follow. In addition, the job description specifies that, when necessary, I will act as the Ambassador's interpreter. Wonderful.

The week before Christmas I will wander off alone into the countryside for a week (as part of my scheduled training) to practice Korean. I plan to visit the South Coast, which in two years I have not touched upon other than my trips to Pusan.

I completed the move into my new Apartment 12-A, about three weeks ago. It has, of course, the same basic layout as old 13-C, except that now I can study my Chinese characters in front of the fire roaring in the fireplace and, come the warm weather, peruse the world from my balcony. Being on the second floor also affords more privacy.

The move teetered on the point of collapse when it was not entirely clear that the piano would make it up the stairs. The operation took an hour, putting immense strains on the piano, the six workers' strength, and my nerves. When it was over, Mr. Kim from General Services said that, when I leave, they'll take the piano out through the balcony. It was not entirely clear whether he meant to use a crane or just to push it over the edge.

A few weekends ago I went to Pusan with Yong-gun and two of his friends. *Han mata ro malhaesa* (in a word), the trip was a disaster. It started out well, with a late night departure by train followed by the consumption of numerous bottles of beer enroute. We had a five-minute pit stop at Taejon at 2:00 a.m. The train disgorged all its passengers who swamped a small booth for bowls of hot noodles.

From there on the trip went downhill, primarily because one of Yong-gun's friends was a Pusan native. We spent the better part of two days waiting in tearooms for him to make contact with old buddies. Instead of sightseeing, we went bowling. I might as well have stayed in Seoul!

But on the other hand, we met some girls on Saturday night and had a drinking party until curfew.

I was at Yong-gun's throat by the end of it and was selfish enough to demand that (since earlier train tickets were sold out) his buddies pay the difference for my air fare to Seoul. Yong-gun even told Korean Airlines that I was on official business so that they bumped another passenger off the booked flight. The trip had cost me $40, for which I seemed to have gotten only immense amounts of unwanted coffee (and the grotesque Korean variety laden with sugar at that) and lots of wasted time.

Somehow our friendship survived.

Notes from Lower Volta

1978

January 1, 1978 Sunday

The Year of the Horse arrives, when I have not quite gotten used to 1977, or even 1976, for that matter. Of all holidays, New Year's Eve and Day seem the most dreadful, since they insist on emphasizing to an unwelcome degree the rapid passage of time.

January 3, 1978 Tuesday

Not a very good start on recording all the memorable events of this year. I have not, in fact, finished detailing the highlights of the year just past. There was, for instance, the unusual air raid drill December 2nd which exceeded all previous ones in both scope and realism, involving both a daylight and a nighttime exercise. Not content with the wail of a few sirens and the clearing of the streets, the government threw in parachutists, jets sweeping down on the city in a simulated attack, the sounds of exploding bombs, gunfire, a nighttime blackout (and Seoul *is* dark without lights!), and sweeping searchlights. Frankly a bit too much like London 1940 for my taste.

Then there was my week-long excursion into the Korean countryside to practice my Korean. I toured Namweon (site of Korea's famous Chunhyang love story), the port of Yeosu, and the fishing village of Chungmu.

I proved that any foreigner can travel in the country if only he knows English. English speakers popped out of the woodwork at me. I did use Korean (for directions, prices, and ticket information, i.e., the type of Korean I've known for 18 months). But then I had a government-paid opportunity to visit parts of Korea not previously seen, including the Hallyo Sudo ("Inland Waterway") which even in winter is as beautiful as claimed.

I almost choked to death on raw fish in Chungmu, committed my supreme *faux pas* by calling a man "young unmarried miss" (*akashi*) rather than "uncle" (*ajawshi* - whereupon he directed me to the women's bathroom), and almost created an international incident in a Namweon wine house when I expressed little interest in the keeper's daughter (she apparently came as a side dish) and even worse somehow conveyed the impression that I did not intend to pay my bill.

I am now in the last week of my three-week school break which, in addition to my trip, I have spent in the Political Section, working valiantly on the arrangements for the visit this week of a Congressional delegation.

The highlight of the past week was a visit to the Ministry of Foreign Affairs when the Park Tong-sun case was approaching its resolution. Consequently, the newsmen gathered in front of the Ministry were willing to latch onto any foreign-looking individuals as undoubtedly the bearers of some new American proposal. Someday. I'm not so sure I want to finish school and go back to the Embassy to work full-time.

The holidays passed with minor incident. They were, in fact, an extended dud, certainly not measuring up to last year's swirl of activities. Oh well. Next year (or, rather, *this* year) I shall plan more carefully.

April 13, 1978 Thursday

Here I am, ensconced in the plush suite of a Korean *yogwan* in the little town of Noryang on the island of Namhae. I am in the middle of another of my language trips. This time I have sojourned so far at Daedunsan, Yeosu, and here. Tomorrow I will go to Pusan before returning to Seoul. This trip has been more successful than the last. The weather is nicer so more Koreans are running around, and my Korean is clearly improved.

By this stage I should have enough sense to realize that, when a tour book describes a view as "breathtaking," the author invariably means it literally as well as figuratively, namely, that the climb is so steep that the only alternative to frequent rest stops is certain cardiac arrest.

Notes from Lower Volta

Such thoughts did not enter my head as I set out to conquer Daedunsan, not even bothering to take along climbing shoes. I quickly realized my error but refused to retrace my steps for fear of the resulting damage to American prestige. So I reached the famed swinging bridge ("Cloud Bridge") and, very self-satisfied and foot-blistered, made my descent.

Not knowing when to leave well enough alone, I made the mistake of striking up a conversation with two guys in their last camping trip before entering the army. They asked me to climb up again the next day with them and act as their photographer. With my reserve weakened by some beer and with the *yoinsuk* proprietor offering to provide tennis shoes for my tired feet, I agreed. The tennis shoes, though, were so tight that they nearly removed my toenails. On the second ascent we quickly passed Cloud Bridge and went all the way to the peak, a truly breathtaking view.

April 14, 1978 Friday

(Now enroute to Seoul – and home – via the wonderful means of the *Saemaulho* train whose ride is not as smooth as could be hoped for.)

Having abandoned Daedunsan at last, I returned to Taejon. I missed by three minutes the last train to Yeosu for seven hours. In the meantime, I camped out in a *yogwan* where I reveled in the glories of a cold bath and boarded the Yeosu express at 11:30 p.m.

I had forgotten, however, that the meaning of an express train in English and in Korean is quite different. In Korean the only discernible difference between a local and an express is that the express only stops at every *other* station. Consequently, I spent seven more hours sitting and sleeping less than comfortably amidst a group of grandmothers.

When at the crack of dawn, we reached Yeosu, I met my first major disappointment of the expedition. I discovered that the tourist hotel (whose Western food and toilets I craved) was booked solid by a convention. Putting myself at the mercy of a taxi driver with the request that he recommend a good *yogwan*, I wound up on the doorstep of the Namdo Hotel, an exceptionally quaint-looking structure from the outside.

When I finally signed the register that night – some things are done slowly in Korea – the slightly middle-aged proprietress offered herself to me for the night. I, proving beyond a shadow of a doubt that my Korean remains far from perfect, completely misunderstood the question and blandly replied that the inside of the room was too dark to take a picture of us. She was so confused that the whole subject was dropped.

While seeing the sights of Yeosu, I ran into (or rather they ran into me) a group of five male grade school teachers from Cheonju on a holiday because of the anniversary of their school's founding. Their idea of a good time was beer and ping pong (this in the early afternoon). I held my own at both.

In such encounters they (namely the Koreans) are ready to pledge eternal friendship from that moment, with all the attendant favors exchanged back and forth. They invited me to visit their school, and to donate to the school some book providing good information on America.

I got off easy with them. At Daedunsan, the *yoinsuk* proprietor apparently felt so out of touch with his own government that he thought it useful to ask a lowly foreign diplomat to intervene with President Park for the sake of developing the area as a major tourist area.

From Yeosu I traveled to Pusan via the Venus hydrofoil boat, with a day-long stopover at Namhae. Namhae's principal attraction is the recently constructed suspension bridge which connects the island to the mainland. The bridge packs the tourists in by the busloads to have their pictures taken in front of an imitation Golden Gate Bridge and to buy their tacky souvenirs at the horde of souvenir stands.

Considering the relative insignificance of Namhae Island, one may wonder why the Koreans have built such an expensive bridge here. Perhaps a propaganda showpiece for the regime?

Notes from Lower Volta

April 22, 1978 Saturday

There has been quite a furor the last few weeks over whether or not the United States bugged the Blue House. The latest twist came when former Ambassador Porter said yes, indeed, there was surveillance in the 1960s which he ordered stopped. The Korean government, to show its displeasure (in spite of official American denials), encouraged / allowed / ordered "spontaneous" anti-American demonstrations at high schools and various organizations (old folks' groups, war veterans). The whole thing was so patently staged (and the choreography was rather weak) that the effect was more humorous than anything else.

Considering the distinct historical importance in this country of college student demonstrations (the 1960 Student Uprising), it was rather pathetic to see the government so afraid of its college students that it dared not let them loose even in government-controlled demonstrations. Instead it relied on their younger brothers and sisters in the high schools to march out onto their athletic field in military precision drills to shout anti-American slogans (sounds like North Korea!).

The only major college "demonstration" was accomplished at Seoul National University by four pro-government student leaders marching onto the platform during military training and unfurling anti-American banners in front of 1,600 students just long enough to get their pictures taken for the evening news.

There is, in fact, less anti-Americanism in this country than in Alabama. There have been reports of Peace Corps Volunteers beaten up in Pusan. From my own prejudiced viewpoint, I'm inclined to think such incidents are more against the people involved than against the United States. I spent the week traveling hither and yon when anti-American demonstrations were "sweeping" the country. Although I was obviously an American and freely admitted my connection to the Embassy, the subject of wiretapping never came up unless I raised it. Then the reaction bordered on: "What do you expect?"

Dr. Loris, the Regional Language Officer from Tokyo, paid a

visit at the end of March and tested my Korean at a 2+ speaking, 2+ reading, which is considerable improvement since I started training. For quite a while I felt like I was floundering, buried under a mountain of new Korean before properly absorbing the old. So it's a rather good feeling to think that something has sunk into my brain these last few months.

The Koreans have recently opened the new King Sejong Cultural Center across the street from the Embassy. As part of their three-month long opening celebration, they've invited such outfits as the Royal Ballet, the Philadelphia Orchestra, and the New York Symphony, along with a large number of other foreign groups and an assortment of Korean artists. I've spent $100 on tickets and will be going to the Center about once a week between now and the middle of June.

I got promoted for the second year in a row! From FSO-7 to FSO-6. At this rate I'll be an Ambassador by thirty-one. The promotion came completely unexpectedly. Best of all is a $2,800 pay raise (to $17,231) and a raise in status from third secretary to second secretary. Besides that, because I've been in Korea so long, I am now the senior second secretary among FSO-6s, so I jump a whole page on the diplomatic list (which sure beats two years in last place).

The Language Student

Once upon a time there was a young Foreign Service Officer who was so entranced by one of the world's most difficult languages that he volunteered to study it full-time. So the wise Department of State assigned him to eight months training to fill a 2-2 consular position. Then, later, when his assignment was changed to a 3-3 political spot, the wise Department, rather than increase his already meager training, curtailed his course to seven months and then placed him into the Ambassador's office for three months, where he neither needed to speak his exotic language nor could spare the time to continue even minimal study of it.

Notes from Lower Volta

August 15, 1978 Tuesday

Since mid-June I have become a national radio celebrity, with a daily twenty-minute program (except Sunday) on MBC (*Munhwa Bangsong*) called *Senghwal Yawngaw* ("Practical English" or "Useful English"). It's on at 6:00 a.m. on the FM and 6:10 on the AM. It is immediately followed by a fertilizer commercial. Pay comes to $80 a week.

I cohost with Kim Sun-ki, a linguistics instructor at a local university. She has recently returned from five years in the States. (Her prolonged absence produces occasional sloppiness in her Korean, a phenomenon which I have noted in my own English.) The producers expect me to speak Korean. An English program and they want Korean? I try my best with mixed results.

The Embassy has kept me fairly busy this summer. I have been the Ambassador's Staff Aide (again!) since the beginning of June and assisted in all the planning of getting Ambassador Sneider *out* of here in June and Ambassador Gleysteen *in* in July. For a month, in fact, the Staff Aide position was actually functional. Now that the Gleysteens are more or less settled in (and determinedly maintaining a slower pace than the Sneiders cared for), the job has once again assumed its usual boring routine. I will have no regrets when I quit the Front Office this week (in favor of Al O'Kelly) to retire to the Political Section.

A word about the Gleysteens: great! If President Carter has chosen his other appointments as well as this one, I cannot fathom what is wrong with the Administration. Both the Gleysteens have made an exceptionally favorable impression since their arrival. Their common Chinese background provides them with an understanding of East Asia perhaps rarely found in American ambassadors. Personally they are very fine people. If the past crises of American-Korean relations can be overcome, the Gleysteens perhaps more than any others can restore the favorable image which seems to have been lost.

The Sneiders were also fine people. Perhaps it would be

accurate to suggest that the Sneiders' way was a more traditional ambassadorial style.

September 4, 1978 Sunday

Today marks the third anniversary of my arrival in Korea. How fast these years have gone by! How much I have learned about Korea, and how much left to learn! Most of all, how my enthusiasm for Korea and its people has not dimmed since that day when I first stepped off the plane! No matter where I go in the world, Korea will always remain my second home and hold memories which perhaps will never be duplicated elsewhere.

In spite of the frustrating aspects of Korean society and the irritating quirks of Korean personalities, in spite of my inability even now to understand so much of the culture which surrounds me, the incredible openness of the people, their dynamic vitality, and their determination to build a modern nation out of war rubble and sweat are all examples of the finest aspects of the human race. The Koreans have a saying to the effect of "Being knocked down seven times and standing up an eighth." That adequately describes their past history, which contains more disaster and tragedy than any nation deserves.

I regret now that the aloofness of my own personality prevents me from telling my friends what I truly feel. Any attempt I make at emotion rapidly disintegrates into sheer sentimentality, which I avoid precisely by avoiding emotion.

Today I visited for the first time the village near Seoul of Oh Young-taek, a young boy whom I sponsor through the Save-the-Children Foundation. It has about five thousand people who, in spite of their poverty, work together for their development. Recently they completed a community center with a day nursery, a bathhouse, and a credit union. Prior to the center's construction the villagers were unable to borrow money except at exorbitant rates, or to take baths unless they rode the bus all the way into the city.

Notes from Lower Volta

1979

January 1, 1979 Monday – Bangkok

    I write this in the Amarin Hotel in Bangkok, in the middle of my two-week swing through Southeast Asia. Margaret came again this year. Christmas in Kyoto at the Three Sisters', a few days in Hong Kong, New Year's Eve in Bangkok, and tomorrow on to Chiang Mai or Singapore.

January 3, 1979 Wednesday – Chiang Mai

    Perhaps I have been in East Asia too long. Things truly exotic no longer fascinate me. I have had my fill of temples and marketplaces. What I want is a quiet place to sit and meditate. Kyoto, as always, offers the visitor endless joys. The sheer artistry of Japanese life in even its simplest aspects overwhelms one. Japanese life is so sensible, the furniture so functional, the cities so livable. It is perhaps Japan, of all nations, before which foreigners feel cultural inferiority. China's civilization dazzles the observer but largely through its sheer weight and garishness.

    Korea has ceased to be a foreign country to me, a fact which came home when I left the security of the Korean peninsula for the unknown quantities of Southeast Asia. The physical beauty of Hong Kong is striking, far exceeding my expectations. Having ensconced ourselves in the Peninsula Hotel, we perhaps saw only some of the more promising aspects of Hong Kong life. The Star Ferry between Kowloon and Hong Kong and the tram to Victoria Peak are experiences I look forward to repeating.

    Whereas the bustle of Hong Kong in the streets and alleys coursing between its gleaming skyscrapers thrilled me, Bangkok appalled me. Two days in Bangkok were two too many. I came expecting to find the pearl of Southeast Asia. Instead I came across Detroit. The incredible dinginess and sleaziness, and over all the incredible heat (this in the coolest season of the year) put Bangkok very low on my list of places to revisit. The problem lies not with its dinginess so much as the fact that its dinginess reflects nothing Thai but rather the worst bastardization of imported Westernization. Bangkok literally looks like Detroit on a hot August day. The few tourist attractions (which can scarcely be enjoyed in the heat) hardly justify the trip. No one would consider a vacation to Detroit. Why one to Bangkok?

Chiang Mai, on the other hand, is truly beautiful. It is what I had expected Bangkok to be. Chiang Mai is much cooler than Bangkok, and Chiang Mai is surrounded by mountains while Bangkok is exceptionally flat.

Having grown up in the American Midwest, I never expected to acquire the unconscious oppression produced by a flat landscape. Having spent the last several years in Korea and Japan (and visited such hilly places as San Francisco, Seattle, Washington, Hawaii, and Hong Kong), I find that flatness depresses me unbearably.

Truly the greatest joy of travel in Thailand derives from the incredible friendliness of the people. I had thought the Japanese unmatched in courtesy and helpfulness. The simple grace and courtesy of the Thai can well be imitated by many other peoples.

March 6, 1979 Tuesday

I discovered on my recent swing though Southeast Asia that all the ugly Americans are not Americans at all. They're Australians, Germans, French, Spanish, and Japanese. On more than one occasion I felt relieved to discover that certain obnoxious tourists I assumed to be Americans were not. We encountered few Americans on the way. We especially noticed the contrast in Kyoto between Christmas 1976 and Christmas 1978. The new order in Asia is perhaps best typified by the sight of two dozen Japanese marching in in a group to take dinner in the venerable Palm Court of Raffles Hotel, that bastion of British imperialism in Singapore.

Northern Thailand reminded me strongly of Korea, both in the physical landscape and the local culture, with its temples, markets, and mountain villages. Margaret and I took one tour up to a Meo hillside village tribe. It was easy to imagine myself thousands of miles away in Korea as we bounced along dusty mountain roads to a primitive village already afflicted with tourist traps but not running water. (The image was heightened by three Thai soldiers hitching a ride part of the way. There is a communist insurgency in the area.)

In the village we witnessed an opium-smoking demonstration, the first time I ever saw anyone *paid* to use dope! We were ourselves offered the chance to puff. We declined with thanks, but did pick up some opium pipes as souvenirs.

Which brings up a tale of how the tourists never win. We espied one particularly attractive pipe in the village whose asking price was $25. Although knowing full well that the price was open to negotiation, we declined to inquire further since we saw no prospect of cutting the price down to any rational level.

After returning to Chiang Mai, we had second thoughts about the whole thing and were pleased to discover the same type pipe in a souvenir shop there. But its price was $37. With no time or inclination to return to the hillside village, we drove an exceptionally hard bargain and each received one for only $25.

Later that afternoon, while waiting for our flight back to Bangkok, we decided to price the same pipe in the airport shop to console ourselves for at least getting it for $25. Imagine our consternation and dismay to find them selling for $18! I thought airport shops were always the most expensive!

Nor was the opium pipe escapade my biggest mistake.

In preparing for the trip, I had been careful to set aside my camera and film. I did not want to miss a single event on the greatest trip of my life. Somewhere between the apartment and the car, the camera got sidetracked. We were on the way to the airport before I realized the oversight. Typical Saturday noon traffic was already so heavy that there was a question whether we would make the flight in time anyway. There was no possibility of going back for the camera. No problem, I thought. This would be my third time to Kyoto, so I certainly needed no pictures there.

In Hong Kong I could pick up a new camera at fabulous Hong Kong prices. That is what I did, an OM-2 with two lenses for $600. (In the duty free shop in Kyoto, the price for the camera body was $500, in Hong Kong $340.) That same evening, I jammed the shutter. I spent the whole vacation without taking a single picture, and had to shell out $40 on my return to Korea to fix it.

Yesterday was the last broadcast of my "Practical English" (*Senghwal Yawngaw*) program on MBC-FM. I quit the program with mixed feelings. Ending something which has become part of one's life (even if an unpleasant part) is never easy. The recognition the program offered will be missed. The immense amount of time required for proper preparation (who would have thought a twenty-minute program could take so much time?) interfered with both my social life and my Embassy activities.

I had told MBC in early February that the end was rapidly approaching (a decision under consideration since before Christmas), but they begged me to stay until the end of March, the beginning of the new "season." It was never clear, though, whether their desperate pleas indicated their confidence in my ability or mainly their lack of a simple alternative for a program in which they had no great interest.

May 20, 1979 Sunday

Perhaps you would like a thumbnail sketch of Korea in the spring of 1979. On the positive side, the economic miracle grinds on almost relentlessly. The streets are clogged with private automobiles driven by the owners themselves, a far cry from the days when most vehicles were taxis and all private cars had hired drivers. Owning a car is no longer the key to prestige it used to be, but *not* owning one is clearly low-class. And what happened to those sturdy old workhorses, the beat up, uninspiring, unsightly blue taxis? There aren't any. Or, if there are, they're lost in the crowd of brightly painted Ponies, Brisas, Rekords, and Geminis.

Notes from Lower Volta

Where does all this traffic flow? (Sometimes it doesn't; on a busy Saturday morning it can take forty minutes to drive from Compound II to the Kwanghwamun intersection.) The city is busy tearing down most of Seoul and building monstrous boulevards and threatening to fine any driver who comes into the city center without a full complement of passengers. The city buses, as always, get more crowded.

When I came to Seoul in September 1975, there was almost nothing on the south side of the Han River. Today that part of the city is mile after mile of apartment high-rises, looking somewhat like an Eastern European capital. The government plan to disperse the population south of the river is taking hold. Downtown, skyscrapers shoot up everywhere. No longer is there only the Chosun Hotel. Now we have the Plaza, the Lotte, the Silla, the Hyatt, all first-class hotels on the Japanese scale and all booked solid.

The visible aspects of economic prosperity are everywhere. On the other hand, the incredible inflation appears out of control and of such concern to everyone that even the dissidents nowadays attack the government as much for economic ineptitude as for human rights violations. A growing number of people believe the government has lost control of the economy, which also appears less strong and resilient than it did after successfully weathering the 1973 oil crisis.

The recent collapse of the Yulsan Group (once held up as a good example of dynamic young Korean business ability) seems to indicate that the phenomenal growth of other companies, even giants like Hyundai and Daewoo, may have involved something less than orthodox business practice.

Politically, the country is quiet. My job in the Political Section is boring and a waste of time. In spite of my upbringing as a good McGovern Democrat and a firm opponent of the government, I wonder more and more why we insist on getting ourselves worked up over subjects which are apparently not that important to the bulk of the Korean population.

The Embassy is practically a private line to Washington for the handful of professional dissidents. Any demonstration that occurs is by definition anti-government, even when directed against school administrators.

The opposition New Democratic Party continues to be the best argument for continuation of the present regime. It is currently in the middle of tearing itself apart in preparation for the May party convention.

Last December's National Assembly election embarrassed the government when the NDP outpolled the government party. It also demonstrated that even in a free election with a chance to send a message to President Park, half the voters still picked Park's party or independent candidates leaning toward him.

As long as Park has his way, there will be no return to democracy. As he insists time and time again, democracy is a Western invention which needs to be "adapted" for use in Korea. Ergo, the Yushin system, which guarantees the rule of one-man, one-vote. For the moment, the one man is the President himself.

Yesterday marked the fifth anniversary of my graduation from Marquette. I never would have guessed then that I would celebrate it by escorting a Deputy Assistant Secretary of State (Evelyn Colbert) around Seoul. We visited the newly reopened Secret Garden (restored to its historic appearance and now maintained as a national treasure rather than a public park), the National Museum, a pottery kiln, and a Buddhist temple.

When I began this year, I had several New Year's Resolutions. Resolutions are something I do not often make and even more rarely keep. Nevertheless, as we approach the mid-year, let us see how well I have kept my resolutions:

Become a more regular correspondent with family and friends. I who once poured out a flood of letters have become incredibly lazy in such matters, preferring to receive rather than to send. My mother sent me my own stationery for Christmas in the hope that it would stimulate me to more correspondence. Presumably she has realized by now that her dream is not to be. I have been faithfully digging through the backlog of letters at the rate of perhaps one a week (every two weeks?). Such a slow approach might not produce much headway, given the continued arrival of new letters. Since everyone except my mother and my sister Margaret has stopped writing, the problem does not rise. Anyway, I shall become a better correspondent. Even if it takes me all year to do it.

Read. The student who used to read forty books a year has become a bureaucrat scarcely able to wade his way through the mass of cables and memos on non-rubber footwear and Law of the Sea Conferences. My passion for buying books has never ebbed, but my patience for getting past the first few chapters in anything which might be termed "intellectual" seemed to have completely evaporated. Last December's trip to Japan provided the catalyst. In Kyoto I discovered the Japanese author Yukio Mishima. Since then I have done surprisingly well. Currently I am immersed in three books of distinct potential: *While Still We Live*, a novel of Polish guerrillas in World War II by Helen MacInnes; *Oscar Wilde* by H. Montgomery Hyde; and *A Distant Mirror: The Calamitous 14th Century*, by Barbara Tuchman. The last falls in the "self-improvement" category. I feared it would join other works of a similar nature in my collection of unfinished books. Surprisingly I, who have never had any taste for the Middle Ages, have been entranced by the subject.

Get some exercise. I have never been a physical fitness cultist. My previous attempt at obtaining regular physical training (spring 1975) was cut short when the State Department issued its summons to duty. Again, under the impetus of Yukio Mishima, I determined to do something to improve my body. Since late January I have been going to the Clark Hatch Physical Fitness Center two or three times a week. No miracles yet, but then I recognize the difficulty of overcoming all these years of inertia.

June 9, 1979 Saturday

I am reclining in my room in the tourist hotel at Songnisan, which is about four hours by express bus south of Seoul. Most of the way runs over the four-lane Seoul-Pusan expressway. The last eighty kilometers carry the traveler along a well-paved two-lane road through some of Korea's most beautiful mountains. (I've long since noticed that whatever part of Korea I have most recently visited strikes me as the most beautiful.)

The underlying reason for this brief weekend trip stems from an ever-present desire to escape the frustrations of Seoul even momentarily and also, in effect, to conduct a "farewell tour" of the Korean countryside in my final year here. In February I traveled to Haeinsa Temple near Taegu, which I had previously visited in 1976 and 1977, with Roz Fisher, Chris Sherwood, an Australian friend, and a couple of Brits.

In early April I returned to Daech'on Beach on the West Coast after an absence of three years, with some friends from the USIS English language group I have monitored since 1977. Most recently (on Memorial Day weekend) I went to Soraksan on the East Coast with two girls from the Political Section and Andrew Sellers from the Australian Embassy.

It is reassuring to discover that, in contrast to what happens so much in Korea (and nowhere more than in Seoul), constant change does not yet seem a way of life. Songnisan and Daech'on both appear identical to the way I last saw them. Daech'on's main street remains unpaved even now.

I was staggered at the transformation of Soraksan. The seedy little village which once huddled at the foot of the cable car route had been swept away, leaving only the old tourist hotel and a spacious park in its place. Farther away, about a kilometer in the direction of the Sea of Japan (or East Sea, as the locals insist on calling it), the Koreans have erected one of their gaudy villages of cheap hotels which they so love to inflict on an otherwise peaceful countryside, this time with some vague gesture toward Alpine architecture.

The Haeinsa trip reminded me that Koreans are always the last persons to ask for directions in their own country. Either they don't know the way and are completely useless; or they don't know the way and give directions anyway, making them less than useless.

Haeinsa can be reached in two ways: either over expressway and paved road all the way, which adds something like a hundred extra kilometers to the route; or the shorter way requiring an early exit from the expressway and a daring (and foolhardy) drive over a road still awaiting the glorious light of the New Village Movement. Our driver, Jeremy Davidson from the British Embassy, elected the latter course, confident that his Land Rover could pass where fainter souls would fear to tread.

When we bid a somewhat hesitant farewell to the expressway at Kimch'on, we determined to find out if the road we were jostling over would lead us to our goal. Armed with our map (and by standards of Korean map-making, ours was a cartographer's delight, actually indicating existing roads and villages), I approached two railroad employees at a railroad crossing to inquire whether we were on the road to the next village indicated on the map as less than two kilometers away.

I worked on the assumption that two men who passed their days raising and lowering the crossing gate for passing trains would certainly have a close acquaintance with the surrounding countryside. After considerable hemming and hawing on their parts, and irritated horn blasts from my own compatriots, these esteemed civil servants of the Korean government suggested that I sit and wait for a passing student who might know the answer to my question. I concluded that not only did they not know where the passing trains were coming from or going to, but quite likely were unsure where the trains were as they passed. We elected to move on.

Our next logical choice devolved on a taxi driver. Even were we willing to excuse the immobile railroad workers their unfamiliarity with their immediate surroundings, surely a taxi driver would know where he picked passengers up, and where he left them off? No. The taxi driver perused my proffered map (labeled in the Korean and Western alphabets, as well as Chinese characters), turned it sideways with a pretense at comprehension, and hailed a bicyclist descending upon us like a *deus ex machina*, who informed us with a rare burst of certitude that in fact we had chosen the right road.

The trip to Soraksan was noteworthy mainly because of the exceptionally relaxed atmosphere in which it was conducted. One of the greatest drawbacks to being a diplomat lies in the fact that others expect me to act like a diplomat. All too often diplomatic actions do not allow much fun.

Added to that is the language and cultural barrier when dealing with foreigners. No matter how fluent in English they might seem, nor how immersed in American styles, the underlying fact remains that I grew up in the United States and they did not. The ease of conversation and humor one naturally assumes with other Americans is rarely there when dealing with foreigners, regardless of the closeness of the personal relationship.

At Soraksan I acted with the kind of abandon and inanity rarely indulged in since graduation from Marquette. I encountered neither the disapproval of my more restrained American colleagues nor the lack of understanding from my Korean friends. Indeed, the four of us (myself, Andrew, Mary Ray, and Judy Benson) engaged in the kind of good-natured verbal matches which regard nothing as sacred.

The weekend was a catharsis. And let's not forget Judy's denting the oil pan on her car, requiring an excursion into the town of Sokch'o. Sokch'o is too small to be interesting and too large to be charming. It epitomized the stereotype of booming Korea, with construction everywhere. The Sokch'o garage was also a fine example of the perennial native disregard for common sense safety. The mechanic had no second thoughts about turning a torch on an oil pan still leaking oil or not wearing a mask and goggles to protect his face from sparks (assuming, of course, he avoided blasting all of us into the sea).

The group of us at Soraksan may well have undermined Korean-American relations and Korean-Australian relations for years

Notes from Lower Volta

to come. (Since all Westerners in Korea are *a priori* Americans, the second possibility may not come to pass.) Unfortunately, an underlying strain of basic anti-Korean feelings found reinforcement in each other's own prejudices. This displayed itself in our childish insistence on responding to all greetings from the student hordes with "Herro!" or, barring that, Burmese obscenities and German proverbs.

The students had the last laugh. Judy inquired at one point whether we thought the sparkling mountain stream water was safe to drink. After a firm consensus that it was, she drank some. A few hundred yards farther upstream we came to the stream's idyllic source in a large pool supplied by a tumbling waterfall where in some far-gone age wood nymphs probably bathed. The modern reality was somewhat less romantic. In place of bathing wood nymphs, we discovered hundreds of chattering girl high school students washing out their socks. So much for Judy's taste of fresh mountain water.

June 12, 1979 Tuesday

This underlying anti-Korean feeling troubles me. On the one hand, I love this country and so many of the Koreans whom I know, and yet I criticize the nation in the abstract. In my more innocent years here, when I still attributed every irritation to the clash between cultures, another foreigner suggested that Koreans on an individual basis are delightful but in a group unbearable. At the time, I dismissed the remark as useless. Some characteristics of many Koreans I find difficult, even taking into account cultural differences.

June 13, 1979 Wednesday

I am somewhat hesitant to pursue the kind of criticism written in the preceding pages, because I realize it reflects as much on my own shortcomings as on those of the people I criticize. For a long time, I have heaped abuse on people for one of two reasons: either because I truly don't like them and wish to make the fact clear; or because I do like them and am afraid to let them know it.

June 16, 1979 Saturday

    During the three and one half years of my residence in Korea, I have been repeatedly assaulted with the litany of weaknesses of American society, beginning with racism, running through our absorption in our own narrow interests, to the shortness of our history compared to that of Korea's. As Koreans view the matter, American history commenced on July 4th, 1776. We have no claim to the achievements of the preceding centuries of Western civilization (as they themselves make no claim on Chinese history). In contrast to this brief, traditionless American history, they boast of their own 5,000 years of Korean history (a curious figure, since archaeologically Korean history can't be pushed back much more than 2,000 years, and their own traditional system only carries us back 4,300).

    Even conceding the indisputable fact that the Korean nation has been around many centuries more than the American, and even granting the doubtful assumption that American culture has no right to claim the traditions of those nations from which it sprang, we arrive at the question which can most simply be phrased as: "So what?"

    It is certainly an understandable tendency for peoples of all nations to see the world in terms which center it around their own country. The American attempt to do so requires considerable less self-delusion on our parts than for the Koreans to do the same. What our history lacks in length it gains in importance. No history textbook of the 35th century will be able to denigrate the importance of the American empire of the 19th, 20th, and 21st centuries.

    That importance derives not merely from the preponderance of military might but from America's pre-eminent position in science, technology, art, music, and political ideas. If we could pass on only one or two items to our descendants, I would hope that they would be the Declaration of Independence and the Constitution.

    Korea, on the other hand, will always remain a footnote in history textbooks, a nation whose major distinction throughout history has been its proclivity to be ravaged by succeeding waves of invaders intent not on the conquest of Korea for itself but for its use as a steppingstone to Japan or China.

Perhaps Korea rates a line or two in the Guinness Book of World Records as the nation most frequently overrun by foreign armies enroute elsewhere, eternally at the mercies of surrounding greater powers, and yet still surviving as a recognizably distinct people. In a phrase, the Poland of Asia.

One would suppose that – considering both the subject matter of the preceding pages and the sudden burst of literary activity after so many months of relative silence – one would suppose that I do not like Korea or the Koreans.

That is not the case. I expect that this outpouring of abuse depends less on the characteristics of the Korean nation itself than on my own excessively critical personality and the outsider's dislike for things foreign, most adequately capsulized in the formula "Only in X," followed by the name of the particular locality. This magical formula explains any activities out of the ordinary, or considered unfavorably by the outsider, by attributing them to the intrinsic nature of the place, whereas the phrase is perhaps most widely used in situations of almost human universality.

It is not the case that I dislike Korea or the Koreans. It is only that they have long since proved themselves quite capable of trumpeting their own fine points that I see no reason to duplicate their efforts here. Perhaps the most striking characteristic is in their relations with others, on the one hand pursuing their friendships with an intimacy and mutual dependence we in the West regard as properly reserved for a relationship between lovers, while on the other hand disregarding those who have no claim on them by blood, friendship, or school ties with a callousness we would regard as inhuman.

As Koreans never cease telling us, America and the West represent a civilization based on material acquisition and conspicuous consumption. Korea, on the other hand, is the embodiment of the mystical, introspective East. Curiously this spiritual people is now engaged in a crass materialism of "Keeping up with the Kims" not seen in the United States since the 1950s. I will prove my case with only one example:

Koreans are willing to spend $1,000 (approximately the annual per capita income) to pay the price and duty of a Japanese color television. I am referring to a set which would cost half that in the United States. Steep price, isn't it? Not only do the Korean networks not broadcast in color, but the government has emphasized again and again that (for the sake of energy conservation and restrained consumption) there will be no color television. So we have a textbook case of consumption for consumption's sake.

June 18, 1979 Monday

Life in the Foreign Service, a notice from the Embassy weekly newspaper of June 1st:

"Beware the Big, Red Strawberry! An article in the Korea Times, Saturday, May 26, stated that farmers are using 'agro-chemicals' containing an antibiotic substance that is harmful to humans on strawberries. Their purpose is to make the strawberries look fresh and to keep them from getting musty. Because of this information, it is advisable not to eat the local strawberries. The Army Food Inspectors also gave this advice. Using Clorox or iodine treatment is not satisfactory on strawberries unless one likes to eat a pale red fruit that tastes like Clorox."

June 19, 1979 Tuesday

On the home front, my old friends drift away. Marriage this year has claimed George, a college roommate, and Val (not, I might add, to each other). I seem to hear less often from my old friends. But then, they don't hear so much from me.

June 20, 1979 Wednesday

Everything at the Embassy has stopped in its tracks to prepare for the arrival June 29th of President Carter and his party of

Notes from Lower Volta

approximately six hundred friends, family, bodyguards, valets, doctors, reporters, and various other hangers-on for a two-day visit.

All rumors to the contrary, I am not little Amy Carter's Escort Officer. I will also not be official interpreter. I might tell Miss Park Geun-hye, the President's daughter, how eager Mrs. Carter is to have intimate relations with her and her people.

That is not to say that I am not intimately involved with the whole thing. There is no one at the Embassy who is not intimately involved with the Carter visit. I am working on Mrs. Carter's schedule, which allows me to participate in a number of mind-numbing meetings where high-ranking and otherwise sensible officers spend an inordinate amount of time discussing Amy's schedule. Perhaps Amy is the brains of the whole administration. That would go a long way toward explaining both its strengths and weaknesses.

The tentative visit schedule was based on a number of outdoor events, geared to media "visuals" and "photo opportunities." If all summits are as incredibly media-oriented as this one, we may wish to spare the principals a good deal of exertion on their parts by substituting look-alikes for most of the events. The continuous rain of the last two days with its hint of an early start on the rainy season has the advance White House staff gnawing their fingernails to the bone.

Rain is only one problem. There are many other equally complex matters to be thoughtfully resolved. For example, a visit to a rehabilitation center by Mrs. Carter will not offer as many "visuals" as a swing through the Secret Garden, where we can stage a "media event" with court musicians and dancers which will look good on American television. And anyway handicapped children are depressing. So Mrs. Carter's deep interest in rehabilitation work notwithstanding, the center is scratched from the schedule and the Garden segment lengthened.

To think all this joy will be over in two weeks!

June 25, 1979 Monday

In selecting my next post, I have three considerations, two of which contradict each other. First, I want an assignment outside of East Asia, for the sake of a little variety in my life, although I expect that my long-range interest will remain here. Beyond that, I would prefer a Washington assignment, both to see how the Department operates (never having been assigned there) and because by that time I will have spent almost five years outside of the United States. If a Washington assignment does not work out, I would like another overseas assignment in a post preferably much smaller than Seoul.

It is hard to defend myself against the commonly heard charge of American diplomats living high on the hog overseas, traveling to all sorts of exotic places at taxpayers' expense. Seoul scarcely qualifies as a hardship post. Yet Seoul is actually the exception rather than the norm. In most places, inflation and the eroding dollar have combined to place comfortable living outside the budget of American diplomats. Even more commonly the place itself is such an incredible hell that only someone with a questionable hold on his sanity would wish to spend two years there.

Going to Europe, for Americans, is like going home. Coming to East Asia – that's like going to another planet. Everything is different. Even so, underneath all the layers of cultural differences, we're still people. I have learned more about life in my few years here than I did in my eight years of Jesuit education. Always my first reaction to something new in Korea is: "How strange a way to think!" Then after a while I consider our own ways of doing things, which I've accepted all my life. I realize that they, too, are strange and by no means more "correct" or "logical" than anyone else's.

July 15, 1979 Sunday

Jimmy Carter has come and gone, having made an amazing impression in Korea. His chances for reelection next year may be nil in the United States. If only he could run here! The Koreans were pleasantly surprised to find that he is not a bull-headed blunderer bent on delivering South Korea into the hands of the communists by withdrawing all the American forces. His very deep humanity and obvious concern for Korea dispelled the distrust of the last few years produced by withdrawals and Koreagate. The spectacle of the American President out jogging with the troops one morning on the Demilitarized Zone and with his wife the next morning in the Secret Garden is still a topic of awed conversation among Koreans.

My own favorite scene of that weekend was President Carter's stopping the arrival motorcade in front of City Hall to push into the crowds to shake hands. President Park, while going so far as to get out of the car, refused to lower himself to shaking hands with the masses. The whole incident undoubtedly offended his every Confucian sensibility.

President Carter can't win. To hear the Korean government describe it, he "harped" on the human rights issue. To hear the dissidents tell it, he "neglected" human rights all together. In my own opinion, he accorded human rights its proper position, even bringing it up in his toast at the state dinner at the Blue House while Park sat there with an unusually stony, distant expression.

July 31, 1979 Tuesday

Perhaps I shall never get used to the transience of Foreign Service life. Having been so comfortably situated in the same post for four years, it disturbs me to wake up one morning to find my familiar surroundings peopled by strangers. Two years in a future context seem so long a time, when in retrospect they seem little time at all. People whom I still regard as newcomers (from my elevated position of seniority) and whom I have scarcely grown accustomed to suddenly pack up and depart post. And due to the realities of Foreign Service assignments, the majority of position movements seem to occur in the summer months. So far this summer I have lost Roz Fisher, Al O'Kelly, the Walkers, Traba Peters, and soon Mary Ray.

Having always been a shy person, I find the amount of time spent meeting new colleagues a tremendous drain on my energies. Although I have become more "outgoing" in recent years, my native tendency remains to avoid conversation or even an exchange of greetings with strangers, unless I expect our future relationship to be of some duration.

August 1, 1979 Tuesday
    I make these scribblings in these pages for my own benefit. My audience is myself, not the person that I am but the person that I shall be in some future time, should he choose to glance into these pages. It is not only what these pages contain, but also the many attendant, unrecorded memories they call forth.

    People may praise the wonderful oral traditions of illiterate peoples and lament our own dependence on the written word. But who will dispute that literacy has always been a central facet of every significant civilization of the human species? Or that the permanence of the written word (barring the casual and constant manipulation of history foreseen in Orwell's *1984*) is the greatest defense against falsification, the weakness of the human memory, and the temptation of a storyteller to improve on a tale he has heard? What would be the contents of the Constitution if it had been handed down orally all these years?

    Since first I learned to read, I have wished to write. For many years my intention in life was to be a world-famous author. Since that desire arose at the same time that my reading centered around a voracious consumption of science fiction, I planned to lift science fiction from juvenile to classical status.

    In fact, in the late 1960s, I wrote a number of science fiction stories. From 1964-1966 I labored on a 200-page novel called (if memory serves) *Ares Paxton on Eron*. Presumably it still sits in the closet in my mother's house, waiting to be discovered for posthumous publication. I have not read it since the day it was finished. The planned sequels – nine in all were plotted out – have yet to see a single chapter composed. I expect, though, that the outpourings of a novice thirteen-year old writer, no matter how talented, may well be literarily revolting. I clearly lifted the general plot, several characters, and a number of key concepts describing the planet Eron from Edgar Rice Burroughs' Martian novels.

My life's ambitions have moved from writer to college professor to lawyer (and potential Chief Justice) to diplomat (and potential Ambassador).

Through it all there has remained the underlying ambition to make some contribution to the world's literature. Perhaps that is one reason why I write the journal of my life, the basis for *The Memoirs of William J. Duffy*, published in 2032, an immediate bestseller and widely-acclaimed achievement.

The more I read, the better I see the difficulty of writing something worthwhile and significant. The problem is simplified when the audience is one, and that the author himself, allowing both author and reader to achieve a complete understanding of each other. These journals will always be worthwhile and significant for me. In a world of four billion souls how should I expect others to find it so for themselves?

August 7, 1979 Tuesday

In my younger years I had no experience with nudity, or at least none that comes to mind. My education came shortly after my eighth birthday, when our family was driving from Colorado to Michigan. We camped along the way.

One morning in a state park in Illinois, I had just finished brushing my teeth in the shower room when three men came in to go swimming. They were young, at least, so far as an eight-year old could judge, perhaps in their early twenties. No one else was in the shower room, and the three ignored me.

I watched fascinated as they undressed, their shirts, their pants, their underwear. Their naked bodies dazzled me. I wondered whether I would ever be so muscular, so hairy, so big as they. Then they put on their swimming trunks and left me alone.

Twenty years have passed. My young Adonises are now approaching fifty. How has time aged them, weakened their muscles, widened their waists, thinned their hair?

Perhaps my entire reference to sexuality is gratuitous and prurient. Sex is too central a part of the human condition to be labeled gratuitous. The prurient aspects of an emerging gay man's life are equaled if not eclipsed in importance by the frustration of attempting to grapple with a difficult situation where gratification is more frequently unknown than achieved.

August 19, 1979 Sunday

I am drunk. I state the fact largely to excuse the execrable handwriting which is certain to follow in the next few paragraphs. I do not state it to excuse the thoughts I hope to express. I think on occasion drunkenness is not without its usefulness in drawing forth the innermost thoughts of the mind. This is my twenty-seventh birthday. Today I am twenty-seven. If a person may not act as bizarre as he wishes on his own birthday, then when may he drop the weight of all the conventions which restrict us?

In an intoxicated state, I may well lack what little eloquence I command when in full possession of my faculties. The lack of eloquence will surely be compensated for by the sincerity of what I write.

I am overwhelmed by the incredible tenacity, diligence, and determination of the Korean people. Here we have a nation fated to lie between the colossi of China and Japan (and, to a certain extent, Russia) as a pawn in big power machinations. The history of Korea has been to react to outside forces, rather than to affect them.

The history of Korea can be described with minimal overstatement as "tragic." Had Korea only possessed sufficient fortune to find itself a European country, its size and population would long since have qualified it as a major power. The tragedy continues today with the division of one of this planet's most long-lasting homogeneous cultures between two irreconcilable doctrines of communism and anti-communism.

I love Korea. Most of my adult life has been spent in this country, and every day of it was through my choice. No matter how many years I spend in the Foreign Service, no matter how many foreign countries I pass through, it seems unlikely that any nation will take possession of my heart the way that this nation has. Next to the United States itself, Korea has provided the single greatest influence on my life.

Both the Koreans I have encountered and the Americans I have worked with would be surprised by such a favorable opinion of this peninsula, given my penchant for criticizing Korea and things Korean. We criticize most and share the least patience with those things which are the objects of our greatest affection. That which we love most is, by its inability to reach perfection, that which disappoints us most.

Today, as I said, was my birthday. I was lucky enough to spend it with three of my closest friends: Lee Yong-gun, Choi Gun-ho, and Kim Ki-yong. I met Lee Yong-gun in May 1977, when he was still a Chinese language major at Kyunghee University. He has since graduated, gone into the optical business, married, and had a baby daughter. Choi Gun-ho was my second producer at MBC (succeeding Kim Il-su) from last October to the program's end in March. I met Kim Ki-yong through Lim Soong-jae, who introduced us one year ago. Kim is an Army Captain currently working in Criminal Investigations at the Ministry of Defense.

How can the world produce the three of them and still be in such a mess? To say that its people are Korea's greatest natural resource is no cliché when the rising generation includes such as Lee, Choi, and Kim. I often think their exceptional friendliness and generosity derives from my position as a foreigner. Then I see them act the same way toward other Koreans, and I know that in fact such profound humaneness is deeply ingrained into their psyches through the dictates of Korean culture.

Do not read these paragraphs as an empty panegyric of superlatives strung together. Let me rephrase the ancient question. Instead of asking, "If there is a God, why is there so much evil in the world?", let us ask, "With so many good people, why is there so much evil in the world?"

There. I have finished the drunken rambling of my twenty-seventh birthday. This time next year, where will I be? My heart, at least, will be in Korea.

>Separation from my love
>is like winter
>(or summer)
>but mostly like winter.

***

>Lady of the falling rain,
>lift me up beyond the clouds:
>raise me from the earth below
>into the cold light of a never-hidden star.
>Put an earth beneath my feet
>on which none but dreamers tread;
>carry me past gravity
>into the cold light of a thousand flaming stars.
>Do for me what you cannot
>for you: break these earthly bonds
>and hurl me skyward, knowing
>through possessing you, I reach for constellations.

August 25, 1979 Saturday

The greatest misconceptions among the American public about what Foreign Service life is like arise from their latching on to its superficially exotic and glamorous aspects. They don't consider that things which in isolated instances are exotic and glamorous become through relentless repetition mind-numbing agonies.

To take only a few examples, Foreign Service personnel travel throughout the world, almost always for free. When we consider *where* they travel to, we may look at the apparent pleasure of world travel differently. London and Paris are the exceptions rather than the rule when it comes to locating embassies and consulates.

Looking at a map of Foreign Service posts, we see that all too frequently they exist in incredibly hot, poverty-stricken, undeveloped backwaters which we refer to, with an incredibly loose use of the term, as "nations." If one of the plagues which Moses called down upon the Egyptians doesn't do the diplomat in, then certainly the next coup, anti-American riot, or mindless terrorist will. No one would choose to live in Cleveland. Why does the fact it exists overseas make it seem more exciting?

As a second example, Foreign Service life is often a mad social whirl of hush-hush lunches with important "contacts" and dignified, stately receptions in the garden of the Ambassador's residence. True, oh, how true! Shouldn't we get extra compensation for sacrificing the privacy of even our lunch hours to put up with the often pointless and unimportant ramblings of strangers and unwanted acquaintances?

One ambassadorial reception is a treat to the young Foreign Service Officer; the second is a pleasure; the third, a chore; the fourth, an imposition; the fifth (and all those subsequent), a quickening descent through the various levels of Dante's Inferno. Week after week, the same guest list is recycled, expanding or contracting as the needs of the moment dictate, but always including the same faces of Cabinet ministers, National Assemblymen, businessmen, professors, military, and other "influential figures."

Virtually all of them know each other, having for the most part participated in the reception merry-go-round since the beginning of the present regime. The flow of inconsequential small talk and hollow conversation closely approximates my vision of Hollywood society ("Dahling! It's been simply ages!" with a foreign accent). Give me the solitude and comfort of my own apartment to the bustle of the Ambassador's residence. Let me have the wisdom of a good book instead of the babble of these self-assured VIPs.

Perhaps the problem lies with me. Perhaps the Foreign Service possesses all the mystique that legend attributes to it, and instead I am the one who does not measure up. For example, a couple of months ago I accompanied John Lancer (my immediate supervisor) on a visit to Kim Dae-jung.

Kim Dae-jung, despite all the efforts of the Korean government to the contrary, remains the single most important opposition figure. When Koreans discuss an alternative to the present President, it is not the leader of the New Democratic opposition party, Kim Young-sam, but Kim Dae-jung of whom they think.

There is also the mightily aged Yun Po-sun, who has a double distinction. He is Korea's only living former President (the immediate predecessor of the incumbent, which probably goes a long way toward explaining the venom the ex- pours upon the ex-to-be). And, he has had the pleasure of my interpreting for him on a number of occasions with American officials.

Visits to Yun's residence are the only time my interpreting skills have been called upon. I suspect that I fill the role because Yun is like a wind-up doll with proportionately predictable responses. Rather than interpret, I rehash what Yun has said before and will undoubtedly say again. I may suggest next time that we dispense with the pilgrimage to Yun's house, since he has become an unnecessary cog in the transmission of his views to Americans. But I digress.

Kim Dae-jung is understandably careful when discussing his political views, given the demonstrated government willingness to kidnap him from foreign countries and/or toss him in prison. So I was not surprised when his wife turned on the television set in the room to confuse any uninvited ears who might just be listening. Here my dilemma arose.

On the one hand, here was one of the most famous men in Korea, one for whom I had waited over three years to meet, one whose every pronouncement was eagerly awaited (or dreaded) by the Korean political world. Indeed, Kim Young-sam's recent election as President of the New Democratic Party was attributed to Kim Dae-jung's support. Here was a man who might very well, right in front of me, utter some statement of crucial importance.

On the other hand, I had been home with a bad cold for three days previous to this meeting. I took advantage of those three days to tune into the U.S. Army's AFKN network and watch that old warhorse soap opera, *General Hospital*.

Like most soap operas, the story had not moved very far ahead in the two years since last I had seen it, right down to the mystery of the missing one-year-old baby (was he now three?). All my friends at the hospital were being engulfed by an African plague. But they didn't know it. All they knew was that they had a lot of people all over town dropping with a unique set of symptoms.

What all the doctors and nurses with their expensive equipment and telephone calls to the Centers for Disease Control couldn't figure out, we viewers already knew. The only question was how long it would take them to catch on. That question had not been answered by the time I returned to work.

Imagine my divided loyalties, then, when Mrs. Kim coincidentally turned on that day's broadcast of *General Hospital*.

Here, providentially, was another chance to encourage my friends to unravel the mysterious disease. Yet duty required me to attend closely to the conversation with Kim, a necessity emphasized by his disconcerting habit of glancing in my direction as he spoke. "Don't look at me! Lancer's your man!" I thought.

What was the outcome of this struggle of conscience? I would gladly share it with you. Diplomatic discretion precludes me from divulging further what transpired in that room.

September 12, 1979 Wednesday

We make much of the so-called pro-Americanism of the Korean people. There are few countries where the local population more warmly welcomes Americans as Americans. This is a recent phenomenon in history, emerging only with the end of World War II. This superficial pro-Americanism conceals the more basic, condescending anti-Americanism which will quickly reassert itself if ever the Republic of Korea does not depend on the United States for its very next minute of existence.

William J. Duffy

What the Koreans like most about us are our military might and our economic prosperity. It is no coincidence that strong pro-Americanism emerged with the rise of American military power in the Pacific, its destruction of the Japanese empire, and its continued function as the guarantor of Korean independence. The frantic clamor for visas to the United States does not arise from any devotion to impractical concepts of freedom and democracy, but from the fervent belief that immigration to the United States is the easiest route to large savings accounts, gas-guzzling cars, and an American passport.

The Koreans scorn us for our institutions, our brief history, our lack of traditions ("a people without tradition"), the perceived superficiality of our personal relationships ("Americans say 'hello' in one breath and 'goodbye' in the next"), our crime rate, our race problem (which to them means not the inability of the races to live together but our passion for mongrelization, in contrast to their own cherished racial purity), our domination by "Jewish interests," and our moral posturing.

I doubt that any Korean perceives that America fights a war with greater determination when the people believe in the war's moral justification rather than merely the nation's national interest. Our involvement in (and disinvolvement from) Vietnam remains an enigma to them.

In contrast to the general American perception that relations between our two nations are a matter of modern history, the Koreans trace the connection back to 1866, when the U.S. ship *General Sherman* steamed upriver to Pyongyang and, for reasons still not clear to me, engaged in battle with the Koreans. It was sunk. I have heard Koreans seriously state that the 1866 incident is not covered in American history books because we are ashamed of such defeats. It does not occur to them that the whole affair was too insignificant to rate even a footnote.

The Koreans blame us for several tragedies in their history. In the Root-Takahara Agreement of 1908, we tossed Korea to Japan in return for the Japanese guarantee of our position in the Philippines. At the end of World War I, we led Koreans to believe we supported "self-determination" for all peoples, and then we refused to deal with the Korean representatives who came to the Paris Peace Conference seeking independence from Japan. Our greatest folly was the 1945 division of Korea at the 38th parallel, conceding half the country to the Soviet Union for no good reason. Finally, the Korean War was the direct result of the 1949 U.S. troop withdrawal.

The unusual appeal of Christianity in this country found its source not in the peace and love of Christ's teachings but in its usefulness as a nationalist tool against the Japanese in such matters as the missionaries' resistance to Shinto worship services.

The embracing of Western concepts of democracy and self-rule received its stimulus from its usefulness in nationalist causes, a function it lost with the end of the Japanese colonization. This is clearly seen by looking at the precarious state democratic ideas have occupied in this country since 1945.

The people out of power harp on "the restoration of democracy," implying that it once was here. It is at best questionable whether any new regime would seriously implement democratization or merely elect to follow what its predecessors did: consolidate its own position and hold on for as long as possible. Were it not for American pressure, I think it inconceivable that the present Yushin constitution would have retained even the bare democratic features that it has.

Even well-educated Koreans confuse the issue by stating that "Western-style democracy" is not compatible with Korea's "unique situation." They identify "Western-style democracy" with "American-style," in distinction to "British-style," "French-style," and – yes – "Korean-style" (i.e., Yushin).

They complain that we Americans want them to replicate our own system in Korea, without considering that there are many way-stations on the thousand-mile journey between "American-style" and "Korean-style" where we would be more than agreeable to have them stop short.

Democracy in their sense is not the down-to-earth job of the people running their own government, but some distant golden age which can only arise under such unlikely conditions (for example, the elimination of the North-South confrontation) that it will never come. Democracy for them is not the surest way to establish the society's stability but a very fragile and volatile substance which, unless existing in a sterile, stagnant environment, will quickly destroy the nation.

Most of all, the Koreans scorn us because they so completely depend on us. They perhaps resent the fate which has consigned such a significant people as themselves to insignificance between the giants China and Japan, while the upstart United States, blessed with resources, territory, prosperity, and strength, has emerged in only two centuries to dominate the world.

September 13, 1979 Thursday

Is democracy not a system under which the people are guaranteed at set times the opportunity to replace one leadership with another? Or, alternatively, a system under which the sudden incapacity of the current leader to lead (such as through his death) poses no threat to the system because a predetermined order of succession exists and the people perceive the system depends on no one man? Dictatorial regimes almost invariably center on the strength of one man and are incapable of preparing the transition to his successor until he is removed from the scene, because it is indelicate (treasonable, even) to discuss a future without him.

***

A newcomer to Korea, unversed in Korean family names, might well one day pick up the phone and, hearing the cryptic statement "I am You" over the wire, conclude that East Asia's mysticism and inscrutability exceed all expectations.

Notes from Lower Volta

September 14, 1979 Friday

When first I joined the Department of State and headed overseas, one of my strongest initial impressions of other Foreign Service people was the degree to which they were out of touch with the contemporary United States. These were people whose notions of the state of current American society derived from whatever period they last spent extended time in the United States. When they discussed the United States of 1975 with foreigners, they were in fact talking about their recollections of 1965 or even 1955. Considering the massive changes in the intervening years, they literally discussed a nation which no longer existed.

Now I wonder whether I too do not face the same fate. My America is that of 1974-75. Except for six weeks' home leave in 1977, the past forty-eight months have been spent outside of the United States. Koreans ask me questions about current American styles which I am unable to answer. I know no more than they do from reading the same *Time* magazine.

From a personal viewpoint, the thought that as long as I remain in the Foreign Service I will remain an outside spectator to America appalls me somewhat. From a professional viewpoint, I wonder about the effectiveness of dispatching diplomats overseas who in their professional and personal activities are expected to represent their nation when every day spent abroad leaves them in greater ignorance of it.

This volume of my life has covered two of my life's more interesting years. It has seen the solidification of my ties to Korea as the second of only two nations in the world where I feel at home. I do not regret the decision which extended my originally scheduled two years in this country to nearly five. Without these two years I would not have such friends as Choi Gun-ho, Lee Yong-gun, and Kim Ki-yong. I might never have…. But why go on? If not here, the two years would have been spent elsewhere. There is little utility in speculation about Alternate Nows. Life is an accumulation of small decisions which, piled one on another, exert a force to push the individual in one direction or another.

As a few examples: What if our move to Denver in 1960 had been permanent? What if I had transferred to the University of Michigan for my junior year as planned? What if Bill McKenny had never suggested taking the Foreign Service exam? What if in 1975 I had turned the Foreign Service down and gone to law school?

How different would my life today be? Recognizing the pointlessness of such imaginings, I end this volume.

The Road Less Traveled
(Korea, Washington, Ghana)
September 15, 1979 - August 31, 1981

Notes from Lower Volta

September 15, 1979 Saturday

    Beginning such an impressive volume as this one leaves me somewhat at a loss for words. Six hundred blank pages stretch in front of me. What words shall I write upon them? The thought intimidates me. Great books require great words.

    Let me capture the moment:

    It is 11:25 p.m. in my apartment in American Embassy Compound II in Seoul, Korea. The incredible rainy season of July and August has given way to my fifth glorious autumn in Korea. The daytime temperatures still remain rather hot, and the evenings are pleasant. The windows are open, allowing some of the sounds of Seoul to filter in as the city races toward the midnight curfew: the sounds of cars speeding past on the road in front of the compound, the blowing of horns, the screech of brakes as accidents are narrowly averted.

    Within the apartment, MBC-FM brings me the sounds of Emerson, Lake and Palmer on Im Kuk-hie's "Eleven PM Visit" program. The apartment is shrouded in darkness, except for the small lamp on the Korean desk at which I sit. By no Western conception would an observer call this a desk: it rises barely a foot off the floor (the tape measure tells me so) and requires me to sit in front of it on a cushion. My Korean possessions surround me: the chests, bookcases, brassware, scrolls, and screens.

    I have returned within the last hour from a birthday party for the Belgian Embassy's secretary, a gathering of a small segment of Seoul's foreign community in which I was the only American. As all such gatherings tend to do, I am left with a nagging sense of inferiority to those who, unlike so many Americans, converse fluently not only in their native language but also in two or three others. When I say fluently, I mean they even understand the differences of nuance in the various slang terms applied to a given subject.

    Within eight months I will have my final parting from Korea and must at long last think seriously about where next I will go in this world.

William J. Duffy

Have I captured the moment? Then I have made my start.

Over the past Labor Day weekend, I made a trip to Haeinsa Temple near Taegu with Judy Benson, Dorothy Bench, and Dan Wilson. (Shall I include names in my recollections if I do not also provide some background on the person behind the name? In twenty more years will even I remember who these people are?)

I have been to Haeinsa a number of times, most recently last February with Roz Fisher *et al.* There is little more to add to my previous notes, except that the weekend remains a pleasant memory and a welcome relief from the pressures of Seoul.

One noteworthy item: on a spur-of-the-moment suggestion by Dan, we abandoned the more direct (five-hour) expressway route back to Seoul in favor of a scenic route up the East Coast. While I had previously been to the East Coast, to Kangneung, Soraksan, and Odaesan, I had never taken a trip down the whole coast. With the recent opening of a good two-lane highway from Samcheok in the North to Pohang in the South, it was a trip I wanted to make. (Considering the small size of Korea, strange that there would still be a part of which I had no knowledge.)

The East Coast, like most of the peninsula, abounds in scenery and charm. An adequate appreciation of its merits would require at least a weekend trip, as opposed to our one-day outing. To make things worse, we did not leave Haeinsa until almost noon. After virtually non-stop driving, we arrived in Seoul about two the next morning. The expressway system has no curfew, but after 10:00 p.m. or so there is only an occasional freight truck. Consequently, late at night is the best time to go traveling. It does impinge on the sightseeing. Despite my expectation that, having sold my car (good Lord, a lot of news I must shortly report), I would do little driving, I drove Judy's car while Dan drove his own. My bed in Apartment 12-A never looked better.

Yes, I sold my car, for $2,000 (which is what I paid for it in May 1977). The Korean who bought it will pay about $4,000 in taxes, making my rapidly aging 1974 Honda a $6,000 automobile. Contrary to my understanding, the five-year period after which the car could be sold tax-free did not date from the time of its importation by its original U.S. Army Captain (and thus become tax-free next month), but from the time of my purchase. Why anyone would still shell out $6,000 for a used car whose replacement parts have to be ordered directly from Japan every time a problem arises is beyond me. The same amount of money would buy a brand new Hyundai Pony. As one potential buyer put it, "Ponies are too common."

September 16, 1979 Sunday

Among my New Year resolutions this year was a decision to read more.

All my life reading has been one of my most constant interests, until by my last year in college I was consuming over forty books a year. In those days I looked somewhat askance at people who read primarily fiction, as if reading fiction was not really reading. The bulk of my consumption was history, biography, and anthropology.

My entry into the Foreign Service resulted in a precipitate decline in my personal reading. I attribute that to the twin factors of being overwhelmed by the volume of reading required in the office and an increased social life which allowed less time for such pastimes as reading. In the first six months of 1978 I read only seven books. Despite an increase later in the year, I finished only twelve more by New Year's Eve.

Already in 1979 I have made my way through thirty-two books. I have followed at least one of my New Year resolutions.

September 23, 1979 Sunday

The Korean political scene, which has been a vast wasteland since my arrival four years ago, has recently assumed a new, more dynamic form. Since the proclamation of the dictatorial Yushin Constitution in October 1972, and the Emergency Measures in 1974 and 1975, it could be truly said that Korea did not have politics, only a politic, President Park.

The recent dynamism commenced with last December's National Assembly election, when the opposition New Democratic Party squeaked by the ruling Democratic Republican Party with a slim 1.1 percent plurality, a smashing psychological victory. The fact the President appoints one third of the National Assembly himself (so the current government was not directly threatened) made no difference.

This was followed by the NDP convention in May, where the party elected to replace the lackluster, pro-government opposition leader (isn't that a contradiction in terms?) with Kim Yong-sam, who has no redeeming features. He would dearly love to be arrested and become a martyr, so he spends his time going out of his way to violate the Emergency Measures in his criticism of the government. Things began to coalesce: the NDP, the Christian activists, the labor unions, and Kim Dae-jung, all who have gone their own ways in the past, started to come together.

The phenomenon reached its peak in the August 11th Y.H. Incident, when police stormed the building where two hundred female workers were staging a sit-in. They were protesting the lack of response from their company and the government over their loss of jobs with the company's collapse. During the assault, one girl died. Police issued a series of conflicting statements on her death. Their only point of agreement was that the police were not responsible.

The police also made the mistake of beating up some National Assemblymen and reporters. This brought down the wrath of the press, undoubtedly less for the Assemblymen's sakes than their own. (Having seen the press in action when President Carter deplaned at Kimpo, I find the police action quite understandable.) For days the news was dominated by the subject of the "Y.H. Incident," as the media defied all government "suggestions" that the coverage be stopped. The government was on the run.

Then the Korean penchant for factionalism and self-interest reasserted itself. Why hit your enemy full in the stomach when you can shoot yourself in the foot? Three district chairmen in the NDP, angered by Kim Yong-sam's heavy-handed leadership (he replaced them in their positions with his own followers) questioned his election to the party presidency in the courts. The case has been described by a "highly-placed embassy source" as "legally correct, but morally it sucks." The court has suspended Kim from exercising the powers of the party presidency until the case's resolution. The NDP appears likely to split into two between Kim's supporters and his opponents.

Kim, showing his pronounced trait for making as many enemies as possible, attacked the U.S. Embassy for not being more involved in the domestic scene and for not talking to him often enough. He had been to lunch at the Ambassador's as recently as three weeks previously. According to Kim, democracy will come to Korea if only the United States tells President Park to do so.

If the spectacle of an opposition leader inviting a foreign power's direct intervention were not enough, Kim then let it be known that the purpose of his statements (printed in the New York *Times*) were to help Senator Kennedy's presidential campaign next year.

September 24, 1979 Monday
From a letter dated September 17th from my mother: "How well I remember September 5th four years ago. I was delighted and happy for you for the opportunity you had, but a little scared as you walked out to the plane with Bill McKenny. Korea seemed the end of the earth and you seemed so young to be going so far away. You certainly have grown in so many ways and have had a great opportunity."

September 29, 1979 Saturday
The other night I unwittingly inflicted one of those fatal jugular thrusts which I can unleash while seeking to win an argument. Choi Gun-ho and I were discussing the long-standing question of "What do Americans think about Korea?" My answer has always

been that Americans *don't* think about Korea. In support of that I produced an American history book, whose index (not surprisingly) offered only three references to Korea, one about the Russo-Japanese rivalry in the early 1900s and two about the Korean War.

Not conceding my triumph, Gun-ho mentioned H.G. Wells' *Outline of History*. The *Outline* possesses some mystical attraction for Koreans based on their notion that it offers a flattering portrait of Korea. I doubt many of them have ever read it. Having by chance a copy of the *Outline* on my bookshelf and not content to let the matter lie, I persisted in looking up every one of Wells' references to Korea.

We had reached only the fourth reference ("We have mentioned a Japanese invasion of China (or rather of Korea) ....") when Gun-ho grabbed the book from my hands and leafed aimlessly through it. When at last he relinquished his grasp, the tears in his eyes showed clearly to my surprise that he had seen nothing in the pages before him, expressed in his answer to my question: "Sometimes I am ashamed to have been born a Korean."

My insensitivity appalled me. How could I understand? How could I comprehend the shame of a man intensely proud of his heritage and yet fearful of its ultimate insignificance?

October 4, 1979 Thursday

In this, my fifth and last fall in Korea, let me recall Korean Octobers, when every day seems crisper and clearer than its predecessor, when for once the gray cloud of pollution lifts its veil from the city of Seoul, and the mountains which enclose the city for so much of the year like hazy sentinels step forward in unmistakable detail. Most of all, the colors of the countryside, the golden glow of the rice in the paddies terraced up the hillsides, the pulsating reds and browns of forests unleashing a final burst of color before the descent of winter.

October 5, 1979 Friday

A restlessness which prevents me from concentrating on

whatever I am doing at the moment afflicts me. I pick up a book to read, and quickly put it down; I consider writing in this journal, but soon abandon the attempt. Letters from my friends crowd my desk drawer and yet I have no interest in answering them.

What shall I write?

Such moods come on me often enough, as often as not (in this case) when I have too much time on my hands and no good plan for using it. October in Korea is a month of holidays: Korean Armed Forces Day, National Foundation Day, Korean Alphabet Day, Columbus Day, and this year (by a quirk of the lunar calendar) Chusok, the harvest festival. This past week the Embassy has been closed as often as it has been open.

I have used the extra time poorly. Even with this four-day weekend, and its beautiful weather, I did not plan a trip. (Of course, the fact that this is Chusok weekend and any would-be traveler must contend with some thirty-five million Koreans enroute to their ancestors' tombs is one consideration.)

When I sit by myself in my apartment doing nothing – and I mean *nothing,* not even thinking – so often people interrupt my reveries to ask what I am thinking about when, in fact, my mind is a complete blank – must a man *always* be thinking to retain his sanity? But, as I say, when I sit by myself, I am not aware of the passage of time and of the fact of my own mortality.

How many years do I have left on this planet? Fifty? And how many of them spent in something approaching youthful vigor? Perhaps twenty? Such intense awareness of the brevity of the cosmic moment which belongs to me makes me wonder whether it is not a tragedy to let even a single day pass by in idleness. Such is our Puritan heritage, even for those of us who have no Puritan heritage. The sense of tragedy is compounded by consideration of all the tasks which remain undone: letters to answer, packages to mail, and work accumulated in the office.

Do other people worry about time as much as I? It is not only the matter of the brevity of my lifespan. The fact is that within eight months my whole life will be overturned and disordered, the cards returned to the deck and reshuffled, when I depart Korea after spending some fifty-seven months here. I sometimes feel like a patient with a terminal disease when I reflect that I am seeing so many things around me for the last time.

I hesitate to embrace the idea that men have the governments they deserve. It suggests a justice in the universe which I do not discern. Perhaps the Germans deserved Hitler in 1933, although I doubt anyone deserved Hitler except Hitler.

Surely the Koreans deserve better than they have had. Their history seems to grow more tragic rather than less. While undoubtedly not as moral or peace-loving as they so often proclaim (my own opinion is that their historic nonaggression against foreign nations is a function of their relative weakness rather than a reflection of their true disposition), the Koreans have certainly received the short end of the stick throughout history.

Even though South Korea (and presumably to some extent North Korea) provides its citizens with a better life than their ancestors knew, it pains me that this people have no better a government than they do. It pains me that American soldiers died here for democracy and freedom, only to have the dream stolen by a dictator whose protestations about his concern for the national security actually reflect his concern for the security of his own position as dictator.

Park Chung-hee's overreaching concern has always been with getting himself in power and keeping himself in power. Yesterday's disgraceful expulsion of Kim Yong-sam from the National Assembly by the government assemblymen, in an assembly building basement conference room cordoned off by policemen to prevent the opposition's participation, exposes the fiction of Korean-style Yushin democracy for what it is, a fiction. The expulsion was not disgraceful because Kim did not deserve to be expelled, or because the government did not have the necessary majority to expel. The expulsion was disgraceful because of the way it was carried out, with tactics more suited to Nazi Germany than to a nation which owes its existence to the United States of America.

In my years in Korea, I have encountered many Koreans, become friends with some, and very close to a handful. None of them deserves the travesty of government which afflicts this nation.

October 25, 1979 Thursday – Pusan

I have come full circle in my four years in Korea. After uncountable sojourns in hotels and inns throughout the countryside whose water taps generally offered a semi-liquid substance only a few degrees this side of ice but no hot water, I find myself in the Bando Hotel in Pusan, unable to extract anything from the pipes except scalding steam. Flip on the hot water tap, and out comes boiling water; flip on the cold, and out comes steam.

Why am I in Pusan? Strictly business, to provide a first-hand account of the riots here and in Masan last week. They compelled the government to proclaim martial law in Pusan and a slightly less stringent "garrison decree" in Masan, and to allow media coverage of student demonstrations for the first time since the spring of 1975. Martial law was declared after a three-minute cabinet meeting the night (11:30 p.m.) of October 17th. Ironically, this first martial law in seven years came seven years to the day since the 1972 proclamation which ushered in the Yushin system.

What were these riots which caused such an extraordinary reaction? I suppose by the standards of many nations, incidents involving no deaths and only a few broken windows and overturned vehicles are scarcely newsworthy. Here their significance must be weighed against past history.

Last week, for the first time in years, college students carried their demonstration off the campus and into the city streets, and not just in the university neighborhood. Students boarded buses and rode seven miles downtown. The government's long-standing policy to prevent just such an occurrence was justified by the consequences. Once downtown, the students were joined by a number of the general citizens (including, no doubt, a share of just plain hell-raisers) who went on a rampage against the police.

In practical terms, the last comparable incidents were in April 1960 during the Student Revolution which brought down the Syngman Rhee government. People already inclined to draw historical parallels did so when the disturbances (which lasted several days) spread to nearby Masan, psychologically important as the location where the corpse of a student killed by police in 1960 was discovered at the time, touching off that revolution.

Rumors of deaths this time around have also popped up. Such an event would likely be perceived as the end for the government. Opposition leader Kim Yong-sam fairly glows when he discusses the possibility of a dead student.

The course of the demonstrations diverged enough from the pattern of the last five years that no one can claim to give an authoritative explanation. Like so many, this began with the three demands: "Down with Yushin! End the dictatorship! Give us academic and press freedom!" But from there they went in new directions (including the fact they took place down in the quiet South rather than the hotbed Seoul universities.)

At best, the recent events undermine the government's carefully cultivated image of a stable society advancing under the Yushin banner. At worst, they call into question the long-term viability of a regime which, even with all the powers of the Yushin constitution and Emergency Measure #9, still requires martial law to maintain order.

October 28, 1979 Sunday

The events of this weekend have left much of what these pages contain on Korean politics useless. President Park Chung-hee is dead. In a scenario which even North Korean propagandists would have been hard-pressed to invent, he was killed in a shoot-out between his chief bodyguard and the Director of the Korean Central Intelligence Agency during an argument at dinner Friday night. The bodyguard is dead. The KCIA chief is in custody as the President's murderer. The nation is under martial law. Prime Minister Choi Kyu-ha has become the Acting President.

Even as I write these words, it is difficult to accept that things which two days ago were unthinkable are now fact. Even more than the suddenness of the event, the manner of its coming defies belief: a drunken argument between two rivals, Park's intervention to quell it, and suddenly a spray of gunfire better suited to the Old West or to a Chicago gangland slaying. No valiant sacrifice for the nation here, no peaceful passing in his sleep with the wish for reunification of Korea upon his lips.

After years of near paranoia on Park's part about the dissidents and the students in the South and the communists in the North, the blow fell not from any of them but from a close friend, from the man in charge of the agency built to safeguard the President. The monster Park had unleashed to control his enemies at last turned and devoured him.

And for what? Some great plan of national salvation? No, only petty jealousies among the courtiers around Park; power struggles among rivals, proving in the end that all their claims for concern about national security and stability really reflected concern only for the maintenance of their own power. Where, after all, has the great threat to Korea's peace and stability come from? Not from the students, or the opposition party, or the Christians; but from a group of men gathered in a KCIA restaurant, more concerned with their own positions than the security of the nation they profess to love so much.

All that is past. The crisis continues. What will happen to Korea? The long-standing question of whether the Yushin system can survive without Park will now be answered, much sooner than anyone expected. The people are shocked and in grief, of course. But isn't their determination to pursue business as usual a little too intense? It is fine not to lose oneself totally to grief, but on the other hand things here seem almost obscenely normal. There is none of the reaction I remember from President Kennedy's death in 1963 in the United States

There is shock; there is sorrow; there is fear. Is there not also relief? By a stroke of fate, the man who perhaps most Koreans believed had stayed in power too long and who gave no indication of stepping aside has now been removed from the scene. Already there is talk that now is the time to move toward democracy, before a new strongman emerges to impose his own brand of "Korean-style democracy" dictatorship.

"*Pulhengchung taheng.*
In the midst of misfortune, fortune."

***

In the few hours since the above paragraphs were written, they too have been overtaken by events. The Korean government announced today that the President's death was a premeditated assassination by the KCIA Director with the assistance of his own agents. Reportedly the director feared Park planned to fire him because of his "incompetence." (The KCIA the last few months has had its share of mistakes and miscalculations.)

The setting supports such findings: the dinner was in a KCIA restaurant near the Blue House and, besides the President, all those killed were members of the Presidential Protective Force and not KCIA agents.

October 29, 1979 Monday

The events of the weekend are potent reminders of the strengths of the American system, which never depends on one man for its existence and which doesn't disintegrate into constitutional crisis with each leader's passing. Such a misfortune to live in any one of so many of the world's societies where the leader's death raises once again even the most fundamental institutional issues: Shall we keep this Constitution? Amend it? Have a direct election? Indirect?

The Founding Fathers have spared the United States immeasurable trouble which would certainly arise, were it not for our

Constitution. The transfer of power – peaceful, constitutional, unquestioned – in 1800 from the Federalists to the Republicans surely stands as one of the greatest achievements of the American experiment.

Perhaps I have drifted to this subject before, but when defining "democracy," is it not easier to avoid abstract theoretical concepts and merely say: Democracy is a system of government which preserves the people's right to change its leadership within certain fixed periods under guidelines established independently of the existing ruling elite?

As a corollary, democracy requires a predetermined system for transferring power from one administration to the next. The transfer must be swift, complete, and unquestioned by all parties as long as it clearly follows existing constitutional requirements.

I still recall the reaction of many Koreans to President Carter's inauguration in January 1977, when with an oath, and a handshake between the two Presidents, power passed from Ford to Carter. No tanks, no soldiers, no blood, but it was still swift, complete, and unquestioned.

How strange that we perceive dictatorships as "strong" and democracies as "weak." The stability of a dictatorship is like the lid of a pressure-cooker, held down tightly by the dictator who dares not peek inside where the pressures build. In a democracy, you have an open pot of water which, even in the most heated of situations, may boil but rarely bubble over. An on-looker's first inclination is to be wary of the threatening turmoil in the open pot and feel safer near the pressure cooker. Experience soon demonstrates that the former derives its stability from its apparent instability. The latter, by its rigidity, guarantees that the accumulated pressure of the ultimate explosion will in one second wipe away its superficial calm.

Only one more point and I will end this half-cooked political theorizing. Many nations face their constitutional crises after the leader has left the scene and the remaining players try to figure out how to go on. The United States, on the other hand, experienced its greatest constitutional crisis in modern history when its leader, Nixon, refused to go, long after his departure was clearly the will of the people. Once he resigned, the constitutional order reasserted itself and the crisis was resolved.

One final postscript (yes, I do not keep my word even from one paragraph to the next): Discussing pressure cookers (as we did) and the relief I perceive among Koreans (as I mentioned yesterday) – I think that Koreans, having seen that the nation has survived the weekend and might even survive the future without Park, are now relieved that he is gone. In a totally unexpected way, the most urgent problem facing the nation (Park himself) has been removed. Granted that his removal gives rise to a host of new problems, they at least appear solvable.

It seems Koreans believed Park would never relax his grip willingly (take the lid off the cooker, so to speak) and that the nation was rapidly moving toward a crisis, another Student Revolution, perhaps. The present situation, while shocking, serious, undesirable, and every other suitable adjective, at least holds hope that a greater disaster – certain so long as Park remained in power – may now be avoided.

The praise, incidentally, that Park receives centers on the Korean economic miracle under his leadership. No one has yet suggested that the Yushin system will be one of his enduring achievements.

November 5, 1979 Monday

The assassination of President Park has not yet become the catastrophe it might have been. They put him in the ground last Saturday. Now there are few reminders that the situation has changed. Flags are at half-mast for a month. Our happy existence under martial law is marked only by a few more soldiers and tanks around government buildings and pages ripped out of *Time* and *Newsweek*. Worst of all, the 10:00 p.m. curfew puts quite a damper on social life.

But at least the radio and television stations have gone back to their regular programming and dropped their round-the-clock funeral music and pseudo-documentaries on Park. It's bad enough being cooped up by the curfew without also sacrificing one's favorite shows.

Koreans have discovered that there is life after Park. That is quite a discovery. For twenty years there was serious debate whether that would be so. In spite of government efforts through the censored press to make it appear otherwise, this is not a grief-stricken nation. Park was respected but not loved.

And perhaps I judged KCIA Director Kim Chae-kyu too harshly. It now seems he assassinated Park not because of his own petty jealousies but because he saw even more clearly than anyone else that Park's continued rule was threatening the nation with disaster. (Curiously, Kim was actually a "soft-liner" who encouraged greater liberalization, only to be overruled by Park.) KCIA reports estimated that, should street demonstrations such as occurred in Pusan take place in Seoul, the demonstrators would number not in the thousands but in the hundreds of thousands, inviting a clear breakdown of all authority.

If Park Chung-hee is the individual most surprised by the events of October 26th, KCIA Director Kim must run a close second, probably wondering why he sits in jail rather than acclaimed a national hero.

Perhaps I have been in Korea too long and see conspiracies everywhere, but there are enough unanswered questions still left to trouble the most trusting soul. One fact the government has neglected to mention in any of its official pronouncements, even though it is an open secret, is that the Chief of Staff of the Korean Army (now, in his capacity as Martial Law Commander, the most powerful man in Korea) was present in the same house in a different room at the time of the assassination. I wonder whether the whole conspiracy does not extend well beyond the confines of the KCIA.

Despite all the protestations from the government about how

"constitutional" the whole chain of events has been and how the civilian government remains in control, the fact remains that the nation now has an Acting President and a Martial Law Commander. I'm inclined to believe the President only acts when so ordered.

The situation ten days into the post-Park period remains surprisingly peaceful. That is a development I had my doubts about that Saturday morning when Mr. Clark, the Political Counselor, called me at 4:00 a.m., said the country was under martial law, and told me to come into the Embassy when it became daylight.

If all that has happened has not been more than enough, the funeral for Park brought Secretary of State Vance to Korea accompanied by Chip Carter, the President's son. Having had such vast experience with Amy and Rosalynn last June and apparently being the resident Carter family attaché, I was chosen as his Control Officer. Thankfully he only stayed twenty-four hours and, the day of the funeral being a national holiday, most of the country was shut up. He still squeezed in some shopping. What official visitor to Korea doesn't?

There was a time when I would have been overawed with the thought of ushering the President's son around. The whole thing was a bore.

November 22, 1979 Thanksgiving

I must mention the recent events in Iran. Student militants have occupied the American Embassy since November 4th and are holding the employees hostage. Their demand is that the United States return the exiled Shah, who is in New York for cancer treatment, to Iran for trial and certain execution. As if these events were not themselves outrageous enough, the ruling Iranian theocracy under the "holy man" Khomeini has supported the Embassy seizure and threatened to execute some of the Americans as spies.

I can barely remain rational while referring to the situation. Even though I am no fan of the Shah, I would rather die than send him back as demanded. The Iranian government, by allowing the continued occupation and threatening spy "trials," is acting like no other government has ever done in modern history – not even the Nazis or the Japanese in World War II.

Life is difficult enough overseas with all the crazy characters willing to use the American government as hate object. It is unbearable with the additional insanity of foreign governments actively supporting their actions.

As far as I'm concerned, we are at war with Iran. President Carter was right to end oil imports and freeze the Iranian assets deposited in the United States. I think he should also order all Iranians (include the estimated 50,000 students) to leave the United States immediately, and order that all trade between the two countries stop immediately. We can do without their oil more easily than they without our food.

The spectacle of Iranian students using the American courts to stay in the United States disgusts me. There is no law which says we violate human rights by ordering citizens of a blatantly hostile nation to get out. On the other hand, there are international treaties, recognized even by Iran, which guarantee the inviolability of embassies and their personnel, in recognition of the fact that such is the minimum requirement for the conduct of foreign relations.

Should the great and God-like Khomeini go ahead and kill any of the hostages, I would hope we would give him a sample of his own "Islamic justice," starting with round-the-clock bombing of Tehran.

(It's lucky I'm not the President. We'd have nuclear war in no time.)

I pray that the remaining hostages are released unharmed. In a great show of Islamic mercy, most of the blacks and women have been let go already. I hope that the American people finally wake up to the fact that all that oil they're so fond of guzzling comes from an area of the world whose stability we cannot predict from day to day. Two years ago Iran was the island of stability in the Middle East. What about Saudi Arabia and Kuwait next year?

Speaking of next year, I recently learned of my next post:

Number One in the two-man Consular Section in the Embassy in Accra, Ghana. I leave Korea in May, as planned, spend the summer in the United States, and go to Africa in August. People ask me how I feel. The transfer is still so far down the road that it is almost impossible to react. Accra was one of my top choices in the list I submitted to Personnel in the Department. I have always wanted to see Africa. I thought it best to do so while still young and relatively resistant to disease. As African posts go, Accra is reputedly livable. None of the comforts and luxuries I have here – but then no threat from a North Korean army thirty miles up the road.

Until I actually set foot in Accra, there's always a slim possibility the assignment might be changed. Ambassador Gleysteen was good enough to send a cable recommending me for a job in the Operations Center of the Department in Washington. For the moment, I regret the two wool suits I ordered made last weekend.

Undoubtedly Mother will not be pleased with the news when she gets my letter. She has often mentioned that she looked forward to my return to the States. But in joining the Foreign Service it was never my intention to stay in the United States.

I will be distinctly unhappy to leave Korea. In many ways, this upcoming move may necessitate ripping apart roots more deeply planted than those uprooted when I came here in 1975.

December 17, 1979 Monday

There is today no issue of more immediate importance to the United States than the safe return of the fifty hostages at the Embassy in Iran. The Embassy occupation has passed its fortieth day, with no prospect of an immediate resolution. The criminals who parade themselves as the "government" of Iran and "men of Allah" and the mobs over whom they may or may not exercise control still discuss spy trials with conflicting statements on whether the hostages would then be killed.

The United Nations Security Council has demanded the release of the hostages. The World Court has ordered their release and the restoration of the Embassy to U.S. control. The madman Khomeini, apparently believing himself to have some special relationship with the Almighty, chooses to flout the demands and requirements of civilization and instead heaps further abuse on the United States and President Carter.

At the same time, the United States has demonstrated its greatness and its unity, two qualities which in the wake of the Vietnam years many doubted we had. The Iranian crisis has brought the American people together. More than that, they have demonstrated their maturity, resisting the temptation to respond to the provocation with an equally uncivilized action. Instead, with great patience and restraint they demand the safe return of all the hostages before a single demand from Iran will be considered. The contrast between the two nations is overwhelming.

Perhaps most of all, our refusal until this point to employ force against Iran – despite our very real potential to do so – offers convincing proof of American greatness. In the history of the world, how often have militarily powerful nations chosen policies of reason and calmness when provoked by weaker powers?

My mother wrote in a letter dated December 9th: "Talked with Joan this morning and she gave me the address in Tehran to send a card to the American hostages. A representative or senator from Pennsylvania has urged everyone to send a card so I got one off in the mail. Also on the news they are urging everyone to display the flag so I got it out and am going to hang it in the front window until the Iranian situation is cleared up. Prayer services are also being held as well as prayers at Sunday services in all the churches.

"The only half-decent item in the news has been the release of some political prisoners in Korea. I hope that means the beginning of better government for the Koreans.

"The Detroit *Free Press* has an article that said the lives of the hostages may take second place to larger considerations. What an awful, agonizing thought."

1980

January 1, 1980 Tuesday – Hong Kong

Can I let this day pass without some comment? I realize that 1980 is the last year of this decade rather than the beginning of the next. Even so, it is understandable that people regard 1980 not only as a new year but also as a new decade, and I will follow suit.

1979 was a good year for me. I was fairly successful in carrying out my New Year's resolutions to read and exercise (and, incidentally, filling these pages at a rate two or three times my previous speed). Perhaps for 1980 I would be best off to continue to pursue my 1979 goals. The more I have read in the past year, the more clearly I have seen how limited (in spite of my Jesuit and liberal arts background) is my knowledge of many areas which have begun to hold a previously unknown interest for me. The background of the Celts and the Irish, and American folklore and folk music are such areas.

Although I have exercised physically more this past year than was previously my practice and consequently have tended to feel healthier than previously, I should try to institutionalize exercise as part of my routine. Regrettably weightlifting and tennis remain things which I do when I have the time, rather than including them as part of my set schedule. My aversion to waking up early in the morning eliminates several potentially useful hours a day from my life.

Perhaps most of all, in view of upcoming events, I must keep in mind that my life goes on and changes constantly. I cannot freeze the present moment and keep it. I should not dread new experiences but welcome them. The past has demonstrated that invariably the future produces memories as happy as those of the present. Separation from friends does not end those friendships.

In that connection, looking at my life in the last ten years, there is no way that I could have or would have predicted on January 1st, 1970 in Southfield, Michigan that on January 1st, 1980 I would be in the Hyatt Regency Hotel in Hong Kong, and in the intervening years would have visited England, Japan, Korea, Thailand, and Singapore. I did not want to lose the security of my college life six years ago; I do not want to lose the familiarity of my Korean life now. But I did, and I must. Each transfer, while containing a difficult transition period, led me to a happier life.

While I paint such a rosy picture of my own life, the world situation continues to unravel. The hostage crisis in Iran drags on, oil prices go up, Vietnam threatens its neighbors, the Cambodian people appear close to extinction, and now the Soviets have invaded Afghanistan.

The Soviet invasion of Afghanistan has had the curious effect of putting the U.S. and the Iranian governments on the same side of an issue. It has caused Jimmy Carter to call Soviet boss Brezhnev a liar and to say his perception of the Russians has changed more in the last week than in the previous two years. It has led Carter's National Security Advisor Brzezinski to make the pointed comment that it was American friendship with Iran that kept Soviet troops out of Tehran for thirty-five years.

January 11, 1980 Friday – Seoul

The gods of weather seem well aware that this is my last winter in a temperate climate until at least 1982. They have blessed Korea with more snow than I have seen here in any of the last four winters. It has snowed on four separate occasions when the snow actually remained on the ground for several days before melting. On the day after Christmas, we received eight centimeters.

At the time my sister Margaret and I were strolling around the grounds of the Kyungbok Palace, located directly behind the Capitol Building near my apartment. It being a workday, almost no one else was around. The thick snowflakes muffled the sound of the traffic from beyond the palace walls. A spectacular sight.

Lest I wax too romantic, however, over the glories of a Korean winter, let me remind myself that biting cold rather than snowfall is its more common characteristic. Yesterday was such a typical day. Most of the snow melted away. Only the drab greys and browns of this dreary city's buildings stood between me and the wind which found every opening through my layers of clothes. Even in my office, the wind swept in through the cracks between the poorly insulated windows. Running the heater at full speed only succeeded in burning up more tax dollars.

I have begun to consider the nitty gritty of actually moving in May – what to take to Ghana, what to ship home, what to dispose of. The piano, my piano, my first major purchase made after arriving here – yes, my tailor-made piano – must go. I really must try my hand at learning some musical instrument of smaller dimensions which will not single-handedly consume a good part of my weight allowance.

I've also tentatively decided to liquidate part of my collection of Korean chests and artwork, with the object in mind of returning to my initial reason for acquiring such things: simplicity in furnishings. While each item in isolation displays a strong statement of simplicity (much as the design of early American furniture), crowding them all together in one apartment makes the place look as junky as a Victorian sitting room.

January 13, 1980 Sunday

I have begun to gear up for the transition to Ghana, with an inventory of things to keep and things to go. I have decided to abandon my stereo system (whose value approaches $600). The climate in Ghana seems to exert such a baleful influence on any instrument of technology that it seems almost pointless to risk such valuable equipment. Additionally, Ghana radio appears to be carried entirely on short-wave frequencies. There seems little point in transporting an FM stereo system around with me. Instead I will depend on my little Sanyo cassette stereo/short-wave radio. If it rots, no great financial loss. Presuming my eighty-plus cassette tapes arrive intact, I should have little trouble filling my musical needs.

What shall I do with my 150 record albums? Some I have

literally not listened to in years. I am such a packrat that I resist parting with anything once I have acquired it.

February 9, 1980 Saturday

Three months to go, and the speed with which the time passes appalls me. How will I ever finish all the things I want to do before leaving Korea? I look forward to Ghana with increasing excitement. All those who have been there with whom I've spoken assure me that, granted the hardships, Ghana is an interesting assignment.

I've even resigned myself to the fact that I must buy a car. Today I priced Jeeps (four-wheel drive with air conditioning) at a mere $8,000. Whatever happened to the days when basic transportation was available for less than $2,000? Or, for that matter, when gas wars drove the price of a gallon of regular down to nineteen cents a gallon (versus the current $1.00 plus and rising)?

How the average Korean family survives escapes me. Here we have an inflation rate which surely approaches fifty percent a year, including two *separate* sixty percent increases in petroleum prices within the last year. The Korean economic miracle, whose spectacular annual growth made the inflation problem only a minor headache, appears to have ended, with projections of three-to-five percent growth for 1980. (Not bad by U.S. standards, but disastrous compared to the usual ten-to-fourteen percent growth rates.)

February 23, 1980 Saturday

So many things I wish to write, both about myself and about Korea, before I leave this country. The task overwhelms me and I do not know where to start. There are so many things and so many people here that I love. Still, I am astounded at the combination of contradictory traits within the Korean personality. Koreans have a facility either to ignore their own defects or to attribute them to some foreign power (usually Japan or the United States).

Part of my own problem may well be that my only substantial foreign experience has been in Korea. I often indict Korea for crimes which many other countries are also guilty of. And yet a large number of Americans with more extensive foreign experience than I have found fault on many of the same points which abhor me. Perhaps I am fortunate to have had Korea as my first overseas assignment, allowing me to overlook many problems, which in the future in other countries will appear unbearable, only because this is my *first* post.

The time has come for me to leave Korea. I have become too involved here, too set in my opinions. Bizarre as it may sound, I do find myself having increasing trouble with English expressions as I become attuned to Korean grammatical patterns.

April 7, 1980 Monday

I occasionally recognize that other people sometimes demonstrate a wit nearly as sharp as my own. Nevertheless, it was with some surprise that I opened the March 17th *Pacific Stars and Stripes*, the U.S. Army paper, to discover "The Ten Most Important Rules While Driving in Korea." If ever I had attempted such a list, the result would have surely been no more succinct and accurate than these rules penned by a Major John B. Smith (could that really be his name?):

"There are no rules.

"On any thoroughfare, the number of lanes depends on the width of the vehicle; that is, six buses equal ten small cabs, equal eight Ponies (a Korean car), equal sixteen bicycles with eight cases of beer on back, or any permutation of the above.

"In traffic, he who hesitates goes second and gets a horn blast from the fellow in back.

"Most pedestrians, who have never driven a vehicle, believe that drivers have mystical powers that enable them to see clearly dark-clothed people crossing unlit highways at night.

"Being close only counts in horseshoes and hand grenades, so an eighth of an inch clearance between vehicles is a sixteenth of an inch too much.

"If a cab driver is caught looking to the left, right, or in the rear view mirror while moving, the passenger gets to ride free. Looking in the mirror during the red light to comb his hair does not count.

"Americans in big cars always give way. And if they don't, American car insurance is the same as winning a lottery.

"Honking your horn loudly and often is the same as driving safely, carefully, and slowly. They were warned, right?

"Playing in the road is always more fun than playing in a yard with Mommy watching.

"The flow of traffic is like Nature, and Nature abhors a vacuum: that is, if there is a space in traffic for another vehicle, another vehicle will fill that space."

I showed the above list to a Korean friend. He failed to see the humor or the accuracy.

April 7, 1980 Monday

Only forty days to go until my departure. Every day that passes leaves me more appalled by the prospect of actually packing everything up – not to mention all the food and the clothes that I will have to buy for Ghana.

April 14, 1980 Monday

I will depart Korea without having eaten dog, snake, or live octopus. One thing I have learned in my travels is that the ability to deal with unusual foods is the price of survival. But the line must be drawn somewhere.

Mine was drawn to include animal intestines and sparrows among the edibles, but the latter only in a state of advanced drunkenness – mine, not theirs. Dogs and snakes are definitely out. And the thought of raw octopus's tentacles writhing on the plate hours after they've been chopped off the body still sends chills up and down my spine. God forbid I ever attempt to eat one and, having used my chopsticks to wrestle it off the plate, fail to swallow it quicker than it can latch onto the roof of my mouth with one of its suction cups!

These last two months have witnessed a flurry of travel on my part through the Korean countryside in one final attempt to fix the sights in my memories. I have visited old sights, seen new sights, and realized once again the difficulty of ever being an "expert" on a foreign country.

On the weekend of March 1-2, I went to Soraksan on the East Coast for the umpteenth time, this excursion in the company of Choi Gun-ho and the MBC mountain-climbing association. Unfortunately, I was recovering from a severe cold and spent a good deal of the trip praying for death. Drinking large quantities of *soju* (Korean-style moonshine better suited to powering lawn mowers) and getting up at 5:00 a.m. Sunday morning (I never even suspected Sunday began so early in the day) also played their part in undermining my health.

The trip offered the opportunity to see the first full moon of the lunar new year (significant to Koreans) shimmering serenely over the East Sea (aka the Sea of Japan). Also, our tour bus did not return us to Seoul via the two-lane expressway. Instead, we went speeding over old country roads through peaceful villages. In one particularly paralyzing segment, we snaked our way up a winding road littered with fallen (and falling) rocks to reach the pass over the mountains.

I remember distinctly thinking at the time, as I stood at the top of the pass (yes, we stopped briefly), that my eyes would never rest on this spectacular view again.

Which only offers convincing proof that any effort to predict even apparently obvious future events is fraught with danger. Four weeks later I passed the same spot, this time in a bus headed in the opposite direction, this time with my Korean friends from the American Cultural Center, this time in a rainstorm. This time, instead of threading our way *up* the mountain, we went roaring *down* it, through one muddy hairpin curve after another. Surely, I thought, such a monster as this road would not allow me to pass by unscathed twice.

Notes from Lower Volta

April 28, 1980 Monday

    Two weekends ago I took a trip with Kathy Sellers and Jeff Morehead. We took off Thursday and Friday for an extended four-day weekend. We descended on Chinhae (famous for its cherry blossoms in the springtime), Pusan, Kyongju (the ancient Silla capital), and Kangneung.

    I may have mentioned: traveling within Korea is fraught with perils. Our *yogwan* in Pusan is a case in point. Having settled ourselves in for the night (in separate rooms because each was no larger than a Munchkin dressing room), I became aware in the midst of my slumbers that a number of people were arguing in the hallway. My first surmise was that it was 6:00 or 7:00 a.m. Such hallway goings-on are not uncommon once curfew ends and the sun comes up. A look at my watch, though, showed it was only 1:30 a.m.

    The argument droned on, with a woman's low, steady voice (the innkeeper's) alternating with a couple of less conciliatory, more inebriated masculine voices. The subject of the dispute apparently centered on whether the would-be lodgers would pay for their rooms now (as demanded by the innkeeper) or in the morning (per the would-be lodgers).

    After some twenty minutes of this exchange, it was clear that the issue was not moving toward resolution. Having reached the breaking point (angered largely by my own reluctance to let the two parties know they were interfering with my sleep), I burst out of my room to pour forth a torrent of English and Korean which compensated for the incoherence of its phrasing by the passion with which I expressed it.

    Kathy immediately burst forth from her room – Jeff elected to sit the matter out. Our mutual outburst – only stirred to new heights by the would-be lodgers' repeated requests that we "Sleep peacefully!" – resulted in their expulsion from the inn, together with the two ladies accompanying them.

    My adrenaline was pumping so hard it was difficult to get back to sleep. I had largely succeeded when bizarre grunts, groans, and squeals again awakened me. At first I thought the walls were full of rats. Then I realized the noise actually originated across the hall, from two (perhaps more) people who were obviously enjoying each other's company. Curiously the gentleman involved seemed somewhat quiet, whereas the lady in question was quite vocal. My own considered opinion is that she was faking it.

Tuesday, April 29, 1980

Tonight I write in the expectation that when in future years I look back on these pages the events here described will have shed the pain and frustration which now cling to them.

An effort to free the hostages from the Embassy in Tehran has failed.

The failure of the rescue effort pains most because it had nothing to do with any action on the part of the Iranians. The rescue team with its helicopters and airplanes entered and withdrew from Iran without the Iranian government even knowing we had been there. Instead, a series of mechanical failures disabled three of the eight rescue helicopters, compounded by the tragic crash of a fourth helicopter into one of the planes *after* the order to withdraw had been given. This prevented even an attempt at the full execution of the rescue plan.

Had it been successful, the hostages would now be enroute to the United States and the crisis for all practical purposes ended. Instead, eight servicemen have died, not in defense of the nation but in the helicopter-airplane accident, and the hostages have been scattered to several cities throughout Iran to prevent further attempts. To add to the disarray, Secretary Vance has gone ahead with a previous decision to resign in protest against the rescue attempt, and the United States (more specifically, Jimmy Carter) has come under attack for the "rash" action which threatens peace.

Why is it that we have threatened peace when, for the first time in the six months of a crisis we played only a minor part in provoking, we have attempted to end it with a quick military operation calculated to inflict minimum injury to Iran to free the hostages? Why should we be criticized for taking action to stop the outrageous detention of diplomats by armed terrorists when the government whose responsibility it is to protect those diplomats not only has failed to do so but in fact encouraged their captors?

I am saddened, not that we made the attempt but that it failed; saddened that those who died achieved nothing by their deaths; saddened that unless Iran returns itself quickly to civilization the only course left open to the United States now is a punitive military action.

We are moving toward war. Barring a sudden burst of rationality from the Tehran government, I think war is coming. Each passing day reduces the chances that the hostages will survive the crisis.

The only humor of recent days comes from the Soviet Union, which finds time to condemn our "aggression" in Iran even as it is still busy liberating Afghanistan from itself.

These are not happy times. I only hope that I live to see better. When was the world situation more bleak than it is today?

July 28, 1980 Monday – Washington

At last after all these years, I close the chapter on Korea. I have hesitated for two months since my May 17th departure to write these lines for fear the words to describe my emotions would not come.

Those last weeks in Korea remain fresh in the memory, the gradual drift into chaos climaxed in my final week there by the large student demonstrations in the streets of Seoul. For days they shut down the downtown area in the afternoon and locked us in our compound due to its proximity to the government buildings. The street demonstrations with their tear gas, rock-throwing, and limited violence terrified the population.

The preceding on-campus demonstrations had set many people on edge. The long-absent spectacle of disorder in the streets conjured up unpleasant memories of the turbulent 1960-61 period.

Since my departure, the news from Korea has been unrelievedly depressing in an atmosphere incredible even for such a nation as Korea used to incredible events. A virtual coup by the military swept away all but the facade of the civilian government. On-going purges of "corruption" and "disloyalty" have netted not only the usual suspects but even caught up long-time government supporters. The capstone of the recent tragedy was the bloody revolt in late May in the southwestern city of Kwangju. The civilian population, enraged by official brutality, momentarily expelled the military before being overwhelmed.

Koreans, it seems, have resigned themselves once again to the military's *fait accompli*. They have once again accepted the argument that resistance against dictatorship in the South risks bringing an invasion from the North. Democracy has again been beaten to death on the Korean peninsula. The tragedy of the situation is all the more intense, coming in the wake of the great optimism of the preceding months that the nation was emerging from the scourge of authoritarianism.

August 17, 1980 Sunday – Washington

Two weeks from tonight I leave New York for Ghana. How quickly the summer has passed! As always, the time which seemed plentiful enough to finish all that was planned for it has passed with many items yet unfilled.

I have been struck during this American sojourn by the basic optimism of the American people. That notwithstanding, the continued high inflation, high unemployment, and foreign troubles offer sufficient grounds for pessimism. When viewed in conjunction with the fact that the election of any one of the three major Presidential candidates this November 4th offers no relief, the future becomes a frightening dream.

Surely our system has failed when it is able to produce the likes of only Ronald Reagan, Jimmy Carter, and John Anderson to vie for the Presidency. Jimmy Carter has demonstrated again and again his extensive political abilities. Unfortunately, these abilities extend only to getting himself nominated and elected. He knows how to get power. He has shown for almost four years that he cannot lead.

Ted Kennedy's bid for the Presidency has fizzled, and yet he delivered the finest speech of the last twenty years at the Democratic convention. It was perhaps a speech which only a man out of the running could have delivered, a powerful reaffirmation of the principles which have guided the Democratic Party for the last fifty years. It lifted the audience for a moment from the unpleasant reality of renominating President Carter.

An observer who had failed to follow the twists and turns of American politics these last months would have assumed, tuning into Kennedy's speech unprepared, that Kennedy had just been nominated. Having heard the speech, the observer would probably have voted for him. Undoubtedly one reaction of Kennedy supporters, even as he thrilled them with his delivery, was: "Why didn't he talk this way earlier in the campaign?"

August 29, 1980 Friday – New York

Labor Day weekend. I am in New York for my Sunday evening departure to Ghana. For most Americans, this weekend marks the end of the summer season and the notification that autumn will shortly arrive. For me, this weekend closes my three-month transition between Seoul and Accra, and begins the two-year summer I will face in Africa.

During these past months, I have visited with most of my friends and family, including old Marquette classmates and Foreign Service friends who had long since departed Korea. I have traveled to Kyoto, Hong Kong, Honolulu, San Francisco, St. Louis, Milwaukee, Chicago, New Orleans, Alabama, Mississippi, Pensacola, Disneyworld, Detroit, Ohio, Philadelphia, Maryland, Washington, Virginia, New Jersey, and New York. The trip to Accra will include stops in Dakar and Monrovia.

My last weeks in Washington were somewhat more hectic than desired, and included shopping sprees of hundreds of dollars for such exotic paraphernalia as candles, Tupperware, hammers, and auto tires.

Two weeks ago I learned that the Ghanaian government has a restricted list of cars which can be imported into the country. Although the specific list was only announced recently (listing five makes), the Ghanaians adopted the general principle a year ago, about the time I received my Accra assignment. The list does not include Jeeps, or any American vehicle. (The Department of State post report for Accra dated 1978, incidentally, recommends bringing along a "small, sturdy American car.") Those foreigners who attempt to bring any but an approved automobile must back its importation with twenty percent of the vehicle's value in spare parts. Considering the Jeep's $9,000 price tag, the idea boggles the imagination.

While not too pleased with the Ghanaian government's policy (which it appears unable to decide whether to enforce), I am upset that neither the Department nor the Embassy in Accra bothered to tell me that all was not well. As of yesterday, when I left Washington, there had been no reply from the Embassy to a cable which I drafted asking for "assurances that the import restrictions will not be applied to Duffy's Jeep."

Getting the Jeep into Ghana is only one side of the problem. Getting it out of the United States is the other. A scant six days before the Jeep was slated to be driven to the port of Baltimore, it died while it and I were moving down the Washington Beltway at the brisk speed of 55 MPH.

The sudden realization that one's vehicle is rapidly losing speed and that a frantic pumping of the accelerator in no way reverses the process ranks as one of life's more dismaying moments. At first the problem was localized in fourth gear, but it quickly made its way down until the Jeep limped along in first gear for one or two blocks between stall-outs.

Having just had the Jeep in an American Motors dealer the

day before to replace the standard fifteen-gallon tank with a twenty-five-gallon tank, I assumed that the mechanics had managed to botch up the entire fuel system. I called the AMC dealer and somewhat incoherently but fervently expressed my predicament. Since he remembered me from the day before, the mechanic did not need much information to realize he had one irate customer and one dead Jeep on his hands, and dispatched a truck to tow me the ten miles to the dealership.

For two days, the mechanics could not duplicate my repeated feat of stalling out. They were about to release the Jeep with a clean bill of health when the car demonstrated how poorly it could perform. The mechanic claimed the juxtaposition of the installation of the larger gas tank and the fuel pump failure was a coincidence.

Did I mention previously that I bought the Jeep? I did refer to the day I *priced* them. Well, the following week, I went back and signed the contract for a Jeep CJ-7 to be built and delivered to me in Michigan. Base price: $6,000. Add options like doors, roof, and back seat and the price really jumped. Throw in air conditioning, a V-6 engine (to power the air conditioner) and power steering (to control the V-6 engine), and we're up in the $9,000 range.

September 21, 1980 Sunday – Accra, Ghana

When a person is about to record for the first time his impressions of a new country, he needs to take care that his comments avoid either extreme of being overly harsh or overly generous. Sweeping judgments derived from a few days' worth of observation may prove to have been totally erroneous, in much the same way that our perception of the interior of a dark room lit by one candle may well bear little resemblance to the reality revealed in the light of day.

In addition, the reader will take these initial words as the most important, indelibly fixing his own impression regardless of what the author may subsequently write. It is with a fair amount of hesitation, therefore, that I have prepared this first entry since my arrival in

William J. Duffy

Ghana September 1st.

The Pan American flight, a fifteen-hour extravaganza variously referred to as "The Red-eyed Special" and the "African Queen," included hour-long lay-overs in Dakar and Monrovia. My first glimpse of Africa at Dakar in the early morning from the airplane window was surprisingly unemotional. "So this is Africa. It looks like I expected it, with flat lands and scattered trees."

In spite of what seemed adequate preparation for the rigors of Ghana, the difficulties of living here have turned out to be all that they were described, and then some. The people are very friendly and the weather nice (or is it the other way around?), the stores empty, the money worthless, the economy bankrupt, the black market supreme, the phones out of order, the city water pumps out of commission, nothing to do except go to the beach or to Togo, and my rest-and-recreation leave still six months away. Those are the good points. The grim details will follow, if only I develop the courage to list them.

The extremes of living in Ghana become apparent in this example: I have an immense two-story house, with three bedrooms and two and a half baths. Two of the three city water pumps, however, have recently broken down. Since no spare parts are available, months may pass before pumped water is restored. In the meantime, water is delivered to my house by truck (heaven forbid it breaks down without any spare parts). The truck pumps the water into a 350-gallon tank on my roof. But the tank connects to only one bathroom, so the others are useless. Well, at least as bathrooms.

September 22, 1980 Monday

The house in which I have taken up residence comes straight out of a turn-of-the-century novel about life in the tropics: whitewashed walls, high ceilings, and a virulently overgrown garden with a hint of decay. It stands in a compound with three others identical to it, giving the resident the added advantage of always knowing where his neighbor's bathroom is when he goes visiting –

provided, of course, that the neighbor has water he will willingly spare. Life in the compound remains surprisingly private while offering the added security of having fellow Americans close at hand. There is the one irritant, however, of the couple across the way whose sole pastime seems to be sitting in their kitchen drinking coffee, allowing them to stay abreast of my own activities.

I have long had an aversion to air-conditioning, except under the most extreme circumstances, because of the sense of claustrophobia it induces and my psychosomatic conviction that sleeping in such unnatural air has a particularly deleterious effect on my allergies. It was, therefore, with some delight that I discovered the house came equipped with ceiling fans. Ghana has high temperatures, but so far has not equaled an August day in Washington for terrifying heat.

The air conditioners grind and wheeze at top speed to cool the air within a foot or so of their grilles. The ceiling fans (with open doors and windows) provide a most refreshing breeze. I am not describing the classic movie image of Sydney Greenstreet in his white suit under a fan lazily circling overhead. Oh no, these fans fly at top speed. Should only they have a wing between them, they might well fly me and the house out of this Evelyn Waugh novel. Whether my love affair with the ceiling fans and open windows will last remains to be seen. Ghana has a particularly dry, dry season which includes Saharan sands wafting down from the North and filling every crevice with dust. At the other end of the spectrum are the mold and mildew, two enemies ever ready to carry their invasions into any book, painting, or expensive object.

October 6, 1980 Monday – Frankfurt, Germany

People who have said that Korea is in my blood may have spoken with greater literal truth than they imagined. On September 26th I left Accra for Frankfurt on a medical evacuation, with a temperature of 102 degrees F and a persistent pain in my right side. The Ghanaian doctor who examined me diagnosed it as a liver abscess, possibly amoebic, which – in view of my recent arrival in Ghana – probably moved in while I still lived in Korea.

Since medical facilities are limited in Accra (shortages of drugs and inadequate laboratory facilities), the Embassy nurse decided it best to send me to the 97th Army Hospital here to try to confirm or deny the diagnosis. All testing so far has produced negative results: x-rays, liver-spleen scan, urinalysis, blood work. I have felt fine since arrival once I slept off the exhaustion of my two days of pain and the long flight. The pain disappeared enroute and the temperature quickly returned to a normal range.

Tomorrow the doctors will look at my gall bladder. They are determined to find something wrong with me. If that examination shows nothing, I might return to Ghana on Wednesday.

I am almost tempted to think that I induced the symptoms subconsciously in order to get out of Ghana. Entering the hospital was like becoming a prisoner-of-war: loss of freedom, restrictions on mobility, orders to follow, and no clear idea when the ordeal would end. It seems unlikely I would make a good hostage, having had in a very small, benevolent way a taste of what the Americans in Iran have gone through for eleven months.

Once I accepted that my release was not imminent, I became resigned to the situation and took the opportunity to read and watch military television (another reminder of Korea). Once the hospital staff realized I was not about to die immediately, the doctor allowed me to leave the hospital on day passes, so I have been able to look around Frankfurt.

This is my first trip to Europe, aside from a month spent in England at Christmas 1972. I had thought in the past that an assignment in Europe would lack interest in comparison with those in Asia or Africa, given the common traditions of Europe and America and the intrinsically "exotic" qualities of every place else. I have seen in this short time that there is a rich divergence between Europe and America, perhaps comparable to the contrast between Korea and Japan, in the way each has produced a different version of the same basic cultural tradition. My month in Africa has already taught me not to discount the sheer comfort of living in the midst of industrial prosperity.

October 22, 1980 Wednesday – Accra

Since my return to Ghana October 8th, life has begun at last to assume a new routine. My household effects arrived from Korea the day before my trip to Germany. (More exactly, the thousand pounds I sent here as opposed to the 1,400 pounds put in storage in California.) Somewhere in their wanderings across this globe, some treasure-hunter forced the lift van open and absconded with the contents of two of the boxes. Presumably the haul from those was disappointing enough to discourage further rummaging. I have unpacked and inventoried what arrived. Having accounted for all the important items, I don't know what is missing. So matters could have turned out less favorably.

The ship with my Jeep and all the other items I bought in the United States this past summer will reportedly arrive in three days. I don't know how long Ghanaian Customs will take to clear them. The prospect of having my own transportation once again will remove one of the major irritants to life in Accra.

Two problems which worried me most before my arrival have turned out to be much more minor than anticipated: the climate and the insects. Although we have not yet reached the hot hot season (not to be confused with the cool hot season), longtime residents assure me that the rigors of a Washington summer hold more terror than Accra's worst.

Hardly any insects at all have presented themselves for my inspection, in contrast to my assumption that the air, ground, and water would swarm with them. The most exotic wildlife so far are the small lizards who run around eating the insects and each other.

There really is nothing to do here socially which people do not organize for themselves. The highlights of the Accra social whirl appear to consist of drinking beer at the Marine House on Friday nights, playing baseball on Saturday afternoons, and visiting the beach on Sunday mornings. (I have not yet availed myself of the first two opportunities.)

I have found only one restaurant (the Palm Court) whose food justifies a follow-up visit. Service in most cases seems to be a lost cause, not because of any surliness or incompetence but because of a general indifference and passivity. The Palm Court, ironically, is a Chinese restaurant.

I've only had the pleasure of Ghanaian food on two occasions. The national dish (or is it a general West African phenomenon?) is called fufu. Fufu is a tasteless blob made from cassava or plantains and shaped like a lump of dough. The trick in eating it is to swallow each mouthful without chewing, in order to avoid the sensation of having a mouth full of plaster of Paris.

All the tests at the hospital in Germany established nothing: no liver, spleen, or gall bladder trouble; no malaria; and no amoebas or parasites. The doctor suggested that perhaps I had a viral infection which ran its course before I reached Germany. Although it was obvious from the day I arrived at the hospital that nothing was wrong with me *then* (regardless of what my former condition might have been), it took the good doctors ten days to confirm that.

They would not release me until I rewarded all their effort by catching a cold. Congestion almost exploded my head when the plane landed in Abidjan enroute to Accra. The tropical weather here, rather than instantly restoring my health, has demonstrated its inexorable ability to make everything flourish (including head colds), and mine still lingers on after two weeks.

October 23, 1980 Thursday

As befits a former British colony, English is widely spoken here. English is rarely a Ghanaian's native language, its use dictated by the necessity of a common medium to surmount the multiplicity of tribal languages. People conduct their business in what is essentially a foreign language, strangers in their own land. The situation calls to mind a high school language class in which the students attempt to carry on conversations in the second language with varying degrees of success and comprehension.

Ghana is not Korea. Even allowing for the natural bias toward Korea caused by its being my first post, I cannot generate anything approaching that level of excitement here. Five years passed quickly in East Asia, with only a few occasions when I wished to be elsewhere. I have trouble accepting that six months from now I will still be in Ghana.

Anthropological dogma that all cultures are equal to the contrary, I have little enthusiasm to delve into the finer points of local culture in Ghana. It is not only a question of East Asia's art, music, and philosophies. It is also that the Japanese, Koreans, and Chinese have built vigorous modern societies. The Ghanaians have used their twenty-three years of independence to turn the prosperous colony the British left behind into an economic disaster. Western influence (Christianity) seems to have worked far more havoc on the local traditions here than in the Far East.

All these nasty comments, incidentally, are directed specifically at Ghana, since I have no other African experience. Even people who have spent years elsewhere on the continent find Ghana appalling.

October 26, 1980 Sunday

It being the first anniversary of the assassination of Park Chung-hee, a few Korean notes are in order. News from Korea filters through even to deepest, darkest Africa: the conviction and sentencing to death of opposition leader Kim Dae-jung; the election of General Chun Doo-hwan as president; and the referendum on the constitution for the Fourth/Fifth/Sixth Republic (check one).

North and South both have embassies in Accra. Some days the local newspapers have articles extolling the socialist workers' paradise in the North, other days they publish articles describing Chun as ideally suited to his new job. The most interesting article combined a South Korean headline with a North Korean text, sending both sides into tizzies.

In two weeks our presidential election will have taken place. Our system seems increasingly incapable of generating leaders of true presidential stature. Instead, we have buffoon Jimmy Carter. He appears likely to overcome his record of demonstrated incompetence in the White House with his very real skill at winning elections. Or we'll get has-been actor Ronald Reagan. Someone once remarked Reagan hasn't said anything original since he starred opposite a chimpanzee in the 1951 *Bedtime for Bonzo*.

November 5, 1980 Wednesday

A strange sensation to awaken this morning to hear the Voice of America announce that Ronald Reagan will be the next President of the United States. Even stranger to hear that the Republicans have taken control of the Senate for the first time in a quarter century.

At first I reacted with satisfaction to the thought that the American public has rejected Jimmy Carter. Then I considered the alarming prospect of a Reagan administration.

No matter what the outcome of the election, I would regard the news as disheartening. The United States has survived for two centuries. Surely the Republic can hold together for another four years (assuming Ronnie himself holds out). Even more to the point, we have survived four years of Jimmy Carter. We should be able to weather anything!

Today marks the 367th day of captivity for the hostages in Iran.

November 7, 1980 Friday

The servant problem, even in this modern age, remains a pressing matter for those of us in the Foreign Service. It is perhaps even more of a problem for those of us who somehow managed to reach maturity without being waited on hand and foot (aside from our mothers) and who early absorbed the notion that all men were equal no matter what their calling. We Americans speak of our "classes." Yet the overwhelming fact remains that we accept all others as our equals or potential equals. This sharply contrasts with the idea I have encountered everywhere in my travels that people do not group into a horizontal equality but into a very clearly defined vertical hierarchy.

Americans may be baffled on how to deal with a servant. Is he a friend? A member of the family? The servant, on the other hand, rarely mistakes his position. He is a servant. Consequently, American democratic ideals and foreign understandings of reality clash, leaving both sides confused and disoriented. The American desire to be a more humane master than foreigners who expect the subservience of servants as a matter of course perhaps results more often than not in a more strained relationship with the employee than the presumably less sensitive employer achieves.

Americans are particularly difficult employers. The servant scarcely knows what to expect next from this unpredictable character. In return he does not know what is expected from him.

I quickly learned this fact the day of my arrival in Korea in 1975. When introduced to the lady who would manage my house for the next five years, Mrs. Yi Song-ok, I instinctively reached out to shake her hand. Even twenty years of dealing with Americans was scarcely sufficient preparation for this gross breach of the social gulf between us. How quickly we adjust! Within a year when my mother visited Korea and shook Mrs. Yi's hand upon their first meeting, I was appalled by this failure to observe social mores.

The idea that the employer runs the household is a myth. Even the most surly and unimaginative servant rapidly takes control of the situation in which the employer's only substantive recourse is the employee's discharge.

I thought in Korea that Mrs. Yi's competence and our mutual language difficulties naturally resulted in her control of all the household details. The effect, in fact, was often to leave me with the sense that I was a guest in my own home, told to "make myself at home" and yet realizing the impossibility of achieving that goal. My concern became to cause Mrs. Yi no trouble; to stay out of her way. That surely turns the relationship on its head.

I became incredibly lazy. Years of relentless Irish Catholic discipline had conditioned me to pick up after myself, to make the bed, to wash the dishes, to decide what to eat for dinner. How quickly all this faded! All the chores which my mother had assured me would be mine to do until my dying day suddenly vanished, done in a twinkling by a very real fairy godmother. Only those who have lived through the experience can appreciate the ecstasy of awakening the morning after a party to discover the dishes washed, the ashtrays emptied, the carpet vacuumed, and the kitchen spotless.

To pay for this I had to accept the little routines which servants impose to maintain their universe. Unable to influence a woman who for years had worked for coffee-drinking, egg-eating Americans, I resigned myself to both. Having conceded coffee with supper one evening, I had conceded it every night for five years. Having conceded eggs for breakfast one morning, I had conceded them every day.

I thought (glorious delusion!) that I could approach the servant problem with a clean slate upon my arrival in Ghana. I had, after all, a number of years of experience which had clarified some of the pitfalls to avoid. I expected that Mrs. Yi was far superior to what could be expected elsewhere.

So it is that I have Yaro. Yaro at times is slow. He and I speak two different English languages. He requires far more direction than Mrs. Yi. (Good Lord, I have to decide what to have for dinner!) But the underlying problem remains.

Yaro came with the house, having worked for my predecessor for two years. In that sense, this is more his house than mine. *He* knows where things are. Worst of all, he is always here. Mrs. Yi had a family to go home to every night. She never appeared on Sundays or holidays. Yaro lives in a room behind the house. He comes in and out every day whether or not he is working. Each evening I breathe a sigh of relief after supper when Yaro finishes cleaning up and leaves. Even then I hesitate to venture into the kitchen, which he clearly regards as his own preserve.

On those occasions when I have made so bold as to venture into it when he is in residence, I can feel Yaro's questioning eyes following me around the room.

I rather think that his service is to the house, not to me, and that I have no more significance to him than the couch or one of the lizards running across the ceiling.

Still, matters could be worse. Yaro is a bachelor. Were he to have a family, I would play the host to them all.

> "As from a bear a man would run for life,
> So fly I from her that would be my wife."
> - Shakespeare, *Comedy of Errors*, Act III

November 8, 1980 Saturday

There is a subject from my American travels this past summer which I have long planned to record and yet knew not how to approach. I scarcely know how to relate it to any other experience in my life. I hesitate to assign an importance to something which time may deny it. And yet the circumstances of *Rocky Horror Picture Show* seem so bizarre as to merit their inclusion here, regardless of their ultimate significance either to my life or to Western culture.

RHPS is a movie. It is a bad movie. The plot is bad. The dialogue is bad. If in fact one is looking for an argument that Western civilization is in decline, the movie provides it. And yet *RHPS* has become a cult movie, playing in theaters throughout the United States for the past several years every Friday and Saturday night at midnight, attended by devotees who worship it week after week.

The plot, to use the term loosely, throws together elements of classic science fiction and other RKO B movies, notably *Frankenstein*, *King Kong*, and *The War of the Worlds*. The action follows this sequence: Brad (the hero) proposes marriage to Janet (the heroine) at the wedding of their friends. They set off to tell Dr. Scott, their professor, the happy news. Enroute, it being a dark, stormy night (the night, in fact, of Nixon's 1974 resignation), their car has a flat tire. And no spare. They walk back (in the rain) to the forbidding castle they had just passed. (A castle in Ohio?)

They arrive in the middle of the annual Transylvanian convention on the very night that Dr. Frank N. Furter (the evil scientist) plans to give life to the creature, Rocky Horror, which he has created. Frank N. Furter is not the run-of-the-mill evil scientist, as he announces in his opening number (did I neglect to mention this is a rock musical?): "I'm a sweet transvestite from Transsexual, Transylvania." He has created Rocky Horror for his favorite "obsession": sex.

Things only get worse, with the pickax murder of Frank's former lover, delivery boy Eddy; the appearance of the aforementioned Dr. Scott who exposes Frank and his entourage as aliens from outer space; the "floor show" in front of an RKO backdrop in which the cast sings "Give yourself over to absolute pleasure" and which ends when Frank's "faithful handyman" Riff-Raff announces that Frank has failed in his mission and Riff-Raff is the new commander.

The movie ends with Frank's death, an echo of King Kong's ascent of the Empire State Building, with Rocky Horror carrying his fallen creator up the RKO tower, and the aliens' blasting off in their spaceship (the castle) to return to Transsexual.

I doubt the above outline conveys the true sense of decadence and perversity the movie offers. But then the movie itself constitutes only one part of the cult. An equally important part is the audience. *RHPS* devotees who view the show week after week are not content to play the traditional role of an American movie audience. They insist on active participation. Knowing every line of dialogue as well as the characters themselves, the audience interjects comments, questions, commands, and rude remarks to complement the screen dialogue so well that one could almost suspect the writer planned it that way.

Having been introduced to *RHPS* last June by the Burtons in

Milwaukee, I became enthralled by it. I saw it again in New Orleans, Detroit, and Washington. Audiences in each city had their own favorite lines, and yet the unity underlying their actions from one city to another was amazing.

I will list a few of the common items. Whenever Brad the hero appears on the screen, the audience howls: "Asshole!" When Janet the heroine appears, they hiss: "Slut!" When the so-called Narrator (who presumably should tie the whole thing together but only succeeds in confusing us more) makes his entrance, his statements are drowned out with a chorus of: "Boring!"

Then there are the audience's anticipatory lines. When Frank first meets Brad ("Asshole!") and Janet ("Slut!"), the audience commands: "Hey, Frankie, say something in French!" To which he obliges: "*Enchanté.*" The audience, eager for education, asks: "What's that mean?" And Frank turns to us and answers: "Well, how nice."

Nor is audience participation confined to verbal antics. People show up with an assortment of props to assist the flow of the movie. Some show up in full costume as the characters.

In the opening wedding scene, the newlyweds are met with a storm of rice thrown by the guests; suddenly too the theater fills with rice tossed in all directions. When Brad and Janet have their car trouble and must walk through the rain to Frank's castle, Janet uses a newspaper (a Cleveland Plain Dealer) for an umbrella. Suddenly, too, newspapers appear over the heads of a large part of the audience – and not only for dramatic effect, since others run up and down the aisles with spray bottles to simulate the rain.

The list goes on.

I only intend here, however, to record this most unusual phenomenon. The aspect of audience participation, which at first appears spontaneous and directionless, soon proves to be completely predetermined. We in the theater are locked into our parts almost as tightly as the actors on the screen. There are books with both the movie script and notations giving the dogmatically approved audience lines.

In that respect, the *RHPS* resembles a Korean masked dance, in which the performance derives a good deal of its vitality from the responses of the spectators. A passive audience would spell death for either.

November 11, 1980 Tuesday

Presumably the impression given so far in these pages is that Accra is a rather boring place. One might compare Accra to a doctor's office. We spend a great deal of time in a doctor's office simply waiting. Now we don't consider waiting for the doctor a particularly enjoyable pastime, and yet we recognize its necessity. Still we crave some escape from the tedium, the boredom of it all. Accra is like that.

How many of us have not had the experience while waiting of desperately reading anything we can lay our hands on, usually year-old copies of some magazine which under normal circumstances we would not bother with? That is how I survive Accra, reading *Time, Newsweek, US News and World Report, Life, Smithsonian, Architectural Digest, Foreign Policy, Penthouse, Fortune,* and *Four Wheel Drive*. I should absorb as much information in two years as in four years of college.

Accra is not a complete social wasteland. There was the Embassy Halloween party, for example, in which I was runner-up in the "Most Original Costume" category for my Japanese kimono and sandals, and Korean horsehair hat, fan, and pipe. Apparently I impressed the judges the most with the fact I shaved off my mustache for the occasion and greased my hair back with Crisco vegetable shortening.

Last night the Marines held their annual ball, commemorating their 205th birthday. It brought out the usual crowd of Americans and other foreigners. I avoided its full effects by volunteering to stand watch at the Embassy from 11:00 p.m. to 1:00 a.m. for the Marines. Shades of younger days, a number of us departed the ball for an all-night pool party at the house of one of the Canadian diplomats.

Today being Veterans' Day and my neighbors having lent me their car while they went to Abidjan, I drove downtown with Virginia Mayberry, the Vice Consul (how has she not appeared here previously?) to look at the market. We visited the main department store, the Ghana National Trading Corporation (GNTC). It was exactly like I have always pictured East European department stores: passive employees, empty shelves, and a few unusual (and unnecessary) items in great profusion.

We then drifted to High Street, where vendors set up shop on the curbside to sell African artifacts of brass, wood, and ivory. The items on display, to my mind, have limited appeal; the short row of vendors reminded me strongly of Korean tourist traps, where each hawker sells the same item as his neighbor, and it is all junk.

My unfavorable view of the wares is influenced by the outrageous prices quoted. They are outrageous only to those (like us) compelled to deal at the official 2.75 cedis to one dollar exchange rate, rather than the black market rate of twenty to one.

The vendors do negotiate. Virginia spotted one small brass case whose price was 300 cedis ($100 legally, $15 black market). She told the salesman that she had seen the same item in an American catalog for the equivalent of 120 cedis. He quickly agreed to sell it at that price and, when we realized we had only 113 cedis between the two of us, he knocked another seven off the price. What kind of profit margins do they have?

November 27, 1980 Thanksgiving

Today I added a new feather to my diplomatic career cap. I crashed the Ambassador's Thanksgiving dinner. This gross breach of decorum resulted not from any premeditated desire to be obnoxious but from incomplete communications between Ambassador Smith and myself. He stopped by my office in the Annex a week ago. In the course of discussing other matters, he asked whether I would care to join his family for lunch on Thursday, or so I understood him to say. I said I would be honored and marked the nearest Thursday on my calendar – Thanksgiving.

I heard nothing more about the invitation and received no invitation card. This did not bother me, since my previous appearance at a non-official lunch at the Ambassador's had also come through an oral invitation. But I had no idea of the time the Ambassador was expecting his guests. So late yesterday afternoon I called the Ambassador's secretary to ask. She betrayed a certain discomposure in her reply (words to the effect: "Are *you* invited to that??").

Doubts bloomed in my mind. Too late now. I had as much as informed the Smiths that they would have me as a guest for lunch. In reviewing my previous conversation with the Ambassador, if it did not include an invitation for Thanksgiving, then I had no idea what we had discussed. Or what I had agreed to.

I left it to the Ambassador's secretary to alert him to put out another plate, and appeared at the time appointed. Mrs. Smith, demonstrating the qualities which have made her an Ambassador's wife and her husband an Ambassador, greeted me with, "Bill, we had this sudden panic when we thought Tom [the Ambassador to his intimates] had forgotten to tell you what time!" Not to mention that Tom had probably forgotten altogether about inviting me.

There were enough plates on the table, and I had a pleasant meal with the Smiths, the Ghanaian Ambassador to the United States and his wife, the German Ambassador, and our Personnel Officer Anita McMurray. (The disparity in favor of the males was further circumstantial evidence that my presence was unplanned.)

November 28, 1980 Friday

My Jeep arrived a little more than a week ago. I doubt any other event short of childbirth could hold me in such a state of suspense and tension for so long. First was the inexactness of the timing of its arrival. From late October on, the message each day came: "The ship should be arriving within a few days." The "few days" became several weeks. I despaired of ever having transportation. Nor did the ship's arrival solve the problem. It merely complicated it. There was the delay in unloading the Jeep off the ship. It was put on the pier along with other arriving vehicles, in an unguarded area in a port notorious for theft and vandalism. Stories began to filter back from Tema of the terrible condition my own and the other cars were in: dents and scrapes, broken windows, flat tires.

I took advantage of my visit to the U.S.S. *Radford* when it arrived in port to swing over to the adjoining pier to examine the evidence firsthand. Damage to the Jeep was remarkably minor, certainly less than expected. The small vent window on the driver's door had been smashed, presumably intentionally (to judge from the small rock inside) by someone who hoped to break into the cab. The lights control knob, the cigarette lighter, and the ashtray lid (but not the ashtray itself) had all vanished. The battery, the spare tire (granted, it is bolted onto the back end), and the mirrors were all there.

I made increasingly shrill inquiries back at the Embassy as to why the cars had been off-loaded days earlier and were still tied up in Customs. Wayne Smith at the Australian High Commission had had a vehicle on the same ship. He was already driving it around town with diplomatic license plates. So the General Services Officer and two of the Embassy's Ghanaian employees accompanied me back to Tema the following day.

From 9:00 a.m. on we shuffled from one office to another with various sheaves of documents to be stamped, signed, copied. Twenty Ghanaian officials had their say about the release of our cars. Some got their say *twice*. Each one wanted to look under the hood, check the engine block serial numbers, quibble over the vehicle's claimed value. Several had the gall to ask me to give them visas to the United States. "Get me my car," I said, "and you'll have your visa." Even such a generous offer failed to speed matters along.

Finally, at 6:00 p.m. we escaped Tema, I in my Jeep, the Ghanaian employees in Virginia Mayberry's Datsun, and the General

Services Officer in his car. I had an appalling ride back to Accra in the dark (the sun sets early in the tropics) along the unlit two-lane oceanfront road. At least my Jeep had arrived. In all the bureaucratic maze through which we had crawled, the subject of the Ghanaian government's vehicle imports standardization policy, the subject which had caused me so much worry my last weeks in Washington, never arose.

One would think such an inefficient system of duplicating procedures would at least limit corruption by preventing any one official from doctoring the papers. Instead it merely multiplies the number of people who want their cut of the rake-off (called "dash") for moving one's papers on one step more.

November 30, 1980 Sunday

Tomorrow I leave with Rod Hawke, the Deputy Ambassador, and his wife Lois, for a twelve-day orientation tour through Ghana. We'll visit all the important places (broadly defined). Rod has solved most of the logistical problems in making arrangements except: Will there be gas? Will there be a place to stay? Will there be food? Will there be roads?

Not much else is happening. There was a coup in Upper Volta last week, which was typically insignificant in the lives of the Upper Voltans, the country's neighbors, and the world at large.

We are remarkably uninformed here. A week passed, for example, before I finally learned the dimensions of Reagan's electoral landslide. We depend largely on Voice of America, BBC, and the Armed Forces Radio for our day-to-day news. Ghanaian newspapers occasionally inadvertently include something important. Radio news tends to give only headlines without too much background. Listening to short-wave radio is not one of the world's more relaxing pastimes. I rely on *Time*, *Newsweek*, and *U.S. News and World Report* to flesh out the news two or three weeks after the fact.

Notes from Lower Volta

December 1, 1980 Monday – Takoradi, Western Region

Road conditions. Accra - Cape Coast: Good. Cape Coast - Takoradi: Bad.

My travel authorization hints at what I should expect these next two weeks: "Travel is authorized to be performed within Ghana as required in the performance of official business by any available means, in any order and at such times as deemed necessary with return to Accra whenever advisable in performance of duties, departing on or about December 1, and returning on or about December 12, 1980."

We spent the better part of today driving west from Accra along the coast to Takoradi, a distance of some 160 miles. Most of the route did not allow a view of the ocean. We passed a number of interesting villages and dusty colonial towns. The road (a two-lane affair) varied wildly in its condition, the solid red line on the map to the contrary. West of Cape Coast (about the last ninety minutes) it sank to an almost continuous state of disrepair. I no longer paid any attention to the surrounding scenery but kept my eyes riveted on the gaping potholes before us.

Travel in Ghana is not a leisurely affair. It requires all the careful planning of an invasion of Europe. One works on the basic assumption that what he doesn't take with him will have to be done without. Besides the obvious objects of gasoline and food, one must not overlook spare tires (plural), extra fan belts and hoses for the engine, drinking water, light bulbs (some places have electricity but no bulbs), candles and matches (some places have neither electricity nor bulbs), soap, towels, and maps. The foregoing by no means represents a comprehensive list, only those items which readily spring to mind.

All this paraphernalia occupies a lot of room, and scarcely leaves enough space in the Embassy van for the Hawkes, myself, and the driver. Most exciting of all is the thought of what a stray spark would do to our mobile gas station. In addition to the fifteen-gallon fuel tank Detroit kindly provided, we have a twenty-three-gallon collapsible tank in the back of the van. The manufacturer more or less guarantees it will not explode on impact. Several five-gallon jerry cans are strapped to the roof. Fifty-five gallons to blow us to kingdom come. The possibility apparently has the Hawkes worried. They spent a good part of the journey chain-smoking cigarettes.

A whirlwind tour through Ghana in twelve days will presumably allow time for only the most superficial exposure to the country. I already feel more at home here; all these remote places no longer seem so strange once I have passed through them.

We visited a construction site in Winneba, in which a seed factory is being built with USAID backing. Its most impressive feature was the huge tree at its center, dominating the countryside for a mile in any direction. Outside of that, there was not too much to see: a few piles of dirt, a few piles of rocks, a few piles of workers, and a couple of surveyors carefully plotting the building site. Perhaps I will have a chance to visit the place again before I leave Ghana, to see if any progress has been made. If they cut the tree down, I'll probably miss the turn-off.

The seed factory (or at least the vision of it) seems representative of our foreign aid to Ghana: nothing much to look at, nothing much to show. After a quarter century of pouring vast sums of money into development projects, we have an economic wasteland.

But then, I thought, the seed factory was the first time I've seen anybody building anything in Ghana.

We also stopped to visit a Peace Corps Volunteer teaching at a girl's secondary school and a Franciscan friar training young Ghanaians for the priesthood. Both were in Saltpond. We gave the Peace Corps Volunteer some fairly recent magazines and the missionary a can of Coke. Surely we can find it in the Bible someplace: "I was a Peace Corps Volunteer and you brought me *Time* to read; I was a priest and you gave me Coke to drink."

Both appeared slightly bewildered by our unexpected appearance, but they had been in Ghana long enough to expect such things. The Peace Corps Volunteer in particular seemed to welcome the interruption of his chemistry lab, although the Franciscan later told us "He doesn't seem very friendly" when talking about his neighbor down the road.

We also stopped at the University of Cape Coast in Cape Coast to visit the Princes, a Fulbright couple. They too received a magazine. I doubted the wisdom of the mission when I noticed the two lead articles predicted a close presidential election and the release of the hostages within days. Perhaps they'll enjoy the advertisements.

The Princes have recently returned to Ghana after a six-year absence. I enjoy listening to old Ghana hands talk about the "good old days." They mentioned that in their last incarnation the economy "had started to go bad."

I was relieved to hear that we newcomers are not the only ones having trouble adjusting to local conditions. The Princes described their return as "culture shock." They were almost ready at the end of six weeks to pack up and head back to the States. As so often happens, the Nigerian example came up, with the refrain that if Nigeria had this country's economy, no foreigner would ever go there; but the Ghanaians make Ghana livable.

There was also more of the growing suggestion that the legendary patience of the Ghanaian people is rapidly running out, and that the present civilian government may not last the time constitutionally allotted to it.

We are spending the night at the Guest House of the Pioneer Tobacco Company in Takoradi.

Aloysius A. Thrabknuckle III

Being excerpts from the diaries of Aloysius A. Thrabknuckle III, late U.S. Foreign Service Officer, who died in the service of his country in the jungles of West Africa, December 31st, 1980.

The family of Aloysius A. Thrabknuckle III have kindly consented to the publication of these *Notes from Lower Volta* as a memorial to their son and brother. His last days were spent in that nation serving as the Consular Officer in the American Embassy in the capital of Aakrid. They wish to dedicate the book to Aloysius, and to all his fellow officers who have given up their lives in the United States for the pleasure of serving their nation in some of the most exotic and exciting locations around the world....

Aloysius's notes end here. Shortly after he made this entry, he died, tragically, on December 31st, 1980, at Ambassador Jones's New Year's Eve reception, gallantly attempting to save the Lower Voltan Foreign Minister's wife from being trampled underfoot. Twenty Peace Corps Volunteers who had arrived from the bush earlier that day were intent on reaching the potato chips. She stood in the way. Unfortunately, both this valiant young American and the distinguished lady perished in this regrettable incident.

As of this writing, the State Department is hopeful that there will shortly be progress towards negotiations on setting up low-level meetings to discuss a working relationship prior to the resumption of full diplomatic relations between the United States and Lower Volta.

On the walls of the Diplomatic Lobby in the Department of State in Washington hang two plaques bearing the names of American Foreign Service Officers who have died in their country's service. One plaque lists all those who died from the founding of the United States to 1967; the second lists those who have died in the thirteen years since. It too is full. Aloysius's name will be the next to be so inscribed.

The American Foreign Service Association opposes the plan to add Aloysius's name on the grounds that numberless other colleagues have suffered severe bodily harm in dealing with Peace Corps Volunteers, and that Aloysius's death, while tragic, does not compare to the deaths of those many others killed in terrorist attacks and Embassy burnings.

December 3, 1980 Wednesday – Kumasi, Ashanti Region

Road conditions. Takoradi - Tarkwa: Good, bad in spots. Tarkwa - Kumasi: Passable, rough, slow going, good four-wheel drive experience, questionable in rain, marked improvement past Dunkwa.

Before departing Takoradi yesterday morning, we dropped in on another Peace Corps Volunteer, also a chemistry teacher, and some American missionaries at St. John's Secondary School. The missionaries were Catholics, one the classic image of the rotund jolly priest and the other of the religious brother a little too slow-witted to aspire to the priesthood but handy around the school with a screwdriver and a wrench.

We turned inland some fifty-five miles to Tarkwa, where Firestone has a tire factory. Tarkwa lies at the edge of the rain forest and adjoins a 17,000-acre rubber plantation. Ironically the factory uses little natural rubber in its operations. Most of its manufacturing involves imported synthetics.

Firestone is the only true manufacturer in Ghana. The Ghanaian government has put so many obstacles in its way that the company will probably pull out within a few more months, leaving the operation to the Ghanaians. Firestone is not very optimistic that the already troubled operation will hold together without American expertise.

The American staff is pleasant enough. Like so many expatriates overseas (of all nationalities) they have carved a little ghetto out of the forest and created a facsimile of suburbia. The overt hostility of the population toward them as they cruise by in their oversized American automobiles bewilders them. During our tour of the facilities, we observed the lack of sympathy and rapport between the American management and the Ghanaian staff. The Americans quite willingly confided that even the highest ranking Ghanaian supervisors were unqualified and uncooperative.

We spent Tuesday night at the Firestone Guest House, another in that system encompassing the country which attempts to remedy the problem of a nation without hotels.

Tonight we are in Kumasi, the old Ashanti capital, at the City Hotel. My 1976 guide book describes the hotel as "a first-class modern hotel with international amenities, and probably the best deep forest hotel in Africa." The definition of "deep forest hotel" eludes me. The building behind the sign is only a shell of what this place might once have been. There is electricity (one light to a room) and running water (cold), lumpy mattresses, a potentially functioning phone, and a pervading sense of tropical decay.

More and more Ghana calls to mind H.G. Wells' novel *The Time Machine*. The Time Traveler hurtles hundreds of thousands of years into the future to find the remains of a great civilization now abandoned and overgrown. Amid the ruins live the Eloi, a gentle, charming folk unable to take initiative or to set their minds to any concrete task.

When looking at the City Hotel, when passing abandoned construction sites in which trees and vines have taken root among the unfinished buildings, when finding fields filled with rusted cranes and other ruined machinery, I see the Eloi.

Tonight we ate dinner at Kumasi's "best" restaurant, Chopsticks. The food was quite good and the service predictably non-existent. Imagine if you can a Chinese restaurant in which only an hour of repeated requests produced Chinese tea, and in which no amount of effort could pry loose a single chopstick. Rather than take the obvious course of informing the guests that the tea or the chopsticks were unavailable, the staff merely responded to each inquiry with: "We will bring it now, please."

Our ride today brought us into the African rain forest. Some things in this world assume mythical and epic images for those who have never seen them. The rain forest is such a thing for me. I have long imagined the closeness of the hot muggy air, the soaring trees blotting out the sun, and the watching quiet broken only by furtive movements in the underbrush and the lonely calls of distant birds.

Perhaps someday I will visit that particular forest. It is not here. The Ghanaian forest has a striking beauty and lushness, but it lacks the expected sense of overwhelming size and menace. Perhaps the fact we passed through it in an air-conditioned van played some role in reducing the mystery of it all.

Notes from Lower Volta

December 6, 1980 Saturday – Mole National Park, Northern Region

Road conditions. Kumasi - Sunyani: Good pavement in spots, reverting to bush elsewhere, improved in Brong-Ahafo Region. Sunyani - Berekum: Narrow but good. Sunyani - Techiman: We got stuck. Techiman - Bamboi (ferry): Excellent. Bamboi - Bole: Unpaved, good surface; slow going (seventy miles in three hours). Bole - Damongo: Unpaved, fairly smooth; slow going.

The impression has continued to grow these last few days that Accra and Ghana are two distinct entities. I guess this phenomenon of capital and country having different identities arises in many developing nations. Korea was that way, with Seoul possessing a wearying dynamism which the provinces lacked. Accra, however, has all the problems affecting large urban capitals with none of the redeeming amenities. Life in the countryside may be difficult for those who live there. A trip to Accra will not help improve the situation.

We visited the markets of Kumasi and Techiman, both huge sprawling affairs which serve not only their own cities but also draw traders from throughout Ghana and West Africa. Accra with its empty shelves and spiritless salesclerks has nothing to compare to the frantic activity and volume of goods found in the Kumasi and Techiman markets. It reminded me of Seoul's Namdaemun Market or the streets of Hong Kong. In Ghana, too, anything can be had, for a price.

Prices are shooting out of sight. A loaf of bread five cedis ($2); an egg two cedis ($1); a chicken one hundred cedis ($33), and a turkey five hundred cedis ($200)!

From Kumasi we drove to Berekum, with a brief stop in Sunyani, one of Ghana's major cultural centers and capital of the Brong-Ahafo Region. The little town of Berekum lies quite close to the Ivory Coast border.

We visited the Catholic nuns who run the Holy Family Hospital, a 130-bed institution opened in 1948. In a number of ways, the hospital seems in better condition than its big city counterparts.

It still has x-ray film. In Accra x-ray film has joined the list of unavailable items.

The sisters were most hospitable, even though they had not expected our arrival. They gave us dinner out of their limited supplies and put us up for the night. I felt somewhat less guilty about imposing on them when I learned that they get to go to the Ivory Coast for shopping quite often and have a rather substantial garden. And they had Louisa sleep in the convent while Rod and I wound up in the men's ward.

It was a delightful time, one of the most informative evenings I have had since arriving in Africa. The surroundings were exactly how I had envisioned a tropical hospital: long, low buildings scattered over a large clearing with the rain forest in the distance.

The major diseases in Berekum, they said, are malaria (did I take my Aralen pill this week?), enteric fever, respiratory diseases (the air is clean but the housing unhealthy), and rabies. Malaria is so common throughout Ghana, in fact, that when medical personnel have conferences malaria does not even enter the discussion. It is a given in the situation.

Nutritional problems also bulk large. It is not that Ghanaians don't get enough to eat (although there have been such bad times). Like fast-food Americans they think a full stomach equals good feeding. The Ghanaian diet has a large starch, low protein content. A good part of the work of all those involved in medical care revolves around teaching the people basic ideas of balanced nutrition.

From Berekum we backtracked to Sunyani and struck north to Techiman. The Sunyani - Techiman road qualifies as the worst we have seen so far, if for no other reason than we got stuck on it. On one particularly bad section where water had worked its worst potentials of erosion, the van slipped off the high ground into two deep ruts, leaving the wheels with nothing to get traction against. The accident occurred within sight of the next village, half of whose inhabitants came running over to view the situation and to offer their advice.

Notes from Lower Volta

After a few community efforts at *lifting* the van out of the ruts (some anthropologist will probably wonder in twenty years' time why all the men have hernias), a few well-placed loads under the wheels, and some shoveling, the van drove free. The village's services cost us one pack of cigarettes. They declined the offer of money because, they said, we were the second vehicle of the day to run into trouble at that spot in the road. The first driver had paid for their help with money, giving rise to dissension in the village over how to split a single 10 cedi note twenty-five ways.

Having vehicles get stuck in the road may well constitute one of that village's daily highlights. Perhaps the villagers encourage the road to fall apart.

We stopped for an hour in Techiman to visit the market (as already mentioned) and to call on the nuns in *its* Holy Family Hospital, bringing with us the greetings of their Berekum compatriots.

A Peace Corps Volunteer (he was up-to-date on his magazines, or at least as up-to-date as we) at the hospital had an interesting project working with the native healers and fetish priests to give them modern knowledge to apply to their own profession. Native doctors still play a significant role in the lives of the people. They occupy an ideal position to undertake the basic preventive health care to head off problems which otherwise will show up in their terminal stages in the missionary hospital's doorsteps.

Traditional training of native healers involves an average of one day, apparently consisting of the instructor's taking the trainee into the forest to say: "This root cures typhoid; this bark is good for colds; this flower is an aphrodisiac." The fetish priests, on the other hand, generally study for as long as three years before going into business. A family history of serving as a native doctor plays a principal role in determining who will become one. A person can also become one after a spirit possesses him (or her, spirits being equal opportunity employers).

North of Techiman the rain forest gives way to savannah land. We are moving toward the Sahara. The Black Volta River divides

Brong-Ahafo from the Northern Region, and the forest from the drier lands. We crossed the river on the Bamboi ferry, a rickety affair of plywood and sheet metal with a sputtering engine. It operates in the shadow of the nearly completed bridge which will take away its business.

As our driver drove up the ramp onto the ferry, I had a sudden vision that the van would miss the track and we would all go crashing into the river. We made the short passage without mishap, however. I jumped off the ferry first on the north shore, ostensibly to take a picture of the van disembarking but actually to avoid riding it down the ramp.

As we went on, trees became sparser and the terrain, which had been somewhat hilly, flattened to a plain. The road was not bad for an unpaved surface. Since we could not go very fast it took three hours to cover the remaining seventy miles to Bole.

I had no clear idea last night and still have my doubts as to why we stopped at Bole. It seems that in the long drive from Berekum to the North, we needed someplace to spend the night. Bole's name was spelled on the map in bigger letters than anyplace else.

The Hawkes and I are pioneers. No one in living memory in the Embassy has attempted such an expedition. Very few people currently assigned to Accra have even ventured forth short distances. Reports of fuel shortages and bad roads have dissuaded them. Upon our return to Accra, we will do our best to reinforce the fears of the foreboding interior, also coincidentally reinforcing the esteem with which our colleagues regard us.

We arrived in Bole after dark. Since the electric power was off at the time, we could not see very much. We only knew we had arrived when a police roadblock brought the van to a halt. We made our way to the Bole Catering Rest House, part of the nationwide, government-run rest house system. Such a system of rest houses is an idea whose time has not yet arrived. Or perhaps more likely in Ghana's case, it is an idea already gone. We had a three-bedroom bungalow with no lightbulbs, no water, no stove, and no restaurant. We sat in candlelight (our light bulbs would not fit the fixtures even when the power came on) in sweltering heat, eating a combination of spam, tuna fish, three-bean salad, and French salad dressing. I supplemented the diet with two beers. I went to bed hungry. The heat only intensified at 10:00 p.m. when the electricity went off (on schedule) and the ceiling fans spun no more.

We were up at dawn. Have I ever seen the sun rise before? Yes, at Kyongju, Korea in 1976 as the sun rose over the Sea of Japan to have its light fall on the face of the Sokkuram Buddha. Hard to believe this is the same sun, the same planet.

After a breakfast of coffee (there being nothing else), we drove on to the towns of Larabanga and Damongo.

Larabanga is famous for an old mud mosque with white walls and wooden beams, and a tower in each corner. By no means should one think in terms of the mosques we are familiar with in the Middle East. Mosques here look much more like African anthills. According to legend (everyone tells *some* version of this story), the architect commissioned to design the American Embassy in Ghana wanted to draw on Ghanaian forms for his work.

He traveled all over Ghana (I now appreciate the depth of that statement) until he reached Larabanga. In a sudden fit of inspiration, he imagined the white mosque – which in a village of brown huts does command one's attention – as the perfect model, with one small alteration: instead of pointing the towers *up*, he would point them *down*. And so it came to be that the Embassy built in Accra in 1957 is up on stilts, an upside-down Ghanaian mosque.

An alternative, and somewhat less flattering, version of the story finds the same architect in a hotel bar in Accra, having had any number of one-too-many. Rather than a fit of inspiration as such, he saw a postcard of the Larabanga mosque and, unwittingly holding it upside down, declaimed: "Thish 'ill be the new Embrashhy."

In Damongo we visited two recently arrived Peace Corps Volunteers working on a project to introduce bullock plowing to the local farmers. The local farmers already do plow with bullocks. So the volunteers have reoriented their program to provide technical expertise on the subject. Until they can buy a couple of bullocks themselves, their activities will be somewhat limited.

"What background prepares you for this?" I asked.

"I worked on a cattle ranch in Texas, and believe you me, Damongo looks just like West Texas!"

The mix-up of introducing something already well-known locally is not the fault, in this case, of the Peace Corps bureaucracy. The bullock project belongs to the Ghanaian-German Agricultural Development Project, the local German version of the Peace Corps. Since the German volunteers expect life a little easier than the Peace Corps Volunteers, the GGADP has been unable to get any Germans to Damongo and turned to Peace Corps for help.

The German volunteers do aid work overseas in lieu of military service. Supposedly Germany sends its conscientious objectors to Ghana. Anybody else would elect to join the army rather than come here.

After saying goodbye, we backtracked a few miles to Mole National Park, a nine hundred square mile game preserve. After our experience with the Bole Rest House, I had doubts about a second night in a government hotel. Mole, however, is one of the country's major tourist attractions (or would be if there were any tourists left).

The facilities at Mole are about the best I have seen in Ghana. Granted the water and electricity are turned on only between 5:00 p.m. and 10:00 p.m., and each room has an air conditioner whose installation is yet "incomplete" and hence unusable. Granted all that, after a day and a half we have washed and had two hot meals. The menu, of course, is whatever is available. The cook did an adequate job on both lunch and dinner (the latter with crepes suzette for dessert!). Although they have no beer, we did get coffee. The electricity will go off in ten minutes. I will stop here.

Notes from Lower Volta

December 8, 1980 Monday – Bolgatanga, Upper Region

Road conditions. Damongo - Wa: Unpaved, rough, slow-going, washboard. Wa - Navrongo: Unpaved, rough, slow-going, washboard. Navrongo - Bolgatanga: Pavement! Without potholes!

The facilities at Mole National Park only look good in comparison to Bole. I overlooked the air conditioner which did not work, the lack of water, and the sightseeing jeeps out of service for lack of spare parts. There was water in the swimming pool, a vile-looking brew covered with a layer of unknown organisms and topped off with an old inner tube and a dead frog. The bill had a space for charges for: "Swimming pool: hours enjoyed."

For all our trouble, I saw a few monkeys and the Hawkes a family of baboons. To give the park its due, December is the wrong season to visit. The rains have recently ended so water for the animals (if not for the guests) is quite plentiful and the high grass offers them plenty of cover. Over the next few months as the dry season develops, most of the waterholes will dry up, driving the animals towards those near the hotel. Nature will help the process with brush fires from the dry heat, and will in turn be assisted by men. Game wardens will light fires to drive the animals to water. Poachers will set fires to drive the animals out of the reserve where they can then kill them.

Considering the heat now, I certainly do not plan to return when it will be even hotter and more miserable, even if that means I miss my chance to see Ghana's elephants and leopards and what-have-you.

From Mole we continued north yesterday to Wa, in the Upper Region. The scenery has little to attract one's attention on the Wa road. Trees and shade are less common. The northwestern part of Ghana has a small population. Traffic on the road was minimal; villages became fewer and smaller.

The mud-walled compounds of the North offer an interesting contrast to the grass hut villages in the rain forest. I would stop short of Lois Hawke's description of them as "cute."

I had heard nothing about Wa previously. There is in fact nothing worth hearing. It is a dirty town in a barren plain under a hot sun. We visited the market (depressing) and the butcher, who would make more money if he charged for the flies rather than the meat.

We called on the Chief of Wa, a singularly dull and uninteresting fellow. Reportedly he stands at the center of some chieftaincy dispute (somebody else wants his job) in which passions rose to such a height that last year twenty-seven people died in a riot. I could hardly imagine dying in his service, or fighting over what they refer to as "the chief's palace." Of such is history made.

The local Peace Corps Volunteer took us to see an Englishman and his snake collection. The Ghanaians avoid him on the assumption anyone who likes snakes must be dabbling in magic. Ghana has thirty-five species of snakes, he said, including some pythons and hooded cobras. Don't go wandering around in the bush.

We passed the night at the Wa Catering Rest House. Another night of no water and no electricity. The locals claimed such things normally worked in the evenings. We would pick the wrong day.

Having driven up the west side of Ghana, we went a little further north from Wa and turned east, covering most of the distance to Bolgatanga near the Togo border by sunset. The route took us through some of the most godforsaken landscape I have ever laid eyes on. No villages, no traffic, just a poorly constructed dirt road cutting through desolation. Curiously the bare trees and brown grass gave the appearance of autumn weather, a mirage belied by the heat. Large sections of the bush had already been blackened by fire. Some still burned.

At the center of the desolation is Tumu, the town from which President Limann comes. One would expect that the President's hometown would find favor with government planners. Tumu has not, except for a cotton ginning mill which, when completed, will have the most up-to-date computer technology available. All it will need will be the cotton to keep it operating. Where will that come from?

Notes from Lower Volta

Tumu has several Peace Corps Volunteers. The two we met appeared overwhelmed by our visit. Since Tumu is in the middle of nowhere and transportation is always a chancy proposition, not many travelers pass through. It has no money economy, but operates on a closed system of barter. A person unconnected to the town could not survive, no matter how much money he might have. It's who you know that counts.

Lois has ceased pointing out the charming villages. The trip has begun to take its toll on all of us, but her most of all. She tends to sit back with her eyes bulging and whimper that the insects are eating her alive. We may yet turn up at the Upper Volta border and ask for asylum.

Tumu was the low point of the day. A seventy-mile drive east brought us to the pleasant town of Navrongo. We had trouble sympathizing with its Peace Corps Volunteers, having just come from their colleagues in Tumu. The eastern and western half of the Upper Region are remarkably dissimilar, with the East looking much more fertile and livable.

From Navrongo to Bolgatanga we rode on our first paved road in days. I realize that my description of road conditions can mislead the reader. I have based my judgment of the roads on how they compare to other *Ghanaian* roads. When I call a road "good," therefore, it has a far different meaning than the casual reader might think. Americans would not generally regard Ghanaian roads as roads at all.

We arrived in Bolgatanga, the regional capital, in the late afternoon and went directly to the government catering rest house. We had heard good things about it, namely that it had electricity and water, both of which we eagerly anticipated after the rigors of the last few days. It was with some dismay and frustration, therefore, that we received the news that the rest house had no empty rooms – not that they were occupied, but only that different government ministries rented the rooms on a permanent basis, leaving none for wandering travelers like ourselves.

With that news, I had reached the end of my patience. But being the junior officer, I left it to Rod to plan our course of action. He led us to the offices of the Regional Ministry, where he dropped the obscure terminology of "Deputy Chief of Mission" in favor of "Deputy American Ambassador" and wondered loudly and frequently whether the Foreign Ministry had not provided notice of our arrival.

The approach at last brought us into the presence of the Regional Minister himself. With a little prompting, he not only graciously offered us accommodations in the guest quarters of his official residence but also offered to provide us with fuel.

We have not seen gas since leaving Kumasi last Thursday. There have been many gas stations on the way. Those with long lines of cars had no gas but expected it within a day or two. Those without lines simply had no gas. We had planned to send our driver over the border into Upper Volta tomorrow for gas. The Regional Minister's generous offer will make that unnecessary.

December 11, 1980 Thursday – Lome, Togo

Patience is a virtue. In Ghana it is also a necessity. Getting gas in Bolgatanga proved more difficult than we had hoped. The Regional Ministry hadn't enough to spare for us, but did assist with a letter to the Mobil station authorizing us to fill both the van's tank and the jerry cans. I don't know which was of greater consequence – the letter, or the government official and soldier accompanying it. The Mobil people were quite willing to oblige, but, the electricity having failed, they could not operate the pump.

Our driver resolved the situation by driving to the electric company and explaining our dire straits. The company agreed to turn on the juice for thirty minutes.

Ghana's electricity problems seem to be less that there is no power than that the available power is insufficient, so the company practices rolling black-outs. We have heard stories of special arrangements with the company to make sure the power is on for a big party, and even one where the customer called up to complain that the power had gone off in the middle of her baking. The company agreed to turn it back on, but asked her to call back when her baking was finished.

December 16, 1980 Tuesday - Accra, Ghana
    Road conditions. Bolgatanga – Tamale: Paved, passable. Tamale – Togo border: Road grows narrower and narrower until it disappears. Lama Kara – Lome: Good, paved 2-lane highway. Lome – Accra: Yes, we're back in Ghana.

    The town of Tamale recently appeared in the news when its citizenry trashed the residence of the Regional Minister because the city had no power or water. Not that Tamalians are hot-tempered people. The city had been without such luxuries for two years before the inhabitants' patience gave out.

    The day we arrived (Tuesday, December 9th) the city had electricity. One had only to manage to be in the right neighborhood at the right time to take advantage of it.

    We stayed at the government rest house, which compared favorably to its counterparts in Bole and Wa. (The proprietor denied vehemently that his establishment had any connection whatsoever to them.) The older units were quite comfortable, built in pre-air conditioning days with ceiling fans and lots of windows. There was one bucket of water per room for washing and flushing the toilet. It was not clear to me how much water we could ask for in the course of a day. The lack of water meant nothing to me, since I was so exhausted from the day's activities that I went directly to bed without even brushing my teeth.

    Our whole trip had begun to wear on me even more than I realized. The farther we got away from such places as Bole, Wa, and Tumu, the more horrible and uninviting those places appeared. The entire Northwest of the country assumed increasingly nightmarish dimensions in my mind of heat, desolation, and inertia.

    In Tamale I went into culture shock. People may argue about what culture shock is. I use the term to describe the condition in which one sees everything surrounding him as totally alien and unacceptable.

My breaking point came in the evening, ironically as the result of the local USAID Representative's desire to make our Tamale stay enjoyable. He had arranged for a dance troupe on their way to Sunyani for the national arts festival to come by his house at sunset and run through their show.

The sun set, they came, they beat their drums, they danced, they sang. And I wanted to be anywhere else. Every hand on a drum hammered on my temples. Every shrill voice stabbed at the base of my neck.

While my colleagues raved over the performance, my cultural insensitivity to the repetitious drumming and the unskillful dancing made me think of an elementary school production.

My negative outlook did not lessen with the following day's events. Enroute to Togo (ah, fabled Togo!), we stopped at the town of Yendi to visit its Paramount Chief, one of only nine in the whole nation. Our friend, the Chief of Wa, is another. Having met two of the nine, I fear for Ghana's future. The man in Wa is called (besides our affectionate title "Mr. Life of the Party") the Wana. The gentleman in Yendi is the Yana.

We called on the Yana in his "throne room." We reached it by passing through his stable. Not much difference between the two, except the latter was occupied by two horses and the former by the chief and his advisers. The Yana sat on a raised platform with his advisors sprawled at his feet and a boy standing next to him with a fan to ward off the flies. His interpreter carried out the usual introductions. There was a polite murmur when he described Rod Hawke as the Deputy Ambassador. There was an audible nod of appreciation when he described me as the man in charge of visas.

We had an inane conversation of pleasantries and platitudes. I remember only that the Yana said he had "twenty-some" wives and "forty-some" children. The advisors clicked their fingers against the sides of their hands whenever something particularly witty was said. I presume it was their form of applause. It sounded very much like snapping fingers. They made their disconcerting noises more often than I thought necessary.

The audience ended when Rod gave the Yana a bottle of gin. We in turn received two bewildered guinea hens and a turkey, as well as five yams large enough to feed the South Bronx. The USAID Representative loaded all the loot in his van, muttering something about finding a suitable charity.

One last comment on the Yana: he chewed gum constantly.

From Yendi the road led east to the Togo border. It grew increasingly narrow, until we arrived in the Ghanaian border town of Tatale. There we encountered an individual about whom I've heard reports in other parts of the world: an illiterate Immigration Inspector. The man could not read his own country's visa. He mistook the date of its issuance (September 1980) as the date of its expiration. He knew he was right, because the visa contained no other date and the words "Valid within 12 months of the date hereof" meant nothing to him. When Rod attempted to explain his own government's forms, the gentleman sputtered: "Oh, sir! I cannot believe you!" He finally let us pass, after making our Ghanaian driver fill out the foreigners' form for himself. Maybe all Ghanaians passing through Tatale somehow forfeit their citizenship. We also studiously ignored the "X-mas Box" he showily placed on his desk, apparently with the hope we would reward him for his services.

We had less trouble with the French-speaking Togolese Inspectors a mile down the road. There were a few tense moments when the Togolese police said we needed a permit to bring in gas in jerry cans. They also viewed our radio equipment with suspicion. I for one refused to go back to Ghana and was prepared to provoke a major international incident. Rod in his best high school French sweet-talked them (that's how you get to be Deputy Ambassador). We drove on.

The first rule about short cuts: Don't take them. There are good and substantial reasons why people build a road forty kilometers longer than a direct route between two points. The reason in northern Togo is the sand. We found this out when we tried to shorten our driving distance to the town of Lama-Kara. We shortened the distance, but not the time. We got stuck in the sand, and extracted ourselves with a shovel. The only way to avoid getting mired was to accelerate through sandy stretches, not a pleasant prospect on a one-lane road in the bush. Those stretches not covered with sand usually consisted of jagged rocks ready to rip out our bottom. We survived, and reached the hotel in Lama-Kara.

December 17, 1980 Wednesday – Accra

Last Thursday we drove from Lama-Kara south to the Togolese capital Lome, a distance of some 250 miles. Considering the distance, it was the longest segment of the trip. Considering the road, it was sheer heaven. Granted Togo's roads do not compare with the American interstate system, being shabby two-lane blacktops. After two weeks on Ghanaian roads, we enjoyed the thrill of racing along at 60 MPH with only the most remote fear that a monster pothole would suddenly leap from the pavement and swallow us up.

Other thrills pleased us less. As in northern Ghana, brush fires were quite common in Togo. The fires often burned right to the road's edge. On several occasions we passed through sections where the flames reached out across the road, with ash in the air and the heat visible. We all thought of the jerry cans on the roof and breathed a collective sigh of relief when we passed.

In Lome we arrived in time to be invited to a reception the Ambassador was having in the evening. We hesitated somewhat over accepting, considering the sorry state of our clothes. (I still have not decided whether to try washing them or just have Yaro burn them.) It turned out to be a reception for Peace Corps Volunteers, so everything worked out fine. Our shabby appearance helped us blend in.

I knew nobody at the reception, the others being Peace Corps workers from all over West Africa in Togo for a conference. Those

Notes from Lower Volta

with whom I spoke seemed suitably impressed by the few cryptic comments I made concerning our trip. They avoided boring me with the usual hardship stories Peace Corps types love to drop on effete Embassy types. A most satisfying situation.

I also ran into our Consular Officer stationed in Lome. He said he has noticed a rise in the number of Ghanaians whom we had refused visas in Accra appearing at the Embassy in Lome with diplomatic notes from their own embassy.

December 18, 1980 Thursday

Such joy to discover that civilization lies only three hours down the road from Accra in Lome: stores with stocked shelves, service stations with gasoline, restaurants with food – everything! People in Accra had described Lome's wonders to me. I hesitated to believe that such an earthly Paradise could exist on this continent.

We spent the morning of Friday, December 12th, on a whirlwind shopping spree. I did not buy too much. I preferred instead merely to stand amidst all the bustle and experience the sensation of a functioning economy once again.

We didn't need the border checkpoints to let us know when we crossed into Ghana. The broken pavement, the long lines of dusty vehicles waiting at service stations for fuel which was not there, and the general shabby appearance of the place left no doubt about our location.

Togo for all its economic glory leaves much to be desired politically. It is ruled by a megalomaniac dictator who has his photograph hanging in every shop and home. The hotel staff at the Sarakawa Hotel in Lome where we stayed even wore little lapel pins with his picture, a la Kim Il-sung in North Korea.

Togo claims that a central event in its history was a 1974 plane crash which President Eyadema miraculously survived. They built a massive neo-fascist monument on the site of the crash to celebrate his deliverance, and renamed one of Lome's major hotels "The Second of February" in honor of the day he was discharged from the hospital.

And so concluded my two-week tour of Ghana. It has satisfied any desire I have to explore the countryside further. Perhaps I might make a trip along the coast to visit the old slaving forts, or back to the Ashanti capital of Kumasi. Perhaps. Or maybe I will just sit in Accra and think about European vacations and my next assignment.

Useful as my four-wheel drive Jeep would be in exploring Ghana, were the mood to possess me, I think its greater value comes from the fact that I can remove its back seat and have immense storage space for all the goodies to bring back from a Lome shopping spree.

We arrived back in Accra in the late afternoon of December 12th. The morning of December 13th saw a heavy rain shower which gave way, strangely, to the harmattan, that mass cloud of dust and sand which yearly descends from the Sahara as the dry season advances. We had expected to encounter the harmattan while up North. Thankfully we did not.

Dust, dust everywhere. Clean the house in the morning, seal the windows closed, and in the afternoon clean, clean again in a losing battle. Dust, dust everywhere, with the sun shining palely through the tons of dirt hanging in the air. What would a thunderstorm do? Turn the sky to mud? Dust, dust everywhere, pouring into my nose, my eyes, my throat. It is like sticking one's face into a vacuum cleaner bag full of what lay on the living room carpet this morning.

I have a flask of water with me constantly. I drink constantly: water, iced tea, juice – anything to wet my lips and clear my throat. If I don't, I cough like a consumptive about to succumb to tuberculosis.

They say, some hopefully, and some proudly, they say that this year's harmattan has already shown itself the worst in the last twenty years. Not often, they point out, is the dust so thick that it forces the airport's closure, as it did over the weekend.

How lucky I am to witness nature in this great display of her majesty! It still beats Milwaukee in December.

Notes from Lower Volta

All through our trip upcountry, Lois Hawke made her way through Steinbeck's *Grapes of Wrath*. I wonder why. We had only to look all around us.

December 21, 1980 Sunday

People ask about the great expedition. What was it like? Did you enjoy it?

How should I answer? I know that some of them, with a little encouragement, would like to try similar trips, although on a reduced scale. Having written as much in this book during those two weeks as in all of the preceding three months, it is difficult to summarize my feelings to twenty-five words or less. Words like "exhausting," "grim," "depressing," and "exciting," "enjoyable," and "fun"? The bottom line of the whole affair is that I would not have missed the trip for the world. Nor would I ever do it again.

Yesterday I typed up my notes with the idea of showing them to interested people here and sending them to friends in the States. They will require some judicious editing. If I avoid remarks offensive to Ghana, there will of course be nothing left. So I will leave them in. I think it best to eliminate some of the less flattering references to the Hawkes. Not only is he the Deputy Ambassador. He writes my efficiency report.

I submitted a memo to the person in charge of rewriting Accra's post report. Post reports provide the information we rely on to find out what a place is like before going there. Ghana's post report was last updated in early 1978. It is consequently hopelessly in error. It begins with a section describing the joys of traveling around Ghana. It even includes proposed itineraries. The whole thing is very misleading. It helped mislead me to Ghana. I suggested that a prefatory warning be added that the uncertainty of fuel supplies, the poor condition of the roads, and the lack of adequate accommodations make travel extremely difficult.

The editor of the Embassy newsletter asked me to write some brief descriptions of possible outings based on my trip. I laughed.

Must send her a copy of my typed notes.

December 26, 1980 Friday

My first tropical Christmas. It's a little difficult to get into the Christmas spirit dressed in short-sleeved shirts and cut-off blue jeans, even with Bing Crosby warbling "White Christmas" in the background. How can you have Christmas without snow? Unless, perhaps, we use all the harmattan dust. It continues to drift in faster than I can sweep it out. I haven't slept through the night for a week, waking up several times with coughing spasms as my lungs try to clear themselves. Perhaps a gas mask would help.

My first tropical Christmas, I say, spent appropriately at the beach with a healthy amount of champagne for refreshment. Hardly the type of Christmas one expects who has grown up in the Great Lakes region. The Australians don't have that problem.

December 30, 1980 Tuesday

I've heard that the best way to pass time in a place such as Ghana is to spend as much time of it as possible *out* of it. So far I've plotted a consular conference in Nairobi for early February, and vacation in Europe for all of June. I've also subtly hinted to my Career Counselor about the Advanced Consular Course next October in Washington. That only leaves one year to worry about.

Things are bad enough here, but I don't find my outlook improved by the fact that I've been here since September 1st and my salary is still not straightened out. In addition to my base salary, I should receive a ten percent cost of living allowance and a twenty percent hardship allowance. I'm getting the cost of living allowance. I've yet to see a single penny of my base pay or the hardship allowance. The blockheads in the Finance Office in the Paris Embassy have messed everything up. How cruel! Insult to injury, they revel in the fleshpots of Gay Paree and screw up my paycheck in a drunken stupor. If the money ever does show up, Uncle Sam won't compensate me with such details as interest.

Notes from Lower Volta

I've had to dig into my savings to pay off the bills I ran up during the summer, naively assuming I would soon have the money to pay. American Express has deluged me with an avalanche of "Personal and Confidential" Amexgrams, each demanding immediate payment, each threatening dire consequences otherwise (they overestimate the threat of cancellation to someone in this part of the world), each asking that I telephone immediately (collect?), each saying what a valued customer I have been (then why do they keep harassing me?), and each with the printed signature of a different individual who invariably has an initial rather than a first name. Maybe computers sign the letters and "B. Finnell," "D. Marrero," "D. Hadden," and "L. Montgomery" are the series names of different machines. That would explain why they continue to churn out their Amexgrams and ignore my several letters which attempt to explain my plight.

The ten percent cost of living allowance we get would be higher, except that the last time the Embassy ran the price survey people checked most items "not available" rather than calculate the cost of shipping such exotic items as potatoes and fresh vegetables from the United States or Europe.

Consular work here is similar to that in Korea, only on a smaller scale. The same push to get visas to the great big coast-to-coast supermarket across the waves. Each day from thirty to sixty Ghanaians apply for tourist and student visas. Maybe one third get a visa. Maybe half of them ever come back to Ghana. The others cannot understand why, on the basis of a thousand dollar a year salary and five hundred dollars in the bank, we question their plans to drop sixteen hundred dollars on a round-trip ticket to visit a brother in the Bronx who went ten years ago on a student visa and who now drives a taxi. If we rashly send off the school records, employment letters, and bank statements submitted to us, half of them turn out to be fakes.

Question: When is a currency not a currency?
Answer: When it's a cedi.

I never studied economics in school, but it takes no genius to see that Ghana's economy has been horribly mismanaged for years. At the center of it all (whether as cause or effect I have no idea) stands the Ghanaian cedi, the legal medium of exchange in this country. The legal, but by no means the *accepted* medium of exchange.

Officially, 2.75 cedis equal one U.S. dollar in value. The current black market rate has pushed that to twenty cedis and more to a dollar. In the legal economy it is impossible for a businessman or a farmer to turn a profit. The cedi is worth less than the paper used to print it. Black-marketing and smuggling have become a way of life. Any product of value (cocoa, cement, tires) is smuggled across the border where it can be sold for CFA, the hard currency of the former French colonies. The CFA then comes back to Ghana, where it is exchanged for cedis at many times the official rate, allowing the smuggler to live quite nicely.

In theory, the government has set controlled cedi prices for most items in the marketplace. In practice, one must pay the black market price or do without. On those occasions when the government inspectors sweep past, the vendors suddenly have nothing to sell. There is the related difficulty that sometimes even the government inspector doesn't know what an item's controlled price is, the listing probably buried with thousands of others in stacks of molding forms in some ministry office.

The government, having set the value of the cedi by sleight of hand, demands that we foreigners, among others, abide by it. To my mind, forcing me to buy cedis at seven times the price I could get them for on the street is legal theft. Even the government recognizes the absurdity of the exchange rate. When Ghanaians buy foreign currency for an overseas trip, they must pay a seventy-five percent "tax," which in effect means they pay five cedis for one dollar, nearly twice the official level.

Every once in a while, most recently in 1979, the government thinks it can solve the problem by closing the borders and declaring all the money in circulation worthless unless exchanged for new cedis (or, perhaps, new new cedis). The hitch is that each person is allowed to exchange only a certain amount of old cedis for new, with the intention of catching currency speculators with large amounts of now worthless money. While dramatic, such currency revolutions (what does one call them?) have no visible effect, because the new cedi picks up where the old one left off: highly overvalued.

The obvious solution is devaluation. Let the cedi float against other currencies. Let it sink like a millstone. Surely the traumatic effects of a sudden devaluation could not wreak greater havoc with the economy than the current Alice-in-Wonderland situation. The government knows that none of its predecessors survived devaluations. Coups replaced them.

And so the smuggling goes on. So does the flight of Ghanaians abroad for employment at real wages. Someday we'll wake up and Ghana will be gone, smuggled out across the border.

1981

January 1, 1981 Thursday

These are my New Year's resolutions: To learn German, French, and Korean; to read, read, read; and not to let Ghana defeat me. I don't like what this country is doing to me, making me passive, depressed, angry, rude. I will not put up with it. I have survived four months here. I have only twenty to go.

January 7, 1981 Wednesday

Some Consular Officers say that one forms a fair impression of a nation's characteristics by paying attention to how much time its VIPs spend in Consular Sections trying to get visas for their friends and acquaintances.

There was the Philippine Ambassador in Seoul, for example. Although the dean of the diplomatic corps, he possessed such strong egalitarian instincts that he repeatedly invited lowly second and third secretaries from the Visa Section to lunch. Such occasions invariably concluded (that is, when the Americans could not find some plausible excuse to decline the invitation) with the sudden appearance of one or two passports belonging to various relatives and other hangers-on of the Ambassador, with the request that they be given visas. Strangely enough, a rather large number of them had previously applied at the American Embassy in Manila and been turned down.

I have encountered the Ghanaian counterpart to the Philippine Ambassador. The Director of Protocol of the Ministry of Foreign Affairs has taken it upon himself to call me at least once a month to inquire about different applicants, all of whom we have previously refused. In all this time he has not even met me. Our total contact has been by telephone.

Although we know almost nothing about each other except the sounds of our voices, it would not be an exaggeration to say that there is no one in this country with whom I have a worse working relationship. That is because he has found me remarkably unbending to his wishes. It is not that I seek to be difficult, only that he asks for visas for the most unqualified applicants. His approach is not to inquire why the applicant was unsuccessful, but to suggest that surely his word should be sufficient to overcome any objections we might have. What does his word have to do with it?

Our most recent conversation ended when Mr. Cicero (heavens, how undiplomatic of me to refer to him by name!) informed me that my performance in Accra has not pleased him. I took that as a compliment, since it indicates that I am doing the job the U.S. taxpayers have hired me to do. Since he could get no satisfaction from me, he huffed, he would have to discuss the matter with Ambassador Smith. He appeared oblivious to the fact that I hold the only keys to the visa machine and the Ambassador wishes nothing less than to enter into a conversation about such things.

Ironically, Cicero's interest extends to every kind of visa except those he should concern himself with. I discovered this in late December when the Ghanaian Ambassador to the United States himself swept into the office with a dozen or so passports for his household entourage. To hear the Ambassador tell it, he had submitted everything to the Ministry's Protocol Office weeks earlier to obtain the visas. Protocol had done nothing, and here was the day the Ambassador planned to leave for Washington. So there stood the Ambassador at our counter, like a messenger boy from the Ministry, filling out the application forms which Cicero's office should have long since prepared and forwarded.

Would that things had followed their proper course! Of the bundle of passports, only the Ambassador's, his wife's, and his children's went out the door that day with visas in them. The others – those of the Ambassador's maid, who has worked for the family since she was eleven without pay; of the Ambassador's nephew the accountant who planned to work as his houseboy; of the Ambassador's other nephew the Civil Aviation Department security guard who planned to work as... well, he planned to work as something; of the student applying to an American college and with an undetermined relationship to the Ambassador; of others, the details of whose histories now escape me – as I say, all those passports were returned with the same number of blank pages as before. I sent off a cable to the Department of State suggesting that our laws don't allow unsalaried servitude and that the idea that the two deadbeat nephews planned to work in the household smelled like a cow pasture, and for the same reason.

The Department, displaying all the vertebrae of an earthworm, found itself unable to understand my concern, given the "sincerity" of all involved (I have no doubt they all sincerely want to go to the United States), and said: "Let his people come!" The Department conceded that we might legitimately question the application of someone obviously overqualified, underqualified, or not qualified for the proposed employment, of someone whose salary will be only room and board (whatever happened to the minimum wage?), or someone related to the alleged employer – but if only they should be sincere, much can we forgive.

I no longer have the Ghanaian Ambassador and everybody and his nephew occupying my waiting room like an enemy army. He has gone on to Washington – but only after stopping off in London to try to get his maid the serf a tourist visa from our Embassy there. I expect that he neglected to mention that he had already applied in Ghana, and had been specifically told *not* to try applying in London.

In a number of ways, diplomatic life does not quite fit the conceptions I had of it in my earlier years.

January 25, 1981 Sunday
The hostages are free. I have nothing to add to that, except thanksgiving that the ordeal is over for them, and for us. Until the final hours of their illegal kidnapping, the Iranians continued to demonstrate the great justice and mercy they have so often shown themselves capable of.

Ronald Reagan is the fortieth President of the United States,

Notes from Lower Volta

General Haig the Secretary of State. What lies in America's future? At almost any other time, I would have looked at this new administration with dismay and fear. These past years of apparent American decline, the exhaustion of the liberal idea, and Jimmy Carter have joined together to cause me to await this administration with a mixture of relief and hope. Have we truly come so far, that a McGovern Democrat looks to California right-wingers for leadership?

January 29, 1981 Thursday

From a letter from my sister Margaret dated January 20th: "Needless to say, this has been a very emotional day in Washington between the inauguration and the hostage release. It was a beautiful day – fifty-two degrees – and I got on my bike and spent the day in town. Saw the swearing-in and the parade, plus got a real *close-up* of Reagan and Bush twenty feet away. Watched the spectacular fireworks off my balcony – better than July 4th.

"Of course, the most moving part of the day was the announcement of the release of the hostages. People were so apprehensive to really let their feeling out in fear that something else might delay the release. But when the darkened Christmas tree was lit, there were many tears of joy shed. We then knew they were all out of Iran.

"As much as I didn't like Carter, I felt very sad for him today, especially with the last delay on the release."

January 31, 1981 Saturday

"How warm and friendly the Ghanaians are!" How often did I hear that refrain from colleagues when they heard of my Accra assignment? How often did that phrase serve as the ultimate explanation, in spite of all of Ghana's other problems, of why I would enjoy my posting?

God could not find ten good men in Sodom. I'm not having much better luck finding a single Ghanaian who has not asked me for something, usually a visa, sometimes only money. In Korea I adopted the guideline that I would disengage myself from all my "friends" who inquired about visas. Even so, I still had a respectably wide circle of friends there.

Applying the same rule in Ghana has left me with almost no Ghanaians with whom I feel at ease in conversation. I flinch at every approach, and mentally calculate how long a conversation will proceed before I am asked for a favor.

My cynicism amazes me. Even more amazing than my cynicism are the shameless requests which confirm it. How can we describe an accurate assessment of the situation as "cynical"? It is my misfortune that what would elsewhere be cynicism becomes in Ghana simple pragmatism.

February 8, 1981 Sunday – Nairobi, Kenya

I arrived in Nairobi early Friday morning, very early Friday morning, like 2:00 a.m. Kenya has lived up to its reputation. Nairobi is quite an attractive city, by far the most attractive among the few which I have seen in Africa. It possesses all the attributes which in the last few months I have come to associate with the basic necessities of life: paved streets, functioning markets, a usable currency, etc. Nairobi has reached such an advanced stage of development that it even has sidewalks, so the pedestrian does not walk in terror of being struck from behind by a taxi.

Kenya appears to depend disproportionately on its European and Asian communities to keep the country's economy running. One quickly gets the impression that all the stores, except for the humblest street stalls, and the hotels are owned and operated by foreigners. Even in those places which appear to be run by Africans, sooner or later a white face appears from behind the scenes.

February 9, 1981 Monday

My depressed mood has improved considerably since the turn of the year. The harmattan has largely disappeared, or perhaps I've merely adjusted to it. At any rate I no longer need continuous infusions of liquids.

    The government finally produced all my back pay. It arrived after I had already dug deeply into my savings account to pay off my American Express bill. Even that action came too late to forestall American Express's cancellation of my account, with the thinly veiled warning that they might refer the matter to a collection agency "in your area." Good luck.

    Yesterday I visited Nairobi National Park in a tour organized by the Embassy. The park is a game reserve right on the edge of the city. It contains an astounding diversity of wildlife. I saw giraffes, zebras, ostriches, wildebeests, antelope, hartebeests, leopards, cheetahs, and a baboon who jumped up onto the hood of our van. He peered in the windshield at us. We peered out at him. We, of course, took pictures. The driver eventually dislodged him by putting the engine alternately into first and reverse gears.

    Kenya's rolling hills and distant horizons were as I imagined Africa's open spaces. In many respects, Kenya and Ghana resemble each other physically. So why do I like the one and abhor the other?

    One can quickly experience my feelings towards Ghana by reading a novel called *The Beautiful Ones Are Not Yet Born*, written by a Ghanaian named Ayi Kwei Armah. I do not recommend the book for its literary value, since Armah believes that he has written something significant if he can only write endless detailed paragraphs about the various excreta which pour forth from every orifice of the human body. No, I recommend the book because it perfectly calls forth the feelings of fury, disgust, and indifference which Ghana raises in me.

February 24, 1981 Tuesday

    While still in Nairobi I successfully eluded all the attempts of self-appointed tour guides to lure themselves into my service. In response to the standard opening line of: "Where are you from?" I came back with: "Ghana." The answer left every one of them disoriented, unable to overcome the mindset which told him that

Ghana and I could not possibly go together.

I did enjoy my ten days in Nairobi. I also had the chance to see Louise Salter, who was the Deputy Ambassador's secretary in Seoul and is now the Ambassador's in Nairobi. We gossiped over old times and traded information on where everyone had gotten. It reminded me again of how I miss Korea. It also made clear that the Korea I know is no longer there.

After all the nasty things I have written about Ghana these last few months, I almost hesitate to record the following story. It certainly undercuts my central thesis that Ghana lacks all social activity.

Mick Fleetwood, of the rock group Fleetwood Mac, came to town with a plan to make an album combining rock and Ashanti tribal music. Not a bad idea.

I first came across Fleetwood and his people two months ago on their preliminary visit. He and his lawyer had their passports, money, and plane tickets stolen. Fleetwood, though British, does have an American green card (the only item not lost), while his lawyer was Californian. We do give American passports to people from that state, foreign as it may seem. Consequently, they looked upon us with favor, and rewarded our efforts on their behalf with free tickets to the benefit concert Fleetwood and his boys put on last Saturday night. Thank God the tickets were free. Fifty cedis may only be $2.50 on the black market, but it's about $20 at the "official" rate.

The concert included performances by a few Ghanaian groups before Fleetwood's appearance. Each group ran well past its allotted time, despite assurances from the show's organizers (who also picked the fifty-cedi admission figure) that they would keep things under control.

There was no recording tape left for Fleetwood's performance, all of it having been wasted on groups indistinguishable from each other for their lack of talent. Fleetwood's appearance had an electric effect. Some of the same Ghanaian performers who had gone out of their way in the preceding two hours to show the audience that harmony and melody were strictly non-African concepts suddenly proved themselves capable of both.

    The only other incident of note at the Fleetwood concert was the diplomatic crisis brought about by the standoff between Ambassador Smith's daughter and the police. Thirteen-year-old Samantha, it seems, had endangered the security of the state by her subversive use of her Kodak Instamatic. I assumed she had snapped a shot of the Ghanaian Vice President. Someone else said she had only taken a picture of one of the policemen. At any rate, the police wanted the film, and Sarah was not about to surrender it. The standoff ended when the Ambassador, somewhat irritated by the conversation behind him without grasping its full import, took the disputed camera and dropped it into his pocket.

March 1, 1981 Sunday

    I seem to have acquired a dog, wrongly named Killer, a small bush dog which I have inherited from an American couple who have returned to the States. Killer was not sure he wished to join my household. He ran off on a number of occasions, usually to his former masters' house. It slowly dawned on him that no one in all of Accra except me had any desire to feed him.

    I returned from Nairobi to find a half-starved animal waiting for a handout. Since then his wandering instincts seem strangely muted. He has run off on only one other occasion.

    His show of independence serves as a cover for the basic insecurity of an extremely neurotic dog. He is unlike any other canine I have ever dealt with. He requires continuous reassurance that I recognize and want his presence.

    He also does not care for other dogs, particularly larger dogs. That is a problem. Virginia Mayberry's Thunder is a good-sized German shepherd. Killer growls at Thunder, and after a while Thunder is so aggravated he barks at Killer. And then they fight.

    Last week Virginia went to Kumasi for the week and left Thunder with me. It was like having two children in the house. I finally brought some discipline into the situation by making Killer understand not to bare his teeth at Thunder. Then I forced the two to lie down together and not move, not make a sound, not even breathe, unless they wanted the wrath of God upon them both. While still far from friendly toward each other, each does tolerate the other's presence.

Their mutual antipathy represented only one facet of my week-long ordeal. Thunder developed a lump in one of his front legs which grew so bad I took him to the veterinarian. And Killer came down with an ear infection. Do dogs have psychosomatic illnesses?

March 13, 1981 Friday

I do miss not being in a climate where spring would be coming about this time of year, *not* that I missed all the cold and snow which has presumably covered the United States these past months. But unfailing hot weather and sunshine day in and day out does become enervating. It clouded over and rained a bit yesterday for the first time since December 13th, so I hope we will shortly arrive at the rainy season. I expect the rain will not cool things off so much as steam them up.

Two good reference books which provide an accurate description of life in Africa: Evelyn Waugh's *Black Mischief* and *Scoop*. He wrote these savage diatribes in a less enlightened age almost fifty years ago. They still provide a taste of the absurdity of life here for those fortunate enough not to experience it firsthand.

Life does have its redeeming features. I've discovered how to make ice cream, or a reasonable facsimile thereof. Our commissary stocks an ultra-pasteurized European cream which requires no refrigeration. Throw a couple of tubs of it into the blender, add Nestlé's chocolate mix and some mint chocolate liqueur to taste, blend, freeze thirty minutes, blend again, freeze, and voila! you have chocolate ice cream. One could dispense with the liqueur, but Lord knows our lives here have little enough excitement as it is. I plan to try the cream with frozen strawberries next. And Drambuie.

Notes from Lower Volta

The Embassy received a rather curious cable from the Department of State today. In line with concern "at the highest levels of the government" the Department will make a special effort to upgrade security immediately at embassies around the world which are considered likely terrorist targets. For some reason Accra is on the list. Granted the Chancery is a wooden box on stilts and the Annex looks like an auto repair shop. But I didn't think we had a security problem.

March 14, 1981 Saturday
Friday, March 6th, being the twenty-fourth anniversary of Ghana's independence and a holiday, I drove down to Lome with Virginia Mayberry. A lot of other Americans and foreigners took advantage of the holiday too, a little disconcerting to discover that instead of getting away from it all it all came along with you. I asked Yaro my steward if he wanted me to bring him anything. I spent most of the time until the stores closed at noon on Saturday shopping for him and his family. I managed to get two dog bowls for myself – or Killer, rather.

Killer has had a traumatic life these last few days. He developed some growths on his more private areas which the veterinarian said had to come off surgically. At the vet's suggestion, he combined the surgery last Wednesday with a second common procedure which may not end Killer's amorous wanderings but will limit his progeny. Killer came home from the hospital looking like a little old man, barely able to walk. His head hung low to the ground, and his tail, which normally curls up like a spring and waves back and forth like a lady's fan, pointed down like an arrow. He has recovered slowly. I hope by next week he'll be back to his usual self. Oh! but the looks of pain and betrayal which he turned on me with his tired, reddened eyes when first he came home!

April 17, 1981 Friday
The days merge together, each indistinguishable from its

successor. Only a look at the calendar shows the passage of time. Nothing much happens to write about.

Well, maybe not locally. On the home front, we've had the shooting of President Reagan, Al Haig's attempted coup, and the long-delayed flight of the space shuttle.

Some Ghanaians made condescending comments about American political violence. I found it somewhat curious, coming from citizens of a nation whose last coup (only two years ago) involved the execution of three former heads of state.

The most excitement recently was the arrival two weeks ago of my $1,400 meat order from the States. One would think that $1,400 worth of meat should suffice for the rest of my tour. Considering freight charges, it amounts to only about $700 at American prices. The meat arrived at a particularly unpropitious moment. The labor unions had planned a general strike for this week which would have shut off the electricity and the water and the fuel. (Cynics would call that business as usual.) I had visions of one of the largest barbecues in West African history as we tried to eat all the meat before it rotted. Fortunately, the government has agreed to the unions' demands and the strike has been called off. Actually, the government agreed to the demands months ago but just didn't bother to do anything about them.

Last weekend we had an annual Peace Corps affair in which Embassy families put up Peace Corps Volunteers in their homes. I took four, considering the size of my house, and never had such an exhausting weekend since my arrival in Ghana. I was in a drunken stupor from Friday night to Monday morning.

The volunteers, anxious for relief from their Ghanaian diet, made themselves sick on gallons of orange juice and powdered milk, pounds of bacon, several sides of beef, and beer, beer, beer. I spent most of the time in the kitchen conjuring up more food than Jesus did with his twelve loaves and fish. The only mishap occurred when Yaro threw a tray of ready-to-serve Sara Lee brownies into the oven to bake at 350 degrees.

Notes from Lower Volta

All my carefully constructed travel plans for the remainder of the year have collapsed/are collapsing. I had intended to vacation in Europe in June and finagle a trip to Washington in October for the Advanced Consular Course. Now the Department has sent a cable assigning me to the course from May 18th to June 5th. So everything is up in the air.

June 18, 1981 Thursday – Zurich, Switzerland
Here it is, six years and a day since Henry Kissinger swore me into the Foreign Service. In the interval, I have passed through Korea, Japan, Hong Kong, Macao, Thailand, Singapore, Ghana, Togo, Kenya, Germany, Switzerland, and Liechtenstein. I added Liechtenstein to the list yesterday, as I wrap up two weeks' vacation in Munich, Berlin, and Zurich after completing the Advanced Consular Course in Washington.

My return to the United States had its moments. Departing Accra the evening of May 10th on Swissair, I flew all night and arrived in Zurich to catch a Pan American flight to New York. Traveling on government orders I was of course required to fly an American flag carrier whenever possible.

Pan American in Accra had written the ticket, but one can hardly expect Pan American to know its own flight schedules. When I presented my ticket at the transfer desk in Zurich airport, the clerk informed me that the flight Pan American had routed me on for that Monday afternoon only flew on Sundays.

The clerk suggested that, since I was traveling at government expense, I could go on to Frankfurt and try to catch an American flight there. No guarantee of success, however. Alternatively, he said, Swissair would accept my ticket and fly me to New York within the hour, since the Pan American ticketing agent had fortuitously neglected to make any limiting endorsements on it.

I agonized over the dilemma. My duty to the United States government, the American taxpayer, and U.S. flag carriers everywhere clearly required that I wander from airport to airport across the European continent in search of an American flight, a latter-day Flying Dutchman. My narrow, unpatriotic selfishness won out, I got on the Swissair plane, and I had a beautiful flight to JFK.

In spite of all the horror stories one hears about JFK, I processed through Customs with a minimal wait and even caught an earlier flight to Philadelphia than scheduled.

After a week in Philadelphia, I moved on to Washington, where I quickly fell into the old round of bar visits and dinners out. The Advanced Consular Course (which had been recommended to me as a good way to spend three weeks out of Accra) did not disappoint me. It was of limited usefulness.

The others in the course (fourteen of us) were interesting personalities. Only one other participant was currently stationed overseas. The rest were Foreign Service Officers currently assigned to Washington, Civil Service employees, and two individuals from the Immigration and Naturalization Service.

One of the INS employees explained in the bar one night she always asks for "a martini, very dry, please," because that sounds so much more elegant than "I'll have a glass of gin."

The second of the three weeks involved an off-site management training seminar at Harper's Ferry, West Virginia, given in a grim, windowless conference room in a "motor inn" on the side of a highway by a management "expert" who fascinated himself with psychobabble ("metagames," "rational paranoia"). He seemed to think we were not as impressed by his expertise as he believed we should be. Our reaction to him was not helped any by his repeated comments on the personality defects of Foreign Service types (who, he finally confessed, are all "mushy"). The week-long session ended with this expert on managing others losing control of the group. On the final morning, we sat him down and offered him a few tips on how he could improve his course and his attitudes.

Having learned all there is to know about managing a Consular Section, I left Washington June 6th for Munich, where I met Don O'Shea, to salvage what we could of our long-planned European excursion. In no time at all Munich rose high on my list of desirable future postings.

We spent the days wandering the city and the nights drinking beer at the Hofbraeuhaus. Under the pressures of the moment, my long-buried German slowly surfaced. In the face of non-English speakers, I still tended to lapse into Korean, or at least to string German words together in Korean word order. All in all, however, it is surprising how far one can go in Germany knowing no more than "Speisekarte" for menu and "zwei Bier, bitte."

One day we took the train out to the village of Dachau to visit the concentration camp. It was obvious who the Americans on the train were. They all got off at Dachau.

Visiting the camp was a sobering experience. The dimensions of the horrors of the Third Reich overwhelm until they numb the brain. I had difficulty imagining that the polite, efficient, orderly people filling the Munich beer halls are the children of people who devised the concentration camp system.

We also took a day tour to Neuschwanstein, mad King Ludwig's fantasy castle in the Bavarian Alps. Last year I had visited Disneyworld, whose castle is modeled upon Neuschwanstein. Little did I suspect then that Disney had not used the model merely to produce some pale plastic imitation. No, Neuschwanstein looks every bit its American counterpart, right down to the fake marble and the painted glass masquerading as precious stones.

Crazy King Ludwig is the one who sponsored Richard Wagner. So the walls of the rooms in the castle are filled with "artistic" versions of scenes from Wagnerian operas. The castle even has an artificial cave to reproduce the Venus grotto in *Tannhaeuser*. The man must have been completely unbalanced.

The Bavarian Alps reminded me of Korean mountains, particularly of the Soraksan chain on the East Coast. That and the fact the tour bus played some German-style Korean bus music made me homesick for Korea.

I discovered that the bizarre hiking outfits for which Koreans display such passion and the tacky souvenir stands outside of tourist spots, both of which I had previously assumed sprang unaided from the fertile Korean imagination, appear to have been copied from the Germans.

From Munich we moved on to Berlin for a weekend. Berlin, both halves, is at best grim. At worst, it is a Kafkaesque nightmare. Even having been raised in a world where the division of Germany has always been a fact, and even having directly observed the continuing division of Korea, I still found my stay in Berlin less a vacation than an ordeal.

What is it like to live in the capital of one's country which is not the capital, which even thirty-six years after the end of the war remains split in two, divided by wall and wire, with uncleared rubble overgrown with bushes and weeds? And where once stood the heart of the city – nothing, except a few restored buildings, and the Wall.

I took an afternoon bus tour of East Berlin. It was even more depressing than the West, all the massive war monuments built with fraternal socialist assistance from the Soviet Union, all the functioning industries built with assistance from evil capitalists.

Our initial plans called for moving on from Berlin to London. There were repeated veiled references in the International Herald Tribune to waves of strikes and flight cancellations in Britain, which left Don paralyzed with fear that he would be late in returning to work and lose his job. I at first dismissed the reports as ordinary indicators of the English sickness. I almost welcomed the prospect of being trapped indefinitely in Britain, unable to return to Ghana.

When Don called up TWA while still in Munich to inquire of the status of their flights, only to have the clerk nonchalantly inform him that London flights had been canceled for three days running, we beat a hasty path to the airline offices. Don elected to return to Chicago directly from Berlin, making his excursion fare ticket valueless and costing him an additional thousand dollars.

I did not have that worry. I was already flying full fare. I elected to spend a few days in Zurich in lieu of London, and a wise choice it was. For one seeking a last fling in the European fleshpots of beer halls, pastry shops, and paved streets, Zurich will do as well as any. Nor could I improve on the beauty of its lake and mountains, and the attraction of its old medieval center. I even visited a Korean restaurant where, given my limited German and the proprietor's limited English, I resorted to Korean without the proprietor's batting an eyelash.

July 2, 1981 Thursday

I returned to Accra Friday, June 19th, to discover things pretty much as I had left them six weeks earlier. More people had been evacuated for medical reasons. The black market rate for dollars had gone from twenty-five cedis to thirty-eight. My entire first floor had been flooded when the water came back on after the maid of the couple watching the place for me left the faucet "on" on a "dry" day. At least it got my turquoise carpets clean.

My great fear, that the electricity would go off and all my meat rot, had not come to pass. My Jeep, which had stood untouched in the garage for six weeks, has somehow managed to break down, with the clutch pedal no longer having any power to disengage the transmission. This comes on top of my camera breaking down two days before I left the United States, with no time to have it repaired. So I have no pictures of my European trip except for those I bought enroute. No luck with cameras.

Virginia Mayberry, the long-suffering Vice Consul, departed on three weeks' vacation in London a week after my return, leaving me in charge of my dog Killer, his two-month old daughter Lady Killer (who, contrary to Ms. Mayberry' reports, is *not* quite housebroken), and Virginia's rather large Thunder. A houseful of children would certainly be easier to deal with.

The night before Virginia's departure I had a party to celebrate the forty-eighth anniversary of the repeal of Prohibition. Having returned to Ghana determined to become the social hub of Accra, I invited sixty people, a good number of whom I hardly know, and then discovered that the commissary had run low on beer and had begun rationing it.

The party still survived and ran on until 3:30 a.m. for the diehards (the Australians).

This week has been rather quiet, helped by the declaration of July 1st as "Republic Day" by the Ghanaian government. Not too clear to me which republic they mean, although I think the original Nkrumah republic. We'll have another Republic Day holiday in September to celebrate the most recent one.

I returned from vacation with a renewed determination to study German and Korean. One may recall that my New Year's Resolutions called for the study of those two languages as well as of French. Since then I have done nothing in the way of studying anything. (Although I have recently submerged myself in Edgar Rice Burroughs' Martian novels for the first time since 1965.) I have dropped French as one of my goals and have decided to concentrate on the two with which I already have a passing acquaintance.

Before arriving in Ghana last year, I had great visions that the lack of social activities here would leave great amounts of time for all sorts of intellectual development, time to the write The Great American Novel, etc. It has instead proven true that the amount of time *wasted* rises *geometrically* as the amount of spare time increases *arithmetically*. That in a nutshell is the sum total of nine months of my intellectual ruminations.

Hard as it may be to believe if one has read all my preceding ramblings on life in Ghana, I find myself faced with an increasing attachment to this place. I was happy to return after six weeks' absence, with the intention to make the best of it.

Part of this attitude derives no doubt from the fact that after living out of a suitcase for six weeks I am happy to unpack anywhere; part that I am quickly approaching the halfway point of my incarceration here and the date of departure becomes increasingly visible; and part that I have grown accustomed to the place.

It does make for interesting letters home.

Notes from Lower Volta

July 5, 1981 Sunday

Since July 4th fell on Saturday, we celebrated Independence Day on July 3rd. The Ambassador hosted one of those mind-numbing noonday receptions where good diplomats are expected to maintain a steady patter of conversation with their counterparts from other embassies and from the local government.

What does one discuss with the Soviet Ambassador, the headaches of waging endless guerrilla war in insignificant Asian countries? Or with the Papal Nuncio, whose English appears limited to: "God bless you, my son"? Or the Korean Ambassador, still resentful of the fact that I impertinently asked him to supply photographs with his visa application?

The reception was not as grim as I might have expected. I received only three inquiries on hopeless visa cases.

Yesterday we had a Fourth of July Picnic at Budweiser Field for the American community. Although I had not arrived in time for last year's celebration, I had read some of the memos written after that event with the view of preventing the recurrence of some of its more egregious irregularities. The list was long, but centered around the complete breakdown of controlled access to the field, allowing every Kwame Mensah and his brother to wander in; the failure on the part of some Peace Corps Volunteers acting as cashiers to distinguish between the cashbox and their own pockets; and the sale of whole cases of soft drinks and hot dog buns which then disappeared into the black market.

Things appear to have been better organized this year. Several ticket booths and food stands were scattered around the field; there was lots of red, white, and blue bunting; a stage; a first aid station; a giant poster of Uncle Sam suspended from the baseball diamond backboard; and a consular information booth.

I neither suggested nor encouraged the latter. Both the Ambassador and the Deputy Ambassador thought last year's had been such a smashing success that I offered no opposition to one this year. It was in such a secluded position that even I, who knew where it should be, had trouble finding it. I dropped off some passport applications and registration cards, and left a note saying that I was wandering around the field. I did not visit the booth again.

The whole field was dominated by a thirty-foot high Statue of Liberty fashioned out of cardboard boxes, crumpled newspaper, and a torch held aloft by an arm fashioned from pantyhose stuffed with newspaper, the whole thing spray-painted with a shade of gray paint capturing the original's authentic coloring. Some poor fool on a flight landing at Kotoka International would look out and dream he was coming into JFK instead.

The Statue did have her own distinguishing characteristics. Due to an insufficient supply of paint, one could see upon closer inspection that her flowing green robes were actually pages of the Sacramento *Bee*. A number of people independently remarked that the expression on her face was definitely a smirk, perhaps thinking of the Emma Lazarus poem in a more modern version:

"Give me your tired, your poor,
Your huddled masses yearning to breathe free,
The wretched refuse of your teeming shore –
And I'll keep 'em that way!"

My own twisted sense of humor almost hoped that the rain which threatened most of the day would come long enough to dissolve Miss Liberty into a lump of soggy newsprint. That did not come to pass.

All in all, the day seems to have passed successfully, climaxed by the distribution of such exotic door prizes as cans of Ghanaian tuna and motor oil, chocolate bars, and six umbrellas, the last donated by Pan American. What? No round-the-world ticket?

August 20, 1981 Thursday

And now I am twenty-nine years old. I celebrated with champagne and a Baked Alaska a la Ghana supplied by Virginia Mayberry and shared with a few friends, Bruce and Sandy Hamilton from our Embassy and Audrey Shockley from the Canadian High Commission. We sat in my little garden in the cool of the evening air, listening to the buzz of insects, the calls of birds, and the discordant shouted exchanges between drivers parked just beyond my wall in a gasoline line leading to the BP station down the street. We followed dessert with coffee and cards, a sophisticated hand of "I doubt it."

I had my birthday dinner a week early, because two of the guests (the Rathers from the Canadian High Commission) were departing on vacation in Kenya August 13th. Virginia Mayberry assembled a sit-down dinner for seven on my rooftop, overlooking the lights of Accra, such as they are. All very elegant, but somewhat exhausting, since everything had to be carried up (and back down) two flights of stairs.

August 25, 1981 Tuesday

An undefinable listlessness drains my energies. I don't want to read; I don't want to write. I come home from work and drift for a few hours until I fall asleep. When I think of writing letters home, no memorable events come to mind. I resent invitations out as invasions of my privacy. I prefer to sit at home and do nothing.

The present dreariness of my social life does not reflect the hectic pace of work. Visas remain of compelling interest to Ghanaians of all strata, if not for themselves then for their nephews, nieces, cousins.

The problem of VIP involvement in visa applications became complicated in the past month with the absence of Rod Hawke, the Deputy Ambassador, on leave and the departure of Ed Perkins, the Political Counselor, on reassignment to Liberia. Whenever someone with a complaint over a visa refusal took it to "higher authorities," it usually wound up with one of those two gentlemen. In their absence, a steady stream of personages passes directly into the Ambassador's Office to press their case. The Ambassador, woefully ignorant of this country's visa problems, reacts to their requests with less than desirable intelligence. He became as much of a problem to me as the visa applicants themselves.

One case should suffice to indicate the dimensions of the

problem. The present Minister of Health's daughter, Perpetual Aswan, went on a three-month visit to the United States in 1978 to her father, who was then an exchange visitor there. Her three-month visit lengthened into a three-year stay, during which she appears to have both enrolled in school and worked illegally. She also applied for permanent residence on the basis of her supposed skills as a housekeeper. She returned to Ghana earlier this summer to pick up her immigrant visa.

Immigration regulations allow a housekeeper with experience totaling one year's full-time employment to obtain preferential immigrant status. Persons with less experience are considered to have no more qualifications than unskilled workers already available in the United States. Ms. Aswan's experience was based on her employment for three years in the home of a friend of her father's outside of Accra. It quickly developed that she attended boarding school in Kumasi during the same period. Kumasi and Accra are separated by five hours of bad roads.

As so many things in Ghana do, this turned out to be a "general clerical error." Ms. Aswan did not actually work in Accra for three years, but only during school holidays. A recalculation of her accumulated experience, even assuming the most liberal amounts of school vacation, quickly showed that she fell far short of the minimal experience required for preferential immigration status.

We refused the visa and suggested she make some effort to explain the discrepancy. She did not.

The next movement on the matter came when the Foreign Minister mentioned it to the Ambassador after a meeting with the President.

I find it incredible even to write the words: The Foreign Minister asked the American Ambassador in the presence of the President about a visa for the Minister of Health's daughter who wants to clean toilets in Maryland.

According to the Minister, he was confident the matter could be cleared up. Anyway Ms. Aswan did not want to work in the United

States but to study. Surely the Ambassador (wink, wink) could be of assistance.

On that basis, we returned Ms. Aswan's immigration petition to the Immigration and Naturalization Service with the recommendation it be canceled.

Yesterday Virginia Mayberry received a call from an official in the Minister of Foreign Affairs' Office. He repeated the explanation that of course Ms. Aswan had no intention to work but only to study. After all, it was inconceivable that the daughter of a leading family should so demean herself. If she had done any kind of household work, it was surely no more substantial than baby-sitting jobs. Our point exactly. I have now spread the suggestion that if we hear any more from Ms. Aswan or from someone on her behalf, I will document her as a fraudulent applicant.

August 30, 1981 Sunday

If I stay in Ghana much longer, I may become so inured to this lazy tropical life that I will finally leave with regret. Here it is a pleasant Sunday afternoon, and I am sitting in my walled garden, drinking fresh-ground coffee, listening to Japanese folk melodies, and writing.

Normally, of course, I pass Sundays at the beach, but the water of late has tended to be too chill, somewhat like the Great Lakes. (It's August. Why is that?)

My mental outlook continues to improve, both because I have now reached the halfway point of my stay in Ghana and because things have gone very well workwise recently.

There have been a few unpleasant incidents, such as last Friday when an American citizen spat at Virginia Mayberry because she refused his friend a visa. On the other hand, several egregious visa cases involving Ghanaian VIPs have recently come to light. They give me ammunition to hold off those who believe we should be more amenable to VIP representations. They give the Ambassador and others in the Embassy second thoughts about inquiring about visa matters.

In addition to the already mentioned case of the Minister of Health's daughter, here are a few other examples.

The Deputy Foreign Minister's brother got a student visa in early 1980 to attend a school in Pennsylvania. He never got farther than the Bronx, where he worked illegally. Now he has applied for permanent resident on the basis of his marriage to an American citizen.

Both the Clerk of the Parliament and the Special Assistant to the Vice President put in a good word for a student applicant who had been accepted by a school in Texas. I had refused him. I doubted he planned to go to Texas, since he presented an airplane ticket to Boston. He did not have a convincing explanation. His guarantors thought his destination a minor point. I did not. They found it more difficult to press the case when it turned out that the student had forged his academic record. He was not the A+ student he had told the American college, but a C- student.

Both the Principal Secretary of the Ministry of Foreign Affairs and the Minister of Agriculture could not understand why I doubted that another student applicant intended to enroll in the school which had accepted him, or that he would return to Ghana after his studies. I sent each of them a letter explaining that the young man had previously spent two years in the United States on a two-week tourist visa. A U.S. Immigration Inspector subsequently refused him entry at Boston's Logan Airport when he attempted to reenter the United States with his brother's passport. Immigration discovered the deception because all of his documents except the passport bore his own name, including a Massachusetts driver's license, a U.S. Social Security Card, and a union card. The last piece of paper, I pointed out, rather conclusively suggested that the man had worked illegally in the United States during his two-year long two-week visit.

September 1, 1981 Tuesday

This volume of my life has covered two interesting years which have seen both high and low points. It divides neatly into my last year in Korea and my first year in Ghana, and yet the bulk of the writing has occurred since my arrival in Ghana a year ago today. Perhaps I saw little new in my last months in Korea to record, as suggested by the fact that a great deal concerns itself with the assassination of President Park Chung-hee and subsequent political developments. Everything Ghanaian, on the other hand, has been totally new and in many ways so disheartening that I could find consolation only by recording it all.

    It is precisely at such moments when I close one book and begin another that I realize again that life continues and all things, good and bad, pass on to something else. In the expectation that I will someday look back on these pages from a better life, I end this volume.

Notes from Lower Volta
(Ghana, Washington, Japan)
September 1, 1981 - 1986

Notes from Lower Volta

The writer seeks his verse,
terse wordings to rephrase
the maze of running thought
caught within the hallways
always of his mind's soul.
Whole days may pass failing,
ailing his mind to sleep,
keeping his mind burning,
turning away from what
but for that he chases,
races to find the way
they might escape his mind
and find a form in ink.
Think you this comes easy,
breezy rhymes neatly got?
Not at all — when begun
the one who writes soon learns
turns of capturing wit
fit the man who better
letters seeks to devise.
Be wise: turn to prose.

September 1st, 1981

William J. Duffy

September 30, 1981 Wednesday
> Lassen wir uns OKTOBERFEST haben!
> Wo: Wilhelm Duffys Haus
> Wann: am 26ste September um 20:00 Uhr
> Kleidung: Lederhosen u.s.w.
> Getraenke und Imbiss!
> Bitte antworten Sie zu 76601, 76944, oder 76785.

***

The Accra social event of the season took place last Saturday night. I turned my little walled backyard into Willis Biergarten and invited eighty people in for an Oktoberfest. Having spent a week in Munich in June researching the idea every night at the Hofbraeuhaus, I felt qualified to put one on successfully. A majority of the guests assumed I had previously lived in Germany and/or was fluent in German. Little did they know that I have been there for only two short visits and derive my minimal command of the language from four years of high school German. The yard, with a few tables and chairs scattered around surrounded by dirty whitewashed walls, made an ideal beer garden.

The guests made their way through the better part of a twelve-pound ham, ten pounds of potato salad, six pizzas, a mountain of cold asparagus and three-bean salad, nine cases of beer, and nine bottles of wine, all consumed amidst a wealth of German beer hall music. All in all, a most successful evening. It went on until 2:00 a.m., when the last of the Australians departed.

October 19, 1981 Monday
> The visa workload, which here as in so many places has always shown such a dreary upward trend, has leveled off of late and (knock on wood) even seems to be dropping. Part of the problem comes from the fact that the Ghanaian government has run out of passports for the second time in three months. Then too the Bank of Ghana seems to have no foreign exchange to give to travelers. All the airlines, including Ghana Air, are reportedly refusing to accept cedis in

payment (in spite of a legal requirement that they do so). So travelers cannot get passports; even if they could get passports, they can't buy plane tickets; even if they could buy plane tickets, they can't legally get any foreign exchange to spend where they are going. Not many people are applying for visas.

That is not to say, however, that we do not have business. A steady stream of would-be consular clients, American and otherwise, continue to stream in. On September 2nd, for example, Mr. Daniel Abdul, Chief Executive of Doha Consultants, West Africa Industrialist and Manufacturer's Representative, and The Son of God, visited me.

According to Him, the United States learned several years ago through our computers and spy satellites that the Son of God had returned to earth and that He was it. He Himself did not at first believe it, until He had a vision of God Himself. Naturally, the U.S. Government wished to acquire The Son of God. Then-President Ford or Carter (he was uncertain which) made an arrangement with the Government of Ghana to transport Him to some unnamed island. There appears to be the added difficulty that every time He travels, there are earthquakes and signs in the heavens and of course there is always the possibility of nuclear war.

He wished to express His concern that no arrangements had yet been made to transport Him to His island, and He wished to make it clear that He felt the U.S. Government should foot the bill. He wished to know to which island He should go, suggesting either Honolulu or Mauritius. In addition, He wished to point out that He is constantly under pressure from the Government of Ghana to leave Ghana. The pressure derives, He believes, from certain nationals of the United Kingdom and members of the House of Windsor who are trying to prevent English republicans from overthrowing the monarchy and joining the United Kingdom to the United States.

He stated that He wished to present His message directly to Ambassador Smith, but that He had been told (truthfully) the Ambassador was out of the country. I assured Mr. God the message would be passed upon the Ambassador's return.

William J. Duffy

Besides the harmless crazies, there are also the people who need help and whom we can help. Mr. and Mrs. Franklin Hamilton arrived in Ghana in early May for a two-year stint as Mormon missionaries. Within days someone stole their $6,800 in Thomas Cook travelers cheques. They had selected Thomas Cook because the Bank of Ghana, an authorized Cook agent, could easily replace any lost or stolen cheques. Or so they thought.

A month after the theft, they came to the Consular Section for assistance in contacting Thomas Cook directly. The Bank of Ghana claimed it had submitted a reimbursement request but that no authorization had arrived. We sent off a cable to Thomas Cook. A month later Mr. Hamilton again came in. The Bank had the authorization, but claimed it could not honor it because it did not come through the Midland Bank in London. We sent a second cable asking Thomas Cook to reauthorize the reimbursement through the Midland Bank.

Thomas Cook responded with a bewildered cable to the effect that it did not understand what the problem was or why the Hamiltons did not yet have their money.

Armed with a copy of that response, Mr. Hamilton marched off to the Bank. When two more weeks had passed without result, I wrote a letter to the Bank's Deputy Governor. I asked for a written explanation of the Bank's apparent inability to pay the Hamiltons. When he delivered it, Mr. Hamilton was told that a Bank official would respond "in due time."

It was on either this visit or another about the same time that the Bank offered the Hamiltons reimbursement in cedis at the official exchange rate or a check drawn on the Bank of America – which has no office in Ghana. It was also about this time that the Bank first put forth the explanation that it had no U.S. dollar travelers cheques and could not get any. During this same period, visa applicants were presenting thousands of dollars' worth of travelers cheques issued locally.

On September 9th I sent a third cable to Thomas Cook. As

written by Mr. Hamilton, it asked for the $6,800 as well as $3,400 damages and twenty percent interest until the refund was made. That message produced early morning phone calls from New York in which Thomas Cook said the Hamiltons should go get their money from the Bank and please call us if you have any more problems.

I sent a second letter to the Bank's Deputy Governor on September 17th (hand-delivered by an Embassy driver) with the suggestion that *he* call Thomas Cook if he anticipated any further delay.

That was the status of the case when on the morning of September 18th, a clerk brought the Bank Governor's passport in for an official visa. In a moment of haste and ill-considered action, I threw the visa rule book out the window. I told the clerk to bring the passport back when the Hamiltons had their money.

In no time at all the institution which had proved so lethargic and indifferent when dealing with Americans was calling up everyone in the Embassy to complain about its treatment. I could not help but see a certain irony in it all. And wouldn't you know it – by one of those very funny coincidences which make life a joy, the Bank suddenly found $6,800 in travelers cheques for the Hamiltons. A problem which had dragged on for four months and thirteen days was resolved in two hours.

October 21, 1981 Wednesday

All the deadbeats in the world make their way to the door of the American Consul. It is bad enough when the deadbeat is a foreigner, and we can tell him to get lost. Worse is when a deadbeat American turns up, a taxpayer, demanding his money's worth in consular service. (Little does the usual irate American taxpayer realize that a Consular Section is often a money-making organization, with all the fees we charge.)

Last month we had a destitute American seaman. He arrived with a one-way ticket furnished by his shipping company to join a ship in Tema Harbor. Michael O'Kelly. Michael O'Kelly, to whom it had never occurred to carry any money at all with him, since the shipping company was responsible for all his expenses. Unfortunately, though, Mr. O'Kelly missed a connecting flight in Paris and then got tied up in Abidjan for four days. By the time he reached Accra, his ship was four days gone.

The local shipping agent (some Dutch Calvinist with an unpronounceable name) refused to have anything to do with him, and claimed he was my problem. That is not how I read the shipping regulations. We did what we could in the way of contacting his union, employer, and family in the United States for spending money and a ticket home.

As an aside, American taxpayers, who so fondly rail against government bureaucracy, tend to be amazed to discover that Consular Officers are not bankers, travel agents, baby-sitters, social workers, or mind-readers. Those who in the United States complain the most vociferously about the interference of the government in their lives seem dumbfounded when they go overseas and discover we are not Big Brothers who will get them out of whatever mischief they get themselves into.

Thus far, a simple case. But Americans abroad have a knack for leaving what wits they have at home, as Mr. O'Kelly quickly proved. He took up with a warm and friendly Ghanaian whom he met in a taxi on the way to the shipping agent's house (this when we still had hopes the agent would be of any assistance). My first glimpse of his Ghanaian friend convinced me the character was about as undesirable as they come, and would remain warm and friendly only as long as he thought he could get something out of our sailor (money and his cassette radio, for starters).

The Ghanaian confirmed my first impression when he presented Mr. O'Kelly with a bill for 1,200 cedis ($400 at official rates) for the first day's activities. It included 120 cedis taxi fare, 360 cedis disco, and a 400 cedi "woman charge." For someone who was destitute, Mr. O'Kelly obviously was not pining away in a flop house. In the week before O'Kelly's ticket finally arrived and he got on a plane to New York, his Ghanaian friend was almost as much of a problem as O'Kelly himself. He stole O'Kelly's radio, although he insisted it was only a surety for his rapidly escalating bill for services, and got thrown in jail.

O'Kelly then had second thoughts and wanted *us* to get *him* – the Ghanaian friend – out of jail. We can't even get Americans out of jail. We're certainly not going to help a foreigner in his own country. O'Kelly somehow got his friend out, who then beat O'Kelly up and threatened to kill him.

It was with great relief we put O'Kelly on the plane. Even then we held our breath until it took off. He insisted on departing with 400 cedis in his shoe. The Embassy clerk who accompanied him to the airport warned in vain that it was illegal to take cedis out of Ghana and, anyway, the money was worthless anywhere else. O'Kelly was adamant and absconded undetected. He no doubt now has one of the more interesting wallpaper patterns in his neighborhood.

November 29, 1981 Sunday

I have tried in these pages to look at my life in Ghana with grim humor. Any other approach would have ended my tenuous grasp on sanity. And things did look better. Today marks Day 456 in this country, with only 274 to go.

It now appears that I may well not complete my tour and equally likely that I will leave the Foreign Service. A week ago I had my resignation letter written. Today the chances are still fifty-fifty that I will deliver it. The background of it all is that my assignment to Ghana has been one problem after another, engendered by both the Ghanaians and my colleagues in the Embassy.

The immediate crisis results from a November 18th meeting between the Foreign Minister and Ambassador Smith. The former complained of my "attitude" and said if it did not improve I would have to leave Ghana. (Being declared *persona non grata* is one way out of here.) He said that I had been insolent to the Deputy Minister in a July meeting the Ambassador and I had had with him.

"Did you think I was insolent?" I asked the Ambassador.

"No," he replied.

"Did you tell the Foreign Minister that?"

"No," he replied.

As a result of the Minister's complaint, I have examined my attitude and my performance. The major change I perceive between myself and my predecessors is that for well-documented reasons I do not believe third-party VIP guarantees are relevant or useful in making a decision on a tourist visa application and therefore disregard them. This does not sit well with the Ghanaians. The current visa workload suggests that some 3,000 Ghanaians will be refused visas between now and my scheduled September 1st departure. Apparently only one or two complaints would be sufficient to seal my fate. The future does not look promising.

I can be impolite, cynical, and impatient with applicants and others. The volume of visa refusals and fraud in applications makes it difficult to remain always even-tempered. My attitude is not improved by matters such as visa fraud involving Ministry of Foreign Affairs diplomatic notes. We have detected six cases so far this year. How many have slipped by? We had, for example, the diplomatic note requesting tourist visas for two Ghanaian chess champions to attend a chess tournament. I do not know chess, but I know what a chess board looks like. The "champions" were each stumped when I asked them to draw me one. Even after discussing with each other, they could not agree on how many squares the board should have. They were also unclear on the names of the various chess pieces. I declined to issue the visas.

I told the Ambassador in a November 6th memo, right after the sixth diplomatic note case came to light, that I thought the current situation was intolerable. Three weeks later he has still not discussed it with the Ghanaians, despite my request that he do so.

The situation is exacerbated by high-ranking Ghanaian government and political figures with no understanding of or interest in the requirements of U.S. immigration law. Such individuals do not hesitate to put forward empty guarantees or to suggest that their word should be sufficient to resolve whatever doubts the Consular Officer may have. The amount of emigration out of this country, as reported frequently in the newspapers, should be sufficiently embarrassing to preclude inquiries about visa refusals. It is not.

I told the Ambassador in a memo (which saw half a dozen drafts of varying degrees of hysteria before assuming its final form November 27th, with my secretary accidentally abridging it further by skipping one of its three pages while typing):

"I trust the Foreign Minister will be as equally upset as he has been by me when informed of the prevalence of fraud in visa applications, particularly those involving his own Ministry. When the subject was raised informally last July with the Deputy Minister, we received the bland assurance that individuals whose applications were supported by diplomatic notes were "beyond reproach." Since then two more frauds have been detected.

"It is difficult to understand why my carrying out my statutory responsibilities is a source of such friction in U.S.-Ghanaian relations and worthy of formal protest at the highest level of government; while the persistence of fraud and deception in visa applications with the witting or unwitting complicity of the Ghanaian government is not."

December 16, 1981 Wednesday

"From eight-thirty in the morning until eleven he dealt with a case of petty larceny; there were six witnesses to examine, and he didn't believe a word that any of them said. In European cases there are words one believes and words one distrusts; it is possible to draw a speculative line between the truth and the lies; at least the *cui bono* principle to some extent operates, and it is usually safe to assume, if the accusation is theft and there is no question of insurance, that something has at least been stolen. But here one could make no such assumption: one could draw no lines. He had known police officers whose nerves broke down in the effort to separate a single grain of

incontestable truth; they ended, some of them, by striking a witness, they were pilloried in the local Creole papers and were invalided home or transferred. It woke in some men a virulent hatred of black skin, but Scobie had long ago, during his fifteen years, passed through the dangerous stages; now lost in the tangle of lies he felt an extraordinary affection for these people who paralyzed an alien form of justice by so simple a method."
- Graham Greene, *The Heart of the Matter*, Book Two, Chapter 2/ii.

December 20, 1981 Sunday

Tomorrow I depart on the Pan American flight to New York and on to Washington. The situation here jettisoned my great plans for Christmas in Germany or Moscow. I need to go home and talk to people, to get away from this very strange, very oppressive atmosphere.

I cannot imagine planning to remain in Ghana until next September. Since a transfer on such short notice hardly seems a solution, resignation remains a strong possibility.

I have disliked my assignment to Ghana since the day I arrived, the heat, the dirt, the poverty, the self-inflicted economic disaster, the resignation to despair, the lies of the visa applicants. This is what much of the world is like, little banana or cocoa republics.

My time abroad has undermined many of the liberal sentiments with which I grew up. I find myself adopting an increasingly unchristian and callous attitude toward the problems of the underdeveloped (and underdeveloping) world.

Why do I put up with this? Is it only the difficulty of quitting a career and starting over? Surely I have not yet reached the point in life where I am afraid to say: "I've had enough of this and I quit!"

I have spent the past week on leave, sitting at home, playing the role of a ticking time bomb. The Ambassador and Deputy Ambassador both know that things are not well. They both know that tomorrow I go to Washington, where I will be thousands of miles closer than they to the Department of State and therefore have a certain advantage in presenting my case.

In spite of several rather obtuse inquiries on the subject, I have declined to indicate whom I plan to see or whether I plan to see anyone. Frankly I don't know. In one conversation, the Deputy Ambassador suggested my trail of unanswered memos to the Ambassador might support a claim of "professional charges" against him. I made no comment.

First I must talk to friends who are removed from the situation, who can say: "You're crazy to put up with that" or "You're making a mountain out of a molehill." (As an aside, the Ambassador has already obtained a certain unpopularity in the Bureau of Consular Affairs because, when the Bureau of African Affairs told him to eliminate one position in the Embassy, he decided to do away with the Vice Consul's position after her February 1982 departure.)

Tomorrow I leave for the United States, my first American Christmas since 1974. I plan to spend some time in Washington, then go up to Philadelphia to see Mother and Joan. I've not planned anything past my Washington arrival. Only my sister Margaret knows I'm coming.

William J. Duffy

1982

January 8, 1982 Friday – Washington

Many people have had their careers saved by coups. I doubt many have had theirs saved in quite the fashion mine seems to have been.

On December 31st Flight Lieutenant Jerry Rawlings overthrew the Ghanaian government for the second time. He also staged a coup in the summer of 1979, later relinquishing power to the democratic government which he has now turned out. It may be somewhat inappropriate and selfish for an American diplomat to welcome the death of a democratically-elected government in a friendly country. The news did not particularly distress me. I also felt a good measure of satisfaction when the news reported the arrest of my friend the Foreign Minister.

Now I am ready to get on Pan American Sunday night to go back to Accra, assuming that the borders have been reopened by then. I think I'm glad I was hiding in Pennsylvania this past week. I've learned that the Department was busy looking for me and those like me who had had the wits about them to be absent from Ghana at an opportune moment. What would have happened had I been found I don't know. As late as yesterday the people in the Department were talking in terms of all of us rendezvousing in Togo and crossing the border by car *en masse* into Ghana after the Ghanaian government's approval.

Today rumor has it that the borders and the airport will open shortly, if they have not already done so.

So here's what happened between the time I left Ghana and the coup solved my problem. I convinced myself on the Pan American flight to New York that I would resign when I reached Washington. Then I reached Washington and talked to friends and people in the Department and decided to reconsider the whole thing again. The general tenor of comments: My situation is not unusual. I only have seven months left in Ghana. The alternatives (either in the Foreign Service or out of it) are not particularly appealing.

Apparently Consular Officers are always being threatened with *persona non grata* expulsions. Some do in fact get expelled. While I could curtail my tour early, it would be unlikely to lead to a better situation. The only jobs available right now are those which people have been trying to avoid for months. A look at the want-ads confirms that unemployment is at its highest level in seven years, and rising. And my "skills" are not among the most marketable.

One last brake on my earnest desire to quit was the information provided by my Career Counselor that I would be assigned to the six-month Midcareer Professional Development course in August, to be followed by a Washington tour.

I went to Philadelphia on December 30th, still undecided, to visit my mother and my sister Joan.

January 18, 1982 Monday – Accra

I returned to Accra Tuesday morning January 12th on the same Pan American flight I originally planned to take. The flight left New York fourteen hours later than scheduled because the new Ghanaian government has imposed an 8:00 p.m. to 5:00 a.m. curfew on the country. (By coincidence, the Korean government recently abolished its midnight to 4:00 a.m. curfew after thirty-six years. Am I fated to live forever under curfews?) Pan American informed me beforehand of the delay so I stayed in Washington at my sister Margaret's an extra night.

Were it not for a few scruffy soldiers waving rifles around the airport, I would have seen nothing on arrival in Accra to indicate that things had changed. In fact, they had not. What excitement there had been ended long before my return. Nevertheless, Vice Consul Virginia Mayberry seemed more glad to welcome me back than on previous returns. It has been a standing joke since my medical evacuation in September 1980 that all the major consular events (such as arrests or deaths of American citizens) happen in my absence. This most recent absence carried the principle to an extreme.

The coup saw only sporadic shooting and looting, and no incidents involving foreigners, except when the Assistant Peace Corps Director insisted on driving past Burma Camp (the army headquarters) not once but twice on the night of a gun battle.

I have it on good authority that my friend the Foreign Minister, who had taken such pleasure in lecturing the Ambassador on visas and other matters, came to the Embassy to ask for asylum. The Ambassador reportedly derived some pleasure in turning him away.

That is not to say the Ambassador welcomed the coup, much less expected it. In fact, he was placed in the position of recalling the draft copies of an annual forecast which he had distributed to different Embassy officials for their concurrence. It forecast for 1982 more of the same of 1981. The Ambassador is now in the unpleasant situation of having no one in the Government with whom to deal, since all the "contacts" he had cultivated since 1979 are either under arrest, in hiding, or in exile. He had carefully avoided any contact with Rawlings or his friends, and instructed others in the Embassy to do likewise.

So we have no idea who is running Ghana, a situation complicated by the fact that the Provisional National Defense Council (PNDC) has not gotten around to appointing officials to replace those ousted, or even to announce the names of all the PNDC members.

I have previously written that a large proportion of Ghana's production is smuggled across the border to neighboring countries where it is sold for hard currency. Consequently, the closing of Ghana's borders appears to have a detrimental effect on its neighbors, causing shortages of such things as fresh fish, eggs, and fruits in Togo, for example. Closing the borders has also caused a lot of headaches for the Embassy here and the American Embassy in Togo. I was not alone in being caught outside the country when the coup took place. About a fourth of the Embassy staff was also away.

Notes from Lower Volta

There were a number of children of Embassy personnel in Ghana for the holidays, as well as other tourist types, including twenty-two Iowa Christians. The two Embassies had to work together to get everybody across the border in the direction he wanted to go. (Here, again, Virginia Mayberry had resolved the problems before my return.)

The 8:00 p.m. curfew has put an incredible damper on all social activity. I remember in Korea after President Park's assassination when curfew was pushed back from midnight to 10:00 p.m. That seemed the limit of inconvenience. Even worse here, people who should know say the curfew will not end anytime soon, and perhaps won't even be shortened. The people in charge, it seems, like the curfew. (The papers have run articles on the curfew's salutary effects. They strikingly mimic the pieces the Korean papers used to run.)

Dinner parties (there have not been many) run from 5:30 p.m. to 7:30 p.m. The Marine House T.G.I.F.s, which usually run to 2:00 or 3:00 a.m., end at 7:00 p.m. Slumber parties may quickly become the preferred method of entertainment. We spent last Friday night at the Marine Non-Commissioned Officer's house with a group of Americans and Canadians playing *Risk* and drinking, until we went to sleep (passed out?) at about 3:00 a.m.

The only other thrill socially in the past week has come from the VHS recording of *Rocky Horror Picture Show* which Mary Ray provided me while in Washington. Sandy Hamilton offered the use of her machine to see it. Before we knew it, thirty people drawn by the mystique of *RHPS* (most of whom had not previously seen it) gathered at 5:30 p.m. in the afternoon (curfew of course eliminating the possibility of the more traditional midnight showing) to watch it. Not a stunning success, given the high percentage of virgin viewers, who had virgin shock. We've planned a repeat engagement and true *RHPS* fans are signing up.

January 19, 1982 Tuesday

My first year-end holidays in the United States since 1974 also proved the most unpleasant holidays I have faced since that year. There was the question of the future of my own career, leaving me more pessimistic about my prospects than I had been since that miserable year following graduation from Marquette. The question was not when I would return to Ghana but whether. Only the coup on December 31st finally convinced me to do so.

What will come? Will next Christmas have all this in the past, or will it have more of the same?

January 25, 1982 Monday

Peggy Black, a Peace Corps Volunteer teaching near Kumasi, came to Accra last weekend with a friend visiting her this past month from the United States. She wanted to take Virginia Mayberry and me to dinner. Saturday night at 8:00 p.m. (the curfew got pushed back last week to 10:00 p.m.), we piled into Virginia's little Datsun with Peggy's friend and Marilee Keenan, another Peace Corps type, in search of a restaurant. Going to restaurants is something I rarely do, and only when I have received an invitation, since I cannot afford the prices. Peace Corps Volunteers, however, exchange their hard currency on the black market. While this violates every rule in the book, the simple fact is that Peace Corps Volunteers would otherwise starve to death. Their allotments are figured according to official exchange rates by Washington bureaucrats who cannot conceive of a fifteen-to-one disparity between a currency's "official" value versus its actual buying power.

Off we went in search of a restaurant, of which only a small number deserving of the name exist in Accra. Peace Corps standards are much laxer than my own (or those of anybody else seriously concerned with the after-effects of a meal). Peggy kept offering the names of establishments which I had previously heard only in connection with dire next-morning consequences. I did my best to steer the conversation toward consideration of those restaurants on my list of acceptable establishments, both of them Chinese. Our expedition came to naught when we discovered that restaurants have

Notes from Lower Volta

only been open between noon and 4:00 p.m.

So we returned to my house and jointly whipped up a spaghetti dinner. In many respects it surpassed any we might have obtained commercially. Given the lateness of the hour, we could not enjoy the repast at a leisurely pace and barely had time to gulp down a cup of fresh-ground Kenyan coffee (imported from the United States) before everyone had to go home in time for the 10:00 p.m. curfew.

While on the subject of Accra social events, I will recall the Juke Box Saturday Night I hosted on "Saturday, December 12th, "1941" (said the invitation), a big band extravaganza attended by some seventy of my most intimate friends, some of whose names I cannot recall because they had not been invited.

I turned the roof of my house into a "make-believe ballroom" under the full moon and stars and lights of Accra. Glenn Miller, Artie Shaw, Tommy Dorsey, *et al.* serenaded the dancers, their sounds coming from the stereo speakers hidden under the water tank. We had turned the tank into a 1941 jukebox with a bed sheet decorated with paint, red wrapping paper, and aluminum foil.

I repeated my Oktoberfest party with only the minor alterations of location (roof versus garden) and music (big band versus beer hall). It came off just as successfully.

January 27, 1982 Wednesday

Monday's newspapers carried the banner headlines "Mercenaries to Invade Ghana?" (*Daily Graphic*) and "Nigeria-U.S.A. Plan against Ghana" (*Ghanaian Times*). The opening paragraphs of the *Ghanaian Times* article gives the flavor of the Kafka world we live in: "Sources in Nigeria have revealed that the Federal Government of Nigeria and the United States of America plan to carry out an armed attack on Ghana in a bid to bring back the overthrown Limann regime.

"The plan was revealed by a group in Nigeria in a pamphlet in which they accused the Shagari Government of 'playing the errand boy of the United States in Africa.'

"According to the group, the news of the overthrow of the Limann regime reached the United States 10 minutes later.

"Predictably, the group said, Ronald Reagan was not happy about the overthrow of the Limann regime so he contacted M.K.O. Abiola to sell the idea of invading Ghana to the Federal Government of Nigeria.

"Abiola thereupon contacted President Shagari and another man called Suleiman Takuma. The three accepted the Reagan proposal.

"Abiola was sent back to tell President Reagan that military and financial aid would be needed to put the invasion plan into effect.

"The group said President Reagan agreed to provide planes, a crew of TV stars, and some mercenaries."

For the last forty-eight hours we have waited for Miss Piggy to parachute out of the sky. The newspaper stories would be humorous were it not that so many Ghanaians appear to accept them as gospel truth.

One of Ghana's redeeming features has been that the Ghanaians are truly a friendly people. The regime's desire to whip up anti-Americanism threatens to remove even that.

I spent the better part of today going through the Consular Section's files and destroying as much material as possible. If things reach a point serious enough for an evacuation, there will be less to get rid of later.

My own increased unease comes from several factors. Foremost among them, Americans who have experienced other revolutions under other circumstances are not taking events as lightly as I would expect them to.

There have been specific incidents. Yesterday, for example, the Vice President of Kaiser Aluminum and its Ghanaian subsidiary Volta Aluminum Company (VALCO) was pulled off the Pan American flight before its departure to New York and taken to Immigration without explanation. I hot-footed it over to Immigration. The officials there could not explain what had caused the action, other than to say the American's name was on a "stop list" issued by the PNDC and his exit permit had been issued in error. Only the PNDC could authorize his departure and the man to contact was not presently available.

The American wandered off to the airport to try to retrieve his luggage before the flight's departure (he failed) while I went off to tell the Ambassador what was going on. (The American in question is well-known to any number of Embassy officials, including the Ambassador.) The Ambassador immediately contacted a friend in the Ministry of Foreign Affairs (a former Ambassador to the United States who coincidentally also knows the beleaguered American) to find out what was going on. The vague response was that perhaps there had been some "technical mistake" but hopefully the situation will be resolved. (The Ghanaians have already been stung by our reaction to their bizarre newspaper reports of imminent American invasion.)

Other irritants include the incident yesterday in which four armed soldiers stopped an American from the USAID Mission on the road. Even after he presented his diplomatic ID, was told to report to the authorities this morning. When the Embassy Security Officer and I showed up at the appointed time and place to make our views known, the Lance Corporal who had given the order was absent and no one else could explain the problem.

There were also reports today that students planned anti-American demonstrations at either the main Embassy or at the Annex. Nothing happened at the Annex. As a precaution, we moved all the employees' cars to the four-house compound where I live, making it look like a used car lot.

There appears to have been some action at the Embassy, but I have not yet heard any details.

February 8, 1982 Monday
That time of year again to do taxes, which brings to mind how much my salary and taxes have risen since 1975, as shown by my

Form 1040s for the past seven years.

In 1977, 1978, and 1980 I was promoted, accounting for the better part of the income increases in those years. The Foreign Service Act of 1980, which substantially raised Foreign Service salaries, and the twenty percent hardship differential for those assigned to Accra explain the leap in 1981 income.

February 10, 1982 Wednesday

Here we are well into 1982 and I have not even come up with any New Year's resolutions, or made any profound comments on the passing of the years.

The unusual circumstances of my own life at the New Year as well as the unsettled conditions in Ghana offer a few good excuses for this omission.

I cringe to think of the New Year's resolutions I made a year ago. I have resolutely ignored them. I did read seventy-nine books in 1981, but that says more for Accra's social life than my own dedication.

What about my resolution to learn German, French, and Korean? It has been months since I gave any one of them more than a passing glance. Most of all, what of Resolution #3, "Not to let Ghana defeat me"? Clearly it very nearly did. It took a coup to salvage the damage. So here it is February 10th. I can only resolve not to make any resolutions for this year, or at most to resolve to handle life day-to-day.

February 11, 1982 Thursday

Notice from the Embassy nurse:

"Schistosomiasis, or bilharzia, is a parasite found in fresh or briny waters throughout much of Africa. The parasitic egg is excreted from infected individuals into a body of water where it soon hatches, liberating a free-swimming embryo. The embryo penetrates a suitable fresh water snail in which it develops and produces thousands of cercariae, or infective larvae. These infective larvae swim about and are then able to quickly penetrate the skin of humans and enter the blood stream where they journey to the gastrointestinal or urinary tract, causing ulceration and abscess which may later become malignant.

"Schistosomiasis hematobium (affecting the urinary tract) and schistosomiasis mansoni (affecting the intestinal tract) have been found in many fresh water areas throughout Ghana. Both species have been found in the Volta River, extending from Kpong to where the river joins the sea, including Ada.

"Drinking, bathing, swimming or wading in these waters constitute a dangerous threat and must be avoided."

February 14, 1982 Sunday – Lome, Togo

Too much time spent in Ghana leads me to generalize from things Ghanaian to things African. The continent may have more than its share of problems, but not every part of it has reached the advanced state of disaster of which Ghana boasts. A three-hour drive east along the coast to Togo quickly reminds me of that fact.

This is my third trip to Togo, each more relaxing than its predecessor.

A long weekend because of Washington's birthday tomorrow, a fair number of Americans from the Embassy have come this way. Many came in two Embassy vans, which provided the convenience of leaving the driving to somebody else, with the drawback that they have to rely on local taxis while here.

I was not keen on the latter idea, so Virginia Mayberry and I drove down in my Jeep yesterday morning. Traffic was light, and there were fewer checkpoints on the road than rumor had described. The Lome road is no exception in the network of Ghanaian highways. We bumped in and out of potholes and over washboard surfaces right to the Togolese border. The ride was rough enough to knock the tailpipe loose. It did not fall off, so I was able to untangle it and put it inside the Jeep.

At the border crossing the Ghanaian soldiers had everything

firmly under control. A man with a gun does have a certain advantage in getting a crowd to do what he wants.

We swept through both Ghanaian and Togolese Immigration with a minimum of delay. The Ghanaian Inspector told me he wanted a visa to the United States.

Things proceeded smoothly until we arrived at the Sarakawa Hotel, where we had reservations. Or so we thought. The hotel had heard of neither of us, nor the friend at the Embassy in Lome who had made the reservations. The staff barely conceded the existence of the American Embassy or of the hotel itself. They had no rooms no way no time and please go elsewhere.

With dismay we went in search of other accommodations, which we found at the Hotel Second of February, a thirty-five-story skyscraper with twenty-three floors (it skips from three to fourteen) done in modern Mussolini, a concrete slab with minimal vegetation and lots of marble around the edges. Somewhat grim, but five stars anyway and certainly paradise to refugees from Accra.

On a previous trip, we had been told the hotel's name referred to the 1974 date President Eyadema got out of the hospital after a plane crash. This time the staff said the name refers to the anniversary of the destruction of imperialism, the year of which no one could specify and the idea of which seems incongruous with the lavish jet-set ambiance.

February 15, 1982 Monday – Accra

A weekend's perspective from Lome has altered my view of recent events in Ghana. What seemed ridiculous is now chilling. What was an irritant is now terrifying. A conversation with our Consular Officer in Lome suggested that the Americans there wonder why we have not all left. Things are grim.

And not helped by events during the forty-eight hours I was absent from Ghana. Saturday morning soldiers descended on VALCO in Tema and arrested four VALCO employees: two Americans, a German, and a Ghanaian. The apparent charge: working for the CIA, based on their alleged recording of certain radio broadcasts connected to Ghanaian military movements (a rather questionable pastime, to be sure).

The Ambassador tried to reach me or Virginia Mayberry. He was unsuccessful since neither of us had our radios on. The crucial moment which saved our Lome weekend (when the arrests occurred we were still in Accra) happened when one of the passengers in the two Embassy vans already enroute to Lome used the radio to report that he thought we had left for Lome early in the morning.

The Ambassador, quick-thinking, soon determined that, even if we had escaped, the two vans had not, and they were in VALCO's neighborhood. He ordered both of them to go to VALCO to see what they could. So up drives a merry crew consisting of the Political Counselor, his wife, and two children; the Budget and Fiscal Officer, his wife and child; the Administrative Secretary and her husband; the Nurse; the Personnel Officer; two Marines; and the two Ghanaian drivers, all set and dressed for a holiday weekend, instead called upon to do – what? They sat at VALCO for two hours, until relieved by our back-up Consular Officer, at which time they resumed their trip to Lome.

This massive show of American Embassy force having failed to spring the prisoners, the Ambassador then mounted an around-the-clock watch by Embassy officers at Police Headquarters. (The VALCO employees were held in a conference room, not a cell.)

With my limited consular experience, I cannot fathom what was the object of doing this. Two possibilities leap to mind. Either the Ambassador sought to lend credibility to the alleged CIA connection, in which case he has presumably been most successful. Or, he feared the Ghanaians could not be trusted to mind their prisoners and someone had to guard the guardians, in which case he was less successful. Although the Police were tolerant enough during the day, they refused to have any protective assistance between 9:30 p.m. and 6:00 a.m.

I trust I will have answers to all these questions – and others –

in the morning. If the Ambassador objects to my absence over the weekend, I will point out that, had he told me of the impending arrests on Friday morning (which was when he learned what would come to pass), I could have changed my plans. Why tell the Consular Officer about something as basically consular as the arrest of an American or two?

As the siren sounds the 10:00 p.m. curfew, let me close with the incredible fact that the Embassy has not yet bothered to notify the Department of State of the arrests. Running off in all directions and bumping into each other when something happens, we neglect to take the most basic commonsensical and required actions.

March 8, 1982 Monday

Ghana celebrated its twenty-fifth anniversary of independence this weekend.

The case of the VALCO Four resolved itself last Friday with the deportation of the two Americans and the German to Togo, accompanied by front-page newspaper and radio coverage of their spying activities.

Only one of the three (one of the Americans) appears to have actually performed the monitoring and recording of which all were accused. His motivating force appears to have been stupidity. We never did figure out how the other two got lumped in with him. The Ghanaians found it very suspicious that the other American had spent most of the last fourteen years in Ghana (who would stay that long?). The whole thing was handled in accord with revolutionary justice. The government never formally charged these criminals with any crime or held any tribunal either to present its case or to allow them to respond.

The Ambassador continued his bungling right up to the end. He nearly acquiesced to a VALCO request that the men go to Togo in an American Embassy vehicle. A VALCO car took them to the border, which they reached about two minutes before its 6:00 p.m. closing last Friday.

Notes from Lower Volta

Things have not been very pleasant here the last two months. The "revolution" has a strong anti-American undercurrent. While more muted than in late January, it still surfaces in such things as anti-American cartoons lifted out of Cuban papers without bothering to translate them from the Spanish. Libya is now Ghana's great and good friend. Newspaper articles talk about all the aid Libya provides, such as a recent shipment of fifteen tons of food. The media glossed over the arrival at the same time of 2,000 tons of U.S. food under the Food for Peace program.

The security situation has improved marginally. The soldiers have not shot anybody in public in days. At least two weeks have passed since they burned anybody to death in the marketplace.

Morale within the American community sinks day by day. American missionaries who first came to Ghana thirty years ago come in to tell me they have never seen things so bad. Within the Embassy there is a growing feeling that the Ambassador is out of touch and living in a fantasy world, refusing to believe that the situation might get out of hand.

After all, these are "a warm and friendly people," even if some of them do set people on fire. He believes that, if the situation deteriorates (it hasn't already?), we will have sufficient "warning signals" to allow us to evacuate everybody in time. Presumably as much warning as we had December 31st. The coup was almost over before we learned about it. And at the first sign of trouble the government (whoever it might be) will close the borders and the airport.

As Consular Officer, I am expected to keep in touch with the private American community, most of whom are missionaries scattered around the country. In spite of several pointed remarks from me on the subject, the Ambassador still acts as if I can contact all Americans in Ghana on a few hours' notice. The telephones rarely worked pre-coup, the postal system upcountry has collapsed (which we learned when a general mailing to all Americans registered with the Embassy never got beyond the Accra area), and the government has shut down the missionary in-country radio networks upon which we have so heavily relied in the past and impounded the radios.

I have suggested that we recommend that all Americans consider leaving the country temporarily, but the subject is not one for discussion. We do not want to send the "wrong signals."

Apparently Washington cannot believe the rosy glow in the Embassy reports. The Department has sent out a security team to look the place over. I would not be surprised to see the Department order the evacuation of Mission dependents. All the families of VALCO, about forty altogether, are reportedly leaving in the wake of the VALCO Four.

Today Virginia Mayberry, the Vice Consul, departed on the Pan American flight to conclude her tour. She very nearly missed the plane because it left an hour early. She had to be driven out to planeside even as they prepared to remove the steps. So diplomatic. Virginia will not be replaced; the Ambassador abolished her position.

On the good side of the ledger, I have received official notification that I will take the Midcareer Professional Development course. It begins August 2nd in Washington. The course lasts until December 17th. I am looking for an onward assignment in Washington after it.

I will leave this place with no regrets. What frightens me more than the situation here is our half-assed response to it. Foreign Service "Africa hands," they say, are a breed apart.

March 18, 1982 Thursday

The consular business has been very slow since Virginia Mayberry's departure. Lucky she left when she did, or else we would have to fire her. Do I really have less work, or is this proof in reverse of the old adage that the amount of work expands to occupy the time and personnel available to do it? I can only pray that my good fortune holds for the next four months.

The Department, incidentally, euphemistically describes my job here as "undersubscribed," meaning nobody wants to replace me.

Notes from Lower Volta

Presumably the word on Accra has gotten out and people are no longer fooled by out-of-date reminiscences of Ghana as the garden spot of West Africa. Besides my consular position, the Economic Officer slot, the Budget Officer job, and one General Services position are also undersubscribed, with the last two already vacant. Reportedly at least one person has resigned from the Department rather than accept the General Services job. It has been vacant since last September.

March 21, 1982 Sunday

Another Sunday spent at the beach. Champagne and orange juice, cheeses and crackers, a thatched-roof beach hut, and the waves of the Gulf of Guinea/the Bight of Benin crashing on the shore. This once a week makes the other six days bearable. My vision of Hell is Ghana without an ocean.

The coup (oh, so sorry, it's a revolution, not a coup) continues its anti-American, anti-West, pro-East, pro-Libya stance. The government wants to get rid of alien cultural influences (including music – musicians should write revolutionary anthems) and wonders aloud whether Ghana needs all these foreign missionaries, since they contribute nothing to Ghana and most are foreign spies anyway.

Government insistence that business be conducted at the (long outdated) controlled prices has ensured that what little was previously available in the market has now disappeared. The country should run out of petroleum products by mid-April. The principal supplier, Nigeria, demands payment for what is already owed and the Ghanaians do not have any money. That should only be a minor problem, since within a couple of months' time food shortages may deteriorate into famine.

People are routinely called before Citizens' Vetting Committees and Preliminary Investigation Teams to explain how they came by their ill-gotten gains, the assumption being that any gains are ill-got and the getter a crook, a not implausible hypothesis in this country where corruption is the one aspect of society which always functions. The newspapers run lists of names of individuals (under the heading "Revolutionary News") to advise them to report to Burma Camp "in their own interest without fail."

I have only 113 days to go. I am tentatively planning to leave Ghana July 12th on Pan American (assuming that I, Pan American, and Ghana are still here then).

March 28, 1982 Sunday

The litany for the week:

Three armed men who appeared to be soldiers (although they offered no identification) stopped Erika Schwartz, the American half of the German-American couple I know in Kumasi, a few blocks from her home. They commanded her to drive them where they wanted. They released her several hours and 150 kilometers later out in the bush. Not knowing where she was, Erika took the rest of the afternoon to find her way home.

A young missionary couple attached to the Institute of Linguistics in the Volta region failed to come down to Accra as expected last Monday. The Institute was unable to reach them by radio and finally contacted another Institute person located about some three hours' drive away to go see what had happened.

What had happened was that the military had come and taken away the couple's two-way radio, which they used to contact Accra, and then came to take away the couple and their four young children. The parents (and a third American visiting them) were kept for two days at the Army Barracks in Ho, the regional capital, before being released on bail to an Institute official who drove up to Ho to look for them. The children were left in the care of some Catholic sisters.

The charge against the missionaries: espionage, on the suspicion that they were using their little fifteen-watt, two-way radio, licensed for their use by the government to allow them to contact Accra (and not always powerful enough for that), to transmit surreptitiously to the United States.

The idea is so absurd as to be comical, were it not for the

seriousness of the matter. To underline the ridiculousness of it all, the missionaries had previously surrendered the radio to the Ghana Police in response to a PNDC directive that all private radios be turned in. The Police examined it and, having satisfied themselves that it was suitable only for internal transmissions, returned it to the Americans for their continued use.

We are sending a diplomatic note to protest the fact that the government never notified us the Americans had been arrested – granted the government in Accra may not even know it themselves, but the times do not suggest giving the Ghanaians the benefit of the doubt is a good idea – and to point out the pointlessness of complying with the requirements of one authority (the Police) only to have another (the Army) take you back to square one.

Diplomatic notes are such wonderful devices, typed on the best paper in the most elegant language from one government to another with no reference in the first person:

"The Embassy of the United States of America presents its compliments to the Ministry of Foreign Affairs of the Republic of Ghana and has the honor to refer to the detention of Mr. and Mrs. Jones, citizens of the United States, and to point out what a silly government you have.

"The Embassy of the United States of America takes this opportunity to renew to the Ministry of Foreign Affairs of the Republic of Ghana the assurances of its highest consideration."

VALCO continues to have its problems. A disgruntled domestic employee reported one of its American employees to the PNDC Information Centre. The employee had grown impatient with the slow pace of justice in resolving her claim against the employer resulting from her injury in a fire in his home. The Information Centre does not give out information; it collects it. That's where you go when you want to turn your neighbor in. The lady's lawyer had previously asked for 18,000 cedis ($6,000). The American had offered 500-5,000 cedis. The Information Centre told him to give her 45,000 cedis ($15,000). Whoops. The fact that VALCO's Ghanaian lawyers prefer not to get involved complicates the American's case.

Americans are not the only foreigners encountering problems. Soldiers picked up two Italians on suspicion of espionage and took them to Burma Camp. One of them was reportedly overheard in a public bar to admit that he was a member of the crew of TV stars Reagan is sending.

The Italian Embassy learned about the arrests from a friend present at the arrest. The Italian Ambassador immediately went down to Burma Camp. The military admitted having the men, but refused to let the Ambassador see them and directed him to the Ministry of Foreign Affairs. When the Ambassador explained the situation to the Ministry, an official told him that the Ministry would *not* get involved. They changed their minds, reportedly, when he threatened an immediate break in relations and the suspension of visa issuances to Ghanaians (the latter always an effective tactic). The Ghanaians released the two men after forty-eight hours, during which time they received no food or water, and were repeatedly beaten.

My replacement was named this week, some guy coming out of Bangkok whom I do not know. He will arrive in July. Thought I would write him a letter. On second thought couldn't think of anything nice to write. Have put letter idea on back-burner.

In reference to my own future, my Career Counselor sent a cable suggesting that a very strong recommendation from the Ambassador would help my chances of getting an assignment to the Operations Center in the Department. Fat chance. He hasn't offered and I haven't asked. After his underwhelming support last year during my troubles with the Foreign Minister, I would not want to see what kind of back-handed recommendation he would do me in with.

I'm still looking for a job post-training. I still prefer one in Washington so I could have time to look for employment outside of the Department.

On a lighter note, a plague of moths has infested us the past week. Sounds like a very bad science fiction film, people having their clothes eaten right off their backs. A number of moths have gotten into the house and flit around. Never fear, however: man's little lizard friends, the geckos, are out in force on the walls controlling the problem. Although it is rather disconcerting to discover how far the sound of crunching moth wings can carry across the room. My dog Killer, who has such a fondness for snapping flies out of the air, has regrettably shown no interest in the moths.

April 4, 1982 Sunday
    Last Thursday evening we received a report from a reliable source that an American citizen was in Burma Camp and had been there for two weeks.
    The Vienna Convention requires that a government inform the appropriate Embassy "without delay" when it arrests a foreign national. The United States interprets that to mean notification within seventy-two hours.
    The Embassy Defense Attaché and I spent Thursday evening at Burma Camp trying (a) to find out if an American was there and (b) to see him.
    We failed on both counts.
    To get in, you need a visitor's pass. You get a visitor's pass from the Information Centre. The Information Centre closes at 4:30. Is there an officer around? No, of course not. All the officers disappear from Burma Camp after dark because they don't feel safe around the enlisted men. And it's not too safe for you either. Come back tomorrow morning. Unless of course you know the password, which we don't. So we leave.
    We renew our efforts Friday morning. The Information Centre is open. But to get a visitor's pass you must have an appointment to see someone in Burma Camp. Go see Protocol at the Ministry of Foreign Affairs.
    The Deputy Ambassador goes to the ministry with me. This is a serious problem, and growing more so. We have now spent twelve hours trying to see the American with no progress. Explain the situation to the woman at Protocol (a woman whom I and almost

everyone else in the Embassy dislike intensely). What, she inquires, seems to be the problem? The problem, as anyone in her position should understand, is that we have a report that you have been holding an American for two weeks and not bothered to tell us.

Oh. Please put it in writing. Back to the Embassy to write another diplomatic note, "presenting compliments" to the Ministry and "requesting" it to determine immediately whether an American is in Burma Camp and if so arrange consular access within twenty-four hours.

Back to the Ministry with note in hand. How soon will there be action? Well of course there are channels and this must go through the PNDC.

We'll check back after lunch. After lunch discover that the Protocol lady and most of the Ministry have gone off to the funeral of a Ministry staffer. Won't be back until Monday. Come back Monday.

Here it is Sunday night, seventy-two hours after the first information on the American. We still have not entered Burma Camp. In the meantime, we have had a second independent report of his presence there, and have even learned his name.

April 24, 1982 Saturday

On the morning of April 5th the Ambassador, the Deputy Ambassador, the Defense Attaché, and I descended on Burma Camp. The Ambassador had been summoned by the Chief of the Defence Staff, the Number Two man in the government, and he intended to raise the question of the detained American.

The Chief of Defence Staff claimed no knowledge of a detained American. The Ambassador said that, if the story were true, it would be a serious blow to U.S.-Ghanaian relations. Meanwhile, as the rest of us waited in the outer office, the Defense Attaché worked through his own military contacts to locate the American in question and have him brought to us. Thus it was that the Chief of Defence Staff, having concluded his conversation with the Ambassador, escorted him out of his office and nearly collided with the American who, he had just assured the Ambassador, was not in Burma Camp.

Some embarrassment in the air with death beams flashing out of the Chief of Defence Staff's eyes at the officer who had not bothered to tell him that they had picked up an American some weeks earlier (exact date unknown/forgotten).

What was the charge? Well, none really, except that the man was acting somewhat suspiciously and had a map of Ghana and might be an invading mercenary. What do you plan to do with him? Well, nothing really. Now that the Embassy is here, he can leave with you.

The Ambassador engaged in a righteous display. He suggested it advisable for the Ghanaians to reexamine their procedures to make sure that the Embassy receives immediate notification of any subsequent detentions.

The Department of State later called in the Ghanaian Chargé d'affaires in Washington and dressed him down for this case, the prior incident of the missionaries in Ho, and a third incident involving the detention of an Embassy van with diplomatic plates at gunpoint. (The Ghanaian Ambassador resigned his position and assumed a teaching position at Purdue in the aftermath of the December 31st revolution.)

All this was not the conclusion of the saga of our Burma Camp American. He was in fact not previously unknown to us. By name Allen Corda, a Californian drifter who has wandered around West Africa for most of the last ten years. He wandered into Ghana shortly before the coup and settled in a small village in the bush where he took up with a twelve-year-old girl.

He claimed they married. The law described it as statutory rape. Eventually the police picked him up (in mid-February) and sent him to Accra. The military did not want to let him into Burma Camp until he took a bath. The Ghanaians released him after a day and told him to get out of Ghana.

They were not pleased to discover him more than a month later back up in his bush village. This time they put him in Burma Camp and forgot about him. After his release April 5th, Corda did not get around to trying to cross to Togo until April 18th. He did so at a remote border post. The Ghanaians let him *out*, but the Togolese would not let him *in*.

Supposedly the Togolese Immigration Inspector thought he should have a visa to enter, not having received the notice issued by the Togolese government a year ago allowing Americans to enter without visas. So there he was, caught between two border posts. He chose the only course of action which always occurred to him when he was not wanted on either side of a border: he struck off through the bush and tried to sneak into Togo. He wandered back into Ghana instead. The Border Guard caught him, brought him to Accra, and he called the Embassy. The man is like a boomerang.

Once again the Ghanaians released him. This time we took no chances. We put him in an Embassy vehicle and drove him to the Lome crossing into Togo (where the officials know Americans don't need visas). I haven't heard anything further, so I take that as good news.

May 8, 1982 Saturday

I hesitate to think that this immortal classic which I have been writing should end as abruptly as it would have, were April 24th the last entry. And yet it might well have been.

Last Thursday Carol Wellman of the Australian High Commission called to invite me to dinner that night at her home with some other friends. I eagerly accepted (social life being what it is).

We had a pleasant dinner, with pleasant conversation. Along about 9:50 I got up to leave, in order to get home by the 10:00 p.m. curfew. I could have taken either of two routes: the Airport Road or the Achimota Road. No, skip the Airport Road, I thought, because there are probably already soldiers and a roadblock in front of the airport. So I went Achimota.

Doing between 40 MPH and 50 MPH, I approached Gifford Circle. No traffic except for one truck approaching me. It slowed down to make the turn into the Achimota Road entrance of Military

Hospital. We were so close I assumed he would wait for me to pass (do I not, after all, have the right of way?). But no, he turned, right into the side of my passing Jeep. Before I fully comprehended what was happening, there was the grinding of metal, the shattering of glass – and we were stopped, I looking out the broken window to my left at the drunken soldier sitting in the cab of a military ambulance truck.

Soon we were surrounded by soldiers on duty at the hospital gate. When do I go into shock? I thought. Why am I still alive? No major wounds, except some throbbing pain in my left side and a one-inch bump on my left elbow.

The Jeep was crushed on the left side from the front bumper to the beginning of the passenger cab. The force of the impact had pushed the Jeep into the drainage ditch beside the road (or had I swerved to avoid the truck, hopeless task?) and thrown the glasses off my face. A soldier found them for me – what could I see? Get the keys, I thought. The car key was jammed in the ignition, so I pulled the other keys free and left it. Get all the papers out of the glove box, I thought, and did so. Why am I so calm, and when do I go into shock?

A doctor leaving the hospital recommended I go in for an x-ray of the arm. The ambulance driver backed his vehicle off (no damage to it except for a broken headlight) and the soldiers told me to go with him. "He's drunk!" I wanted to protest, but then figured why bother. While waiting in the emergency room for treatment, I called the Marine Guard on duty at the Embassy. His reaction ("Are you shitting me?") apparently derived from the absurdity of being hit by a drunken ambulance driver outside of a hospital, rather absurd even by current revolutionary Ghana standards. An Embassy car came to pick me up.

The doctors and x-rays agreed that nothing was broken, although everything was bruised or scratched. I was given tetanus and penicillin injections. Given the hospital's sanitary standards, each seemed more likely to cause what it was intended to prevent. I also got some unidentified white pills with the instructions: "Take two when in pains."

I arrived home about midnight, after agreeing to transport half the emergency room occupants to their homes, and waited for shock/hysteria to set in. It did not, although whenever I turned the light out I felt rising tenseness. I eventually sat up until 2:00 a.m. reading Waugh's *A Handful of Dust*, a story about a man lost in the tropics and presumed dead by his family in England. Appropriate. By 2:00 a.m. I was too tired (and, presumably, sedated with pain killer) to be upset by the events of the preceding four hours. I slept well with no unpleasant dreams. The only one I remember with any distinctness involves tricycles hanging from the ceiling of the Consular Section waiting room.

May 9, 1982 Sunday

Each day I feel better. My lump has almost gone and the use of my arm recovered. Friday I had difficulty writing my name. Yesterday I could write in these pages.

By coincidence, on the day of the accident I had signed the papers for the Jeep's sale. The potential buyer, an Embassy Ghanaian employee, is now trying to determine whether the vehicle can be salvaged. It appears that no major damage was done to the chassis. Because of its height, the ambulance drove *over* the frame and tire. But it is unclear whether the engine escaped serious damage. In my own opinion that seems quite unlikely, although the ambulance presumably was moving rather slowly when it drove into my side. Had contact occurred a second later and twelve inches farther back, the question of engine damage would be of no concern to me.

Apparently the ambulance driver (who, according to a doctor at the hospital, had earlier in the day delivered a corpse to the deceased's family and been given a bottle of gin for his services) thought that I would stop and wait for him to turn. Why I would do that is as unknown to me as how I could have stopped short of the ambulance, given the laws of physics. Why he would expect me to stop, since he had no flashing light or siren to indicate he was an ambulance or any patient on board to justify his appropriating the right of way, I also find incomprehensible.

Had the accident occurred in a more normal, civilized setting, I think it would have affected me more traumatically. Rather than be overwhelmed with nausea by the thought that I almost died, I am consumed with the sense that this has only been one more aggravation.

May 18, 1982 Tuesday

I have almost recovered from the accident. My left elbow bone seems to stick out at a sharper angle than before, although I have been told it is not uncommon for the more frequently used arm to have a bigger elbow. Perhaps. Almost no pain, except that every night all the pain collects in the joints and I awaken in the morning feeling like an arthritic old man.

The Jeep has not fared as well. It is not repairable. In addition to the body and engine damage the steering column was broken in two. The man who agreed to buy the Jeep is still buying it. He leaves next Monday for the United States on an already scheduled holiday. He will take along with him a list of parts to buy, one and a half single-spaced typed pages.

Because of Ghana's Alice-in-Wonderland currency, neither one of us suffers in the sale. He pays me 30,000 cedis, which I convert at the official rate to $10,000 (the original purchase price). In reality those cedis cost him only about $1,000.

May 23, 1982 Sunday

This being beach day and this being the rainy season, it rained, a good, heavy tropical rain which fell out of the skies faster than the earth could absorb it. For the third of four Sundays we missed the beach, never mind that the weather was sunny and hot all week.

The pleasures of the beach have dimmed somewhat these past months. First the commissary ran out of orange juice, a major blow to our champagne-and-orange juice beach brunches which we remedied by a methodical assault on all the neighbors' store rooms. Now the commissary has orange juice in stock again, and has run out of champagne. This deficiency has proved insurmountable. Somehow the beach is just not the same without champagne and orange juice served in big wine goblets.

As I say today we could not go. Gloria Nelson, Gil Mar, and my new neighbors the Harrises came over to my house to play cards. Our game was momentarily interrupted in the early evening shortly after the rain stopped. As so often happens, this produced a swarm of flying insects, this time four-winged termites. First attracted by the porch lights, they soon found their way into the house under the doors and through rips in the screens. They swarmed around the lamps. We only successfully repulsed the invasion by turning off all the lights, making liberal use of flyswatters and spray, and calling the vacuum cleaner into action. The living and dining room floors are littered with crushed bodies and torn wings. Even now I am sitting with a fly swatter at the ready, as the flutter of wings still comes from darkened corners. Killer, my ever faithful watchdog, made himself exceptionally useful as he discovered that twitching termites are as satisfying to the palate as his more standard fare of houseflies.

I have always felt electrically insecure in Ghana. It is not simply the ever-present possibility that the power might go off. It is the power fluctuations, the inadequate grounding of electrical equipment, the makeshift wiring, the multiplicity of outlet plug types within the same building or even within the same room.

Even the best electrician cannot repair without parts, so equipment slowly deteriorates. Its use becomes increasingly dangerous until even the cleverest juggling of wires cannot save it. The house across the way has had two electrical fires in the last six months for such reasons.

I have been much more cautious since the time several months ago when I attempted to turn off one of the air conditioners and 220 volts surged up my arm and left it throbbing for several minutes.

May 31, 1982 Monday
	Another Memorial Day weekend with nothing to do. I had planned to drive up to Kumasi this weekend to visit the Schwartzes. The loss of my Jeep negated that plan. Yesterday the beach was ruled out by a second Sunday in a row with rain (the fourth of the last six). Those foolhardy enough to attempt an outing anyway reported that the mud on the beach road was knee deep.
	The Calendar of Events published in this week's Okyeame (the Mission newsletter) reads:
	"Wed Jun 2 1630-1900 Embassy Club Happy Hour
	"Thu Jun 3 1700-1745 Slimnastics
	"Sat Jun 5 1400 Softball
	"Mon Jun 7 1700-1745 Slimnastics
	"Wed Jun 9 1630-1900 Club Happy Hour
	"Thu Jun 10 1700-1745 Slimnastics
	"Fri Jun 18 School ends
	"Sat Jun 19 1400 Softball
	"Sun Jun 20 Father's Day
	"Mon Jun 21 1700-1745 Slimnastics
	"Wed Jun 23 1630-1900 Club Happy Hour
	"Thu Jun 24 1700-1745 Slimnastics
	"Sat Jun 26 1400 Softball"
So much I have to look forward to in my final full month in Accra! Only forty-two days and seven Pan American flights to go, with the seven to become six within the next few hours.

June 1, 1982 Tuesday
	An important anniversary this month: Henry Kissinger, then Secretary of State, swore me (and ninety others) into the Foreign Service on June 17th, 1975. Sometimes it seems like only yesterday, but more often like the life story of a total stranger.
	If I had to do it all over again, I would still choose the

Department of State. That says quite a bit, since the last two years have been pretty miserable, even counting the year I spent in Detroit after my 1974 graduation from Marquette.

I considered suing the Ghanaian Government to recover the loss of the Jeep, or to ask the Embassy to put pressure on Ghana to pick up the tab. Instead, I will put it all behind me. I will not suffer any financial loss since I still sold the Jeep for its full value. The Police learned about the accident, went ahead and investigated it, and lo and behold fixed the responsibility on the nitwit soldier driving the other vehicle.

Still, I became a bit angry today when, in the weekly staff meeting, the Ambassador referred to my "minor" traffic accident.

June 3, 1982 Thursday

My attitude regarding these remaining weeks provides an interesting contrast to my feelings prior to departure from Korea in May 1980.

I regretted leaving Korea and would have willingly stayed. Realistically the future of my Foreign Service career made it necessary to move on. My last months in Korea I made a special effort to experience as much of it as possible, including going on long weekend trips throughout the countryside. I regretted leaving my Korean friends. I envied those Americans whose tours would keep them in Korea for years more. When at last I got on that Japan Air Lines flight to Osaka on May 17th, I carried the burden of depression which comes upon us when it seems everything has fallen apart. It did not help that Korea could scarcely note my insignificant departure, then involved in the tragic political events following the assassination of President Park Chung-hee.

In contrast to all this are my feelings towards Ghana.

Undoubtedly my intense bond to Korea would cause me to compare any subsequent assignment to it and judge the latter rather harshly. I have certainly done that to Ghana. I had scarcely even deplaned at Kotoka Airport September 1st, 1980 when I began to regret the prospect of two years here.

I dislike those aspects of Ghana which others find so intriguing. Yes, the people are friendly. That does not balance the inability of a nation over twenty-five years to establish a political or economic framework within which to assure peace and prosperity. The people's high level of education and the country's abundant natural resources suggest this objective is achievable.

I am embarrassed by such failure, compared to the economic miracles which East Asians have produced from the rubble of war, working with far fewer natural resources but more ambition.

This is not to say that I wish Ghana had never happened to me. The last twenty-two months have been, as they say, an experience. Suffering is, as they say, ennobling. Rather than regret the past I anticipate the future.

The Department recently announced the delay of the Midcareer Professional Development Course from August 2nd to August 30th. This gives me an extra four weeks of leave, time to find a house of livable size with my $25,000 in savings. Still no word on my assignment after the course ends (January 28th). Why worry about that now?

June 27, 1982 Sunday

Two weeks from tomorrow I depart Ghana. Fourteen days, two Pan American flights, July 12th. There have been times when I doubted I would ever reach this point.

Packing boxes surround me; all the paintings are off the walls. The movers come on Wednesday to finish whatever I don't.

This past week I learned that, after the Midcareer Professional Development course, I will either work in the Operations Center or receive an assignment to Japan. The Operations Center is the nerve center of the Department of State, truly "where the action is." By no means an easy job, but ideal for an understanding of how the Department operates. From a career viewpoint, an assignment to the Operations Center is very desirable.

Ghana has taught me that my personal satisfaction in an assignment overrides career considerations. Ghana has taught me that my desire to remain in the Foreign Service is not so strong that I will endure any assignment which might come my way.

I requested a consular position in Fukuoka, Japan. My Career Counselor has told me the assignments panel is also considering an Osaka, Japan assignment. I would accept either eagerly.

We have a group of inspectors at post last week and this, to check to see if we are doing everything correctly. They also look into such things as post morale. Prior to their arrival, every section and every employee filled out questionnaires on a variety of topics. One of the questions for individual employees was: "How is your morale?" To which I replied: "Bad to worse."

The Personnel Officer received the task of characterizing the morale of the Mission staff at large. Her response, not too surprisingly, suggested that morale was bad. The Ambassador (also not too surprisingly) was incensed that she should dare characterize morale at his post as poor. As he told her, we are all professionals. If we do not like the conditions under which we work, we should find a different line of work. In other words, the morale of Foreign Service Officers is by definition good. Why then bother asking the question?

I try my best when around the inspectors to put my best foot forward. Not an easy task, as the foot often winds up in the mouth.

"Do you use the American employees' clubhouse much?" asked one inspector.

"I used to, when I still had a car," I replied.

"Oh, you sold it?" he asked.

"No," I answered, and after a moment of expectant silence on his part added, "A drunk soldier drove into it."

The inspectors seem to be having their own morale problems. I thought we should place them in either the Continental or Ambassador Hotel, to get the full flavor of life in Ghana. Instead, they have rooms in the employees' association guest house. While only a third-rate Holiday Inn, it is still the best lodging in Accra.

Notes from Lower Volta

Two of the inspectors have wound up in the guest house annex, a small building two blocks from the main one, to which they must walk for meals and such. This is, as I may have mentioned, the rainy season. The heaviest rainy season, they say, in six or seven years. The electricity has also shown an even greater tendency than usual to go off in certain neighborhoods. There apparently have been whole nights at the guest house with no lights or air conditioners. Tsk, tsk.

August 29, 1982 Sunday – Arlington, Virginia

No, I have not discontinued my *Notes from Lower Volta*. But it pleases me no end that while I still may scribble about events in Ghana, that phase of my life ended July 12th at about 7:30 p.m. when I got on Pan American's Accra-Monrovia-Dakar-New York flight, determined not to deplane until I had the United States firmly underfoot. (The 747's radar difficulties, which delayed and almost prevented our departure from Dakar, very nearly defeated that resolution).

I had meant to write sooner than this, had even expected to write some more before leaving Ghana. One thing led to another, and here I am, renting a room in Arlington, anticipating the start tomorrow of the Midcareer Professional Development course.

I had thought I might record my sentiments after all my things were packed in late June and my big house stood empty except for its aging government furnishings, including the faded pea-green couches and sea-blue carpeting. It was not until then, I think, that the realization of my imminent departure finally took hold.

I still had other problems to contend with. Notably, finding a home or homes for Killer and Lady Killer. The market for mutts was not as promising as one might have hopes. Killer, in spite of all his virtues, apparently has acquired a reputation as a rather neurotic canine.

He at least could pose as a watchdog, with a very convincing bark and growl. Lady Killer, however, had nothing going for her except her cuteness. She complicated the issue by getting herself pregnant (this in spite of my efforts to keep her penned up when in heat in May – her uncontrollable lust won out). I tried to believe that she was not pregnant and was merely losing her young girlish figure. It became very obvious the last weekend of June that her weight gain was strictly maternal.

On July 7th between lunch and the end of work she delivered six puppies (five living), in the garage. The garage was not her choice for a maternity ward. She much preferred the living room, ideally the couch.

It was obvious at lunch that her time was near. She was running around in circles, whimpering. It became apparent that she knew next to nothing about building a nest. I got a box, covered the bottom of it with a bath towel, put it in the garage and her in it. She found my efforts adequate. When I returned at about 5:00 p.m., she was mothering her five puppies.

I did not know until the next morning that there was also a dead puppy under all that squirming life. When I discovered it, I moved the family to a bigger box and told Yaro to dispose of the corpse as well as the box, which was soaked with whatever a birth box gets soaked with.

The dog crisis ended well enough. Gloria Nelson, who recently extended for another two years in Accra (poor girl, but her alternatives were three years in Nigeria or Zaire) took Killer as a watchdog; and Marilee Keenan in Peace Corps took Lady and her pups. Marilee had offered herself as a home of last resort, since she had known Lady when she was just a puppy herself and was loathe to see me carry out my threat to have the local veterinarian destroy the whole family if I had no alternative.

My replacement arrived the evening of the day that Lady Killer delivered. (Here I have always complained about the dullness of life in Accra!) He set out making a bad impression with almost everyone, starting with me. He asked whether I still planned on departing the following Monday or whether I would stay longer. I assured him my travel arrangements were set.

From talking to him over the subsequent days, I got the impression he is knowledgeable about consular work. But he is not the sort of person with whom I would want to socialize. As Carol Flanagan at the Canadian High Commission remarked after meeting him: "He's no Bill Duffy." I took that as a compliment. I did leave with quite a bit of sympathy for his position. It was obvious in my final days that the summer rush of visa applicants (we do forty-five percent of our business in July, August, and September) had begun.

Compounding this, the back-up consular position (which the Ambassador had assured me last year would be available full-time when needed) seems to have vanished. Vacancies elsewhere in the Embassy caused by vacation and transfer schedules have led to the back-up officer's assignment elsewhere. By the time I learned this, I had only four days to departure.

Several people remarked on July 12th that they had never seen me smile so much. I replied that I usually smiled. "Yes," they agreed, "but this is a sincere smile."

August 31, 1982 Tuesday

Two years ago tonight I got on a Pan American flight at JFK and headed off to Africa. When I woke up that morning in a New York hotel, I considered intentionally missing the flight. Ghana never had a chance.

It has been almost seven years since my September 1975 departure from San Francisco for Korea. Then too I had a momentary qualm about whether or not I really wanted to do what I was about to do.

My other major recent anniversary was August 19th, when I turned thirty years of age. I celebrated in, of all places, Carmel, California. At the time it seemed appropriate to record my feelings at having reached this landmark but the Muse failed to inspire me to write anything. (Not that she is doing much better right now.)

I did not find my thirtieth birthday traumatic. Occasionally it feels that life rushes past and I have scarcely begun to make anything of it. On the other hand, I welcome the passage of time and my continued maturation. I do not envy teenagers or people in their early twenties. I sympathize with them for having yet to pass through some of the hurdles I have already overcome.

The Ghana aberration aside, each year of my life seems better than its predecessor. Even the appearance of gray hair does not dismay me as much as it pleases me. Will I always have this relaxed attitude toward aging? Where will I be in 1992? Or 2002 (is it really less than two decades to the next century?)?

What most I fear about aging is the possibility of senility or debilitating disease, which would deprive me of the independence and control over my own life which I value so much.

September 2, 1982 Thursday

Excitement in Ghana continued right up to my departure. There was, for example, the Princeton University student the Department sent out as a summer intern. The Embassy had tried its best to discourage receiving an intern because of the situation. Last summer's intern stayed on long after the end of his assignment and did not depart until this April, doing what, it was never clear.

This year's intern was working on his *third* internship. Not bad, considering that most students would consider themselves lucky to get even one such assignment.

The intern quickly established himself in everyone's mind as somewhat eccentric and rather a pain in the neck. He treated the Embassy motor pool as his private taxi service, in spite of several attempts by the Administrative Officer to disabuse him of that notion. It soon became clear, however, that his use of official vehicles was the least of his problems.

I don't know what the final breaking point was. Several possibilities come to mind. He threw himself off his second story balcony in response to a command from God (he survived unharmed). He interpreted events in Ghana in light of the Book of Revelation. He informed the Deputy Ambassador that he had vital information regarding U.S. security and his life was endangered by both Ghanaian and American officials.

The Security Officer persuaded him to depart Ghana the same day as the last event, telling him it was necessary to convey this vital information in person to the Department. Diplomatic Security subsequently sent a team out from Washington to interview *everyone* who might have talked to him during his stay, in an attempt to determine if he had compromised any classified information.

Crazy? Perhaps. Difficult to tell in the Ghanaian environment, where craziness is normal.

The Fourth of July weekend was marred by the discovery of the mutilated corpses of three of Ghana's Supreme Court justices. Who could have done it? Someone able to move without difficulty during curfew and dump the bodies on a military post. But surely not anyone associated with the government! The Justices, incidentally, were known as critics of Jerry Rawlings' 1979 regime.

September 14, 1982 Tuesday

Ghana did have its uses. I came home with $25,000 saved up, more than enough to make the down payment on a house even at today's prices. Buying a house stood out for two years as one major consolation. Upon arriving July 13th, I felt a temptation to forget buying a house and quit the Foreign Service instead. Surely $25,000 would be sufficient to tide me over until I had made arrangements for my future.

Too late for that now. For I have bought a house. Several months ago while still in Ghana I wrote to several realtors in the Washington area, explained my financial situation, and said I was looking for a one- or two-bedroom condominium apartment very close in. I arranged with one, who scouted out a number of possibilities. No sooner did I arrive in Washington July 20th than I was out house-hunting.

The person who started out looking for something small and

practical had within five days arranged to buy a three-story, three-bedroom, two-and-one-half-and-one-quarter bath townhouse complete with fireplace, marble foyer, and oak hardwood floors. Out of perhaps twenty-five places of varying prices, sizes, and locations, this house was the only one which I wanted to buy as soon as I saw it. The two-and-one-half-and-one-quarter baths? A powder room on the first floor, a complete bath on each of the upper levels. On the second floor, the bath connects the two bedrooms on that floor, and each bedroom has its own sink. The "one-quarter" bath is to let me know I have an extra sink.

The cost of this little palace? $101,000 (including $2,000 to have the builder finish the attic level as a third bedroom), financed with an FHA mortgage of $89,500 at 13.5 percent for thirty years, monthly payments totaling approximately $1,200. Am I out of my mind?

September 22, 1982 Wednesday
I move into my house Friday. Settlement is at 9:00 a.m., the movers with my things from Ghana will arrive later in the day (hopefully after I do), three bookcases and a gateleg table which I bought in Georgetown are scheduled to be delivered on Saturday, and my Sears washer-dryer next Tuesday, the same day the telephone man comes to hook up my line.

My Korean things which have been in storage for two years are enroute from California. They should turn up early in the week.

The first weekend in October I plan to drive to Philadelphia to pick up a stereo system, two lamps, a gateleg table, and some of Grandmother O'Callaghan's dishes (God rest her soul these past twenty years). Within two weeks I hope to have a reasonably functioning household.

October 23, 1982 Saturday – Alexandria
My revenge on Ghana is complete following the appearance of my name on the most recent promotion list. I have now, in seven

years, moved from a lowly FO-8 to FO-7 (1977), to FO-6 (1978), to FO-5 (1980), to FO-2 – not as dramatic a rise as it might appear. The grades were renumbered in 1980, automatically moving me from FO-5 to FO-3.

This latest promotion came as a complete shock. Supposedly the average time in grade for an FO-5/FO-3 is four or five years. I had spent only two years at that level. The time factor aside, my last evaluation report hardly seemed of the sort to produce a promotion. Rod Hawke gave me an "excellent" rating and the Ambassador threw in a few obscure paragraphs, but I ignored the common wisdom that says writing more than a sentence or two in the space allotted for the rated Officer's comment is the kiss of death to any promotion. I added a two-page single-spaced statement in which I made clear my feelings about consular work in Ghana and the Embassy's (the Ambassador's) role in helping or hindering me.

The first hint that I had made the promotion list came when I received a telephone message slip from Jay Bookman reading: "Congratulations! When's the champagne?" When a copy of the promotion list turned up at the Foreign Service Institute and included William J. Duffy, I called my Career Counselor to confirm whether it was me. A check of personnel listings showed that, indeed, the Department has only one Foreign Service Officer by that name.

Wouldn't it have been interesting if I had come home and quit the Foreign Service?

It has been all very satisfying. I wonder whether I would do Ghana again, even knowing I could get a promotion and a house out of it?

Promotion does not entail automatic graduation from the mid-level course. But now I am the second-ranking class member.

I have moved into my house and am very happy thus far with the role of Henry Homemaker. Settlement was on September 24th. All my things have arrived, except for one of the eight boxes from Ghana which no one seems able to find. It contains my Korean crown, mahogany chopsticks, an ivory carving from Togo, half my dishes (including *all* the serving pieces), as well as the legs to my butler's table, field bar, and writing desk (on which I had in Ghana kept the coffee and tea pots, also missing). Of the Ghana things which arrived, those I packed came unscathed. Those packed by the movers suffered a thirty percent breakage rate.

In ten months I will pack everything up and put it back into storage. As soon as I finish the Midcareer Professional Development Course I start thirty weeks of Japanese language training at the Foreign Service Institute and go to Fukuoka next September.

Notes from Lower Volta

1983

January 3, 1983 Monday – Alexandria

What is this? Have I allowed the New Year to begin without my making some world survey? Is it that I don't feel myself an active participant in the sweep of world history in my present position as suburban homeowner? (Does that mean in Ghana that I did feel like a participant?) What has become of New Year's Resolutions? This year I have none. I will avoid the yearend disappointment of reviewing misplaced resolutions.

Life plods on. It revolves around going to classes at the Foreign Service Institute, coming home, making dinner, cleaning up, doing homework and housework, and watching a few choice TV programs (the News, *M*A*S*H*, and *Soap*).

I have practically no social life, my natural bent for solitude reinforced by two years of monkish existence in Ghana and the pressures of being both a homeowner and a student. I did hold a Champagne Open House on New Year's Day. About twenty friends came, a pleasant mixture of colleagues from Korea, Ghana, and Washington. Margaret was kind enough to handle the food preparations. It was a successful party, comparing favorably with my 1981 Oktoberfest and Juke Box Saturday Night.

January 5, 1983 Wednesday

The Midcareer Professional Development Course concludes at the end of the month. It has offered an interesting exercise in people, claiming to teach us how to manage others, failing themselves to manage us. The "time management" specialist got so far behind his schedule he left it to us to read an article on effective time use on our own rather than discuss it in class. An "expert" on Islamic law came and lectured at us for two afternoons. He succeeded only in reinforcing my anti-Mideast prejudices, being boring and hostile at the same time. The "expert" on dealing with prisoners put a new perspective on the matter by saying: "We are all criminals. The only difference between us and those behind bars is that they have acted upon their criminal desires." About as succinct a description of the difference between barbarity and civilization as one could hope for.

My missing box of things from Ghana has surfaced. It was in the storage company warehouse all the weeks the company insisted it did not have it. All the things I had given up as lost have turned up (greatly complicating my decorating scheme).

February 2, 1983 Wednesday

How does one spend five long months in a Midcareer Professional Development course and escape with no clear recollection of what has been learned or even of what was taught? The course ended last Friday. My most vivid memory is the graduation ceremony held on the eighth floor of the Department of State, vivid not for the ceremony itself, but because of the antique, historical, and *very plush* decor of the eighth floor, the fabled crown of the Department normally reserved for state occasions. I last saw it in 1975 when Henry Kissinger swore in my entering class.

This week I have taken annual leave to complete all the little errands which I have successfully avoided since returning to the United States: dentist, eye doctor, driver's license, travel voucher, *et al*.

Monday I begin Japanese language training. As the time draws closer, I wonder whatever induced me to think that I could attempt to learn such a language. How little I will know at the end of seven months! This week I'm watching the TV miniseries *Shogun* in preparation. That should bring me up to the one-one speaking-reading level. *Konnichiwa*.

I remember still that September morning in 1975 when first I began the study of Korean. How far away that all seems now.

Notes from Lower Volta

February 6, 1983 Sunday

The third snowfall of this winter, this rather mild winter, came today. Like the other two, it fell on Sunday. I spent today in front of the fireplace, doing not much of anything except to read the Washington *Post* and the *Economist* (the latest addition to my list of subscriptions).

Tomorrow, Japanese training. What have I gotten myself into? (Not that I have any grounds to complain. Of the fifty-seven people in my midlevel group, *ten* did not have on the Friday of our graduation an assignment for the following Monday. Grim.)

February 11, 1983 Friday

Happy Lunar New Year! And so arrives the Year of the Pig. But maybe not in Israel or Islamic countries.

The airports are closed, I-395 is a parking lot, and I am so happy to be in my own warm house with a fire in the fireplace and coffee on the stove. Washington has received its second worst snowstorm in history, with more than twelve inches of snow on the ground being whipped into drifts by the wind.

I spent an hour enroute to work this morning, most of it waiting for a bus. Right as I decided that staying home was the wiser course, three buses pulled up in a row. So I made it in.

At 11:00 a.m., with snow still falling and wind still blowing, the Word Came from On High to allow us to go home. It took me more than two hours to retrace my steps, including an hour-and-a-half wait at the Pentagon bus stop for one of the buses which supposedly run every twenty minutes. It is now 8:30 p.m., and the snow is still falling. The winter (my first since 1979-80 in Korea) may have been mild, but this is not an auspicious start to spring.

I am ecstatic about Japanese language training. I forgot how much I enjoy learning languages. My knowledge of Korean has been very helpful, more than I expected, as has my previous exposure to East Asian ideas and ways of thinking. There is only one other person in my class. He has not been to East Asia nor studied foreign languages since college. Japanese clearly confuses him more than me.

Probably the biggest thrill of learning Japanese is that it will take me to Japan. I don't think studying Bengali to go to Bangladesh would have quite the same impact. I've often had second thoughts about the Foreign Service. But I have no skills which would convert to another job, certainly not at my present salary. With national unemployment at eleven percent, this is not the best time to look for another job, even in Washington. I am so happy with the house and the prospect of going to Japan that I have no complaints right now.

March 4, 1983 Friday

Only three weeks since the blizzard of 1983, and it appears that summer has arrived. Temperatures went above eighty degrees today; I've turned off the heat and the house is still warmer than it has been since last September. Good news, that. My electric bill last month came to $200, apparently because the electric company underestimated my power use the previous months, when I paid only $20, $60, $80, and $100.

Advancing age (can someone who is only thirty years old write about "advancing age"?) continues to bring changes in the music I listen to. The rock music which ten or twelve years ago seemed to me to represent the ultimate in listening pleasure now rarely gets put on the turntable. In more recent years, I have had a growing interest in American folk and traditional music. My years overseas taught me a new appreciation for American things paralleling my appreciation of things foreign. It seems appropriate that an American diplomat learn as much about what makes America America as well as what makes Korea Korea or Ghana Ghana. This even led me to buy the Smithsonian's eight record collection of the history of country music, and I *hate* country music.

I have discovered the beauties of opera. Previously my only exposure to opera came in Korea, where I saw two productions of *Aida* and one of *La Boheme*. Then when I was in Ghana, my mother sent me a few cassette tapes of operatic excerpts. Grand opera in the midst of the West African jungle touched a receptive area of my shell-shocked brain. Since returning to the United States, I have taken advantage of the Book-of-the-Month Club's opera series to acquire recordings of *Aida, La Boheme, Carmen,* and *Madama Butterfly*. How appropriate to have *Butterfly*, since the story takes place in Nagasaki and gives a major role to the American Consul.

March 14, 1983 Friday

What does it say about Western culture that the opera heroine, but rarely the hero, dies at the end of the opera? What does it say about me that the death scenes are usually my favorites?

Japanese progresses nicely, some days better than others. From next Monday, I will be on my own. My fellow student and I are clearly progressing at different rates, with the gap widening rather than narrowing as we go along.

May 6, 1983 Friday

Exactly one year has passed since a drunken Ghanaian soldier drove into my Jeep, demolishing it and providing me with one more sour memory of Ghana. Even though I have left Ghana, it has not left me. The April 1st *People's Daily Graphic* (it used to be just the plain old *Daily Graphic*) exposed CIA plots in Ghana, based on secret documents purloined from the West German Embassy. Buried deep in the text was the sentence: "Consul William Duffy was also involved in these discussions."

My first reaction was satisfaction that at least the reporter had spelled my name correctly. My second thought was, what discussions? The context was not entirely clear. I think the connection was my involvement in the aftermath of the February 1982 arrest of VALCO employees. The article left the implication that the discussions involved a counterrevolution (as if *I* would have wanted to bring back the previous government).

I am sitting in my recently finished garden, complete with

dogwood tree, azaleas, heavenly bamboo, and cotoneasters. Not that I know anything about gardening in general or these plants in particular. When I hired the landscaper (name picked at random from a classified ad) I specified I wanted a vaguely East Asian design which would require minimal attention from either me or a renter. For $838 I got exactly what I wanted.

Although hesitant to mention this, the garden brings back fond memories of my little patio behind the house in Accra. With the beach, it constituted my only satisfying refuges in Ghana. All that is needed to complete the picture is Killer curled at my feet. Killer, alas, carries on his life in Ghana, where he recently proved his value as a watchdog by driving off a would-be burglar from Gloria Nelson's house in the dead of night.

Japanese studies go on. On Wednesday I had a test, since I recently completed Volume II of the textbooks. I got a rating of "one" on a scale of one to five. So I would not starve to death in Japan or die for lack of a restroom. My prior knowledge of Korean continues to be a great boon.

Several weeks ago, I took the Foreign Service Institute Korean test. The Foreign Service Institute has recently come up with new testing procedures, and wanted to test the test. Korean students are not a common commodity, so the instructors prevailed upon me to act as a guinea pig. Such an ordeal!

I could understand fairly well what the instructor said to me, but it was difficult after three years to express any ideas in Korean, and easy to interject Japanese terms. Even something so basic as "yes" or "no" consistently popped out of my mouth as the Japanese "*hai*" and "*ie*" rather than the Korean "*ne*" and "*anyo*."

An observation of generational change in Korea: The senior Korean instructor knew enough Japanese to follow me when I wandered off; the junior instructor was completely baffled by even a simple Japanese "no."

Even during the one hour the exam lasted, I felt Korean flooding back into my head. Words which I had forgotten I had ever known reappeared. Best of all, I got 2+ plus rating for my efforts – a decline, to be sure, from my 1979 peak of three, but not as precipitous a decline as I had assumed.

May 24, 1983 Sunday

My social life has always left a good deal to be desired. Whether being a loner is the cause or the consequence of a lackluster social life is unclear, but clearly my being gay has imposed strict limits on it, particularly when overseas. I returned to the United States last summer determined to correct that situation. Not being a person who enjoys going to bars alone or cruising for companionship, this turned out to be a more formidable task than expected.

So I placed a personal ad in two issues (March 18th and 25th) of the Washington *Blade*, reading as follows: "GWM, 30, 6'1", 165, professional, likes backgammon, tennis, hearts, folk music, opera, pre-1964 rock and roll, Orient, travel, good wine, cuddling."

Having surveyed the personal ad scene for some time previously, I wanted to word mine in such a way as was likely to produce a response from someone I would be interested in getting to know. All too often the only thing another gay man and I have in common is our gayness – essential, perhaps, for sexual purposes, but not much upon which to build any other kind of relationship.

In all I received about fifteen responses. Most did not merit a second reading, although the literary difficulties of writing a response under such circumstances may constitute a reasonable brake on Shakespearean touches.

One of the first letters interested me the most. It was literate, sexy without being direct, and suggested the writer had actually considered the meaning of my ad rather than just picking it out at random.

I called the number given, had a pleasant conversation, and arranged to meet the evening of March 27th at his apartment. I took a bottle of champagne with me, we finished it off with grilled cheese sandwiches at midnight, and the rest is history.

We have been together almost continuously since. I knew by the end of that first night together that it had not been a casual encounter but the beginning of the most significant relationship in my life.

As firm a believer in first impressions as I am, I still thought that I might have read too much into our meeting. So I went ahead with meeting two other respondents. Each of those meetings, while not unpleasant, reinforced my conviction that fortune had dealt me a winning hand when it brought Ken to me. I have never met another like Ken, and think it unlikely that fortune will easily give me a second chance.

Ken, for his part, did not rush wildly into our relationship. He certainly enjoyed our acquaintance, and doing all those things men like to do with each other. But at first whenever I hinted at the prospect that ours could be more than a wild fling, he resisted with pointed references to the rareness of true love and the desirability of giving a relationship time to bloom. I wore his resistance down. He casually made reference to us as lovers one evening (April 14th), amazing himself at his lack of restraint.

We go happily along, our relationship constrained only by the prospect that come September off I go to Japan.

I celebrated our new-found relationship by turning to the catalyst of our meeting, the *Blade,* and ran an ad quoting Carmen to Escamillo: *"Je t'aime, KMP, je t'aime et que je meure si j'amais aime quelqu'un autant que toi!* WJD"

September 16, 1983 Friday

Fifty-one weeks ago today I moved into 416 West Glebe Road. Today I leave it. I begin my trip to Milwaukee, San Francisco, Tokyo, and Fukuoka. I leave the house and most of my furniture in Ken's hands, a concrete manifestation of the link between us. He, having bought a small one-bedroom apartment in the District, has realized that not only is it too small to live in. It is also cheaper for him to rent it out, stay here, and find a roommate. Thus our "temporary" cohabitation of mid-May until late July has gone on, and will continue.

I also leave behind Killer, my Ghanaian bush hound, whom I had left in Gloria Nelson's hands upon my departure from Ghana. When her tour was curtailed because of the situation in Ghana this June, she decided to bring Killer with her because, as she wrote, things had become so bad it wasn't fit even for a dog. Since Gloria had to find a place to live, as well as take some leave, before she began Serbo-Croatian language training at the end of last month, she asked me to dog sit Killer.

On Friday June 23rd I took the day off from school and drove out to Dulles Airport to meet the poor creature. By the time he reached Washington, he had been traveling thirty-six hours, flying from Accra to Amsterdam to New York (where he spent the night under the care of the ASPCA). He was pleased to see me, and clearly remembered our past association.

Contrary to my fears, he has adjusted to the different smells and sounds of America and the greater restrictions on his freedom to wander the streets without difficult. And my doubts about having the dog in the house with Ken were laid to rest when it quickly became apparent what a soft touch Ken is.

It hurts to leave. It is not the uncertainty of my first flight to Korea in 1975, or the despair of going to Ghana in 1980. It is the pain of being separated from the person whom I love the most in the world, and who loves me, even as I go to the assignment and a country I have long eagerly sought.

If this time it were Ghana, I would quit the Foreign Service and stay. Instead, I hope to have both worlds: my marriage, and my trip to East Asia. In two years I will come back, and we will see about alternatives.

The Foreign Service is no life for such as we, and at age thirty-one I already find myself tired of the transience and rootlessness of this life. I have had eight very good years (yes, even counting Ghana in some ways), but no desire to go on like this for twenty more.

I must go back to East Asia. I left in 1980 with the need to see it again. These two years will give me that, and in 1985 I will leave Japan knowing that I will not return there again to live. Instead, I will make my life in this house with my lover.

September 24, 1983 Saturday – Tokyo, Okura Hotel

Coming back to East Asia brings back many happy memories. When I left Korea in 1980, it was with considerable reluctance. I knew then, even before Ghana reinforced it, that I would not be happy until I returned. I wish so much that Ken were here with me to see it all. I cannot wait until he comes to see it for himself.

I miss not waking up in the morning with him at my side. I miss not coming home in the afternoon, knowing that he will soon be there.

It is raining in Tokyo now, weather which never fails to put me into a sentimental mood.

For some reason I never did fall asleep on the flight here, even though I usually have not much trouble to do so. Last night I slept only four hours before waking up at 2:00 a.m. completely and irreversibly.

September 25, 1983 Sunday

I had dinner with Ken tonight. I went all dressed up to one of the hotel's restaurants, thinking all the while of how happy I would be to have done it together with him.

At my request the pianist played "Sakura." It reminded me of an evening at the house when we lay on the couch together listening to Rampal's "Sakura" in front of the fireplace. Ken said he would never forget that moment. Has he?

The dinner cost as much as if the two of us were having it in the United States. It was worth the cost to watch the staff fall over each other to provide service.

Notes from Lower Volta

October 6, 1983 9:20 p.m. – Fukuoka

Sometimes I come home in the evening from work and feel so lonely in this house. I would give so much to have Ken in my arms right now, even as I know that he is probably just arriving at work. It takes willpower to resist the temptation to pick up the telephone to call him.

Today I went to the Navy commissary at Sasebo to buy food, three hours there, three hours back. Only one hundred kilometers, but no expressway, only two-lane roads with 50 KPH speed limits! I thought of Ken while I was shopping. I missed arguing about his buying the more expensive orange marmalade for himself and the cheaper strawberry preserves for me.

October 16, 1983 Sunday

I am slowly getting into the groove of life in Japan. Work is easy and slow-paced, the office very attractively furnished. I almost feel guilty working in such splendid conditions when I remember what things are like elsewhere.

Columbus Day was Sports Day in Japan, a waste of a duplicate holiday. I was invited to a tennis tournament put on annually by the president of the Iwataya Department Store. I declined the offer to play, but did go along and look American, for which I was rewarded at the awards banquet afterwards with the *Kokusai Kyooryoko Shoo,* "International Cooperation Prize." Almost everyone received a prize for something, including those who lost 6-5 matches!

At the banquet I sat next to the oldest participant, an eighty-nine-year-old woman who surprised me with her perfect English. When asked how she knew it so well, she said that she had lived in the United States for seventeen years and returned to Japan forty years ago ("before you were born"). Given the math, I did not inquire further into her history, merely observing that she had known English longer than I had.

The banquet concluded with a series of "*banzai!*" shouts by all present, myself excluded. The *banzais* showed the fellowship of the tennis association's members. My dictionary translates the word as "cheers." Americans associate *banzai* with less pleasant memories.

I have signed up for tennis lessons, with the incentive not only of learning tennis but also of putting myself in a position where I will have to speak Japanese. My attempt to fill out the registration form only avoided disaster because I was familiar with such forms from Korea, everything such as "name, address, telephone number" being written in Chinese characters common to both languages.

It was only by a burst of inspiration, however, that I figured out to write my birth date as 27.8.19. I knew the East Asian practice of writing dates as year-month-day. I was momentarily nonplused by the unexpected presence of the Roman letters M-T-S in the "year" space. Then I remembered that Japanese rarely use the Anno Domini system within Japan, the years instead being numbered according to the Emperor's reign. The country has had three emperors in the past century: Meiji, Taisho, and Showa (the present Emperor, Hirohito). This is now Showa 58. So my birth year of 1952 was Showa 27. A gremlin in my left hand almost had me circle M for Meiji, which would give me a birth year about 1895.

Friday night the Consulate staff made an overnight trip to Nokonoshima, a small island in Fukuoka harbor largely covered by a park. Somewhat curiously (to me, at least) none of the staff (other than the other two Americans) elected to bring along either spouse or children. We consumed vast quantities of food and drink. Some of the women had taken off early from work and had everything ready by the time the rest of us arrived about 7:00 p.m. We stayed up to midnight, by which time the cumulative effect of beer and sake did us all in. I spent most of yesterday recovering, going so far as to go straight to bed after getting home about noontime.

October 29, 1983 Saturday

Has this year had more than its share of unsettling news? In Lebanon terrorists blew up the American Embassy in April, and last week the Marines' Beirut headquarters, killing hundreds of people.

Notes from Lower Volta

In August the Soviets shot down a Korean Air Lines 747 out of the sky, killing 269 people, including a U.S. Congressman.

Early this month a bomb blast decimated the Korean government in Burma where President Chun was visiting (the work of North Koreans, perhaps?). Chun himself escaped being blown up due to the fortuitous chance of being delayed in a traffic jam.

Now the United States has invaded Grenada (who can even find it on the map?), together with six Caribbean mini-states, after the thugs in power on the island started shooting each other.

The Burma incident occurred shortly after my arrival in Fukuoka. Dick Morley, the Principal Officer (he arrived in July), and I combined our introductory courtesy calls with a condolence call to the Korean Consulate General, the only other diplomatic representative in town. The Koreans ushered us up several flights of stairs into the room they had rigged up as a memorial shrine with a small altar. Each of us paid our respects, including lighting sticks of incense, everything filmed by a local TV crew which the Koreans had arranged to appear. That concluded, we returned to the Consul General's office for the obligatory cup of tea.

I had wondered about the propriety of combining our introductory and condolence calls. Reality quickly brought me back to my senses. There in the Consul General's office sat the father of a Korean student visa applicant whom I had refused. The Koreans were not about to forego the opportunity to make another visa pitch to the American Consul just because half their government had been blown to pieces.

Returning to our Consulate, I almost alienated the Japanese staff by neglecting to purify myself at the door with a handful of salt over the shoulder. They had placed a small tray of salt outside in anticipation of our return.

October 30, 1983 Sunday

My household effects are in Japan. They may well be in the Fukuoka area. I hope to have them within a few days, everything unpacked and in its place. Until then I feel like I'm living in a hotel room. I never feel "at home" until I'm surrounded by my books, and I am desperate to have my stereo and records. Japanese TV can be fascinating, but I can't wait until I can blast out a little Verdi or Glenn Miller.

I am toying with the idea of buying an upright piano, only 700,000 yen for a Yamaha (about $2,900 at present exchange rates). I'd have to forego putting any money into my IRA this year. I've missed having a piano ever since I sold the Horugel in Korea.

November 26, 1983 Saturday

Jane Cartwright and her friend Bonnie Wrigley visited Veterans Day weekend as part of a three-week holiday in Japan. They picked the weekend of the Consulate staff outing, when we all went together to Yufuin, a resort in eastern Kyushu famous for its hot springs. (I have yet to find a place in Kyushu not famous for its hot springs.)

We left Fukuoka Friday the 11th on the 7:47 a.m. train. Trains, subways, and buses all run on such exact schedules that one can set one's watch by them. To catch the 7:47 train from Hakata Station, for example, we had to arrive at Tojinmachi Subway stop for either the 6:57 or 7:01 train. (Fukuoka Station is called Hakata Station for historical reasons, which are of minimal interest to the foreign traveler in Tokyo or Osaka Station dismayed to find no train to Fukuoka.)

In spite of my inability to comprehend why we have to get out of bed earlier on a holiday than on a workday, we did so, after breakfasting on donuts picked up at Mr. Donut the night before.

The train ride to Yufuin strongly reminded me of a fact which I often forget while living in the middle of a city: Japan is full of mountains. Rarely can one stand in a spot, unless surrounded by the buildings of a city, where he cannot see mountain upon mountain.

On the way, we stopped at a place called El Rancho Grande, an incredibly authentic dude ranch lifted right out of the American

West and dropped lock, stock, and barrel in the highlands of Kyushu. Aside from the Japanese cowboys, the neighboring Japanese-style farm house, and terraced rice fields, we could have been in Colorado, which was where most of the equipment, including the horses, came from.

After eating lunch in the Saloon (and after making a suitably dramatic entrance through its swinging doors), we went horseback riding. I, who had never been on or near a horse in my life, felt compelled to put aside personal preferences and uphold American prestige by joining the ride. The Japanese could not believe that any American was not an experienced cowboy. How many times in the past eight years have I done things which, left to myself, I would never have bothered with, except that it seemed expected of me as an American?

From El Rancho Grande we continued on to the hotel where we had reservations. After convincing the management that this *gaijin* barbarian could sleep on the floor, eat with chopsticks, and use a Japanese-style toilet (I fudged on the last point), we adjourned to the bath to partake of its medicinal and/or sensual benefits.

The custom of mixed bathing among the sexes has pretty much disappeared in Japan, and so it was at Yufuin. Not, of course, that I would be likely to derive any pleasure from seeing a member of either sex naked in the bath. The moment I remove my glasses in the dressing room I become functionally blind.

The Japanese style of bathing, identical to the Korean, is worth a description. After taking off one's clothes, one enters the bathroom. It has one or two very large tubs of standing hot water (and sometimes a tub of very cold water – such was the case in Korea). The difficult thing for Westerners to remember is that one does not get into the tub until *after* all the dirt has already been scrubbed off. In that respect an East Asian tub resembles a Western swimming pool. You should be clean when you enter.

To get clean, you squat yourself on one of the very low stools to be found in the area in front of any of the water faucets on the walls. The stool will dump you on the floor with the most insignificant shift of your weight in the wrong direction. The faucets, emerging from the wall only about a foot from the floor, are marked "hot" and "cold" but invariably produce only cold water.

Using the faucet water, tempered with hot water scooped out of the tub with a small bucket (another item universally present), you scrub and scour yourself in an intimate fashion you would probably not try under normal circumstances even in the privacy of your own bathroom. When thoroughly clean, you rinse all the soap off.

Then and only then do you dare enter the bath, there to be scalded by temperatures more suitable to boil fish. Once you overcome the initial shock to the system, what pleasure engulfs the body and warms the soul! The East Asian bath is a luxury Westerners have foolishly deprived themselves – the perfect preparation for a good night's sleep, the best way to wake oneself in the morning, an incomparable salve to the pounding head of a hangover.

The Japanese somewhat detract from the pleasure of all the bathing experience by persisting in the belief that a single hand towel is sufficient for both washing and drying. I have yet to master the technique of drying myself with a wet hand towel (or even a hand towel which is dry to begin with). Japanese assure me it can be done by repeatedly wringing the towel out. Not likely.

Our evening bath was crowned with heated sake placed in small bottles left to float on wooden trays across the steaming water's surface. The real enthusiasts could, if they so wished, take advantage of the *outdoor* bath. In November mountain air, the curious combination of hot water and cold air left one's senses uncertain which was the exact cause of the very real assault on the body.

After the bath, everyone gathered in a large private dining room for a Japanese dinner. We all dressed in yukata robes provided by the hotel. Consequently, we all dressed exactly alike. Japanese food comes in small portions but lots of different courses, some of which a Westerner may recognize and some of which he won't. The rice comes last. This puzzles many Westerners. We grew up thinking Japanese always eat rice, and assumed it was eaten with the rest of the food.

There is very little Japanese food which a foreigner will not find edible. Cooked fish with the heads still attached leap to mind as one exception. Or maybe my point of view reflects five years' experience with Korean food, a good deal of which Westerners are apt to find quite unappetizing.

Entertainment followed dinner. I became accustomed during my Korean days to the idea that every participant at a party was expected to provide entertainment, usually singing a song, regardless of personal ability. One's ability to sing or not seems to have minimal bearing on how well the listeners receive the song, they being as likely to applaud the effort as heartily as the quality of the product.

As in so many things, the Japanese have carried this idea to technological refinement within the past few years. It is not enough merely to sing. One must do so with microphone in hand and amplifier, whether or not the size of the room suggests amplification is necessary. This is *karaoke*. It happens not only at private parties but also in public bars, where bar patrons take turns singing songs (preferably sad and sentimental), picked out of books provided for the purpose, while a recording of the melody plays in the background. The most up-to-date places have video *karaoke* machines, which provide the song lyrics as subtitles to a short film which may or may not have any connection to the song.

The fact that I do not know any Japanese songs, and the hotel did not have any English titles, did not save me from a performance. The audience demanded a song, so I obliged with a spirited rendition of the old folk song "Keep Your Hand on the Plow" without musical accompaniment.

The following day we had a pleasant Japanese breakfast (including more fish heads and raw eggs) before visiting a local folk art village. The craftsmen included smiths, glassworkers, and potters. What struck me as I watched them was the similarity between their techniques and the way Europeans developed the same items. The technology was basically the same, with only the added cultural veneer distinguishing this place in Kyushu from its counterpart at, say, Jamestown.

Observing these workmen also brought to mind the overwhelming importance that fire has in our lives and in our race's rise to civilization. Without fire, where would we all be?

We caught a noon train back to Fukuoka. On the way Jane commented on the fact that there is no Japanese counterpart to the British practice of businesses' bearing the claim: "By appointment to Her Majesty." For reasons not entirely clear, but probably best explained by the draining effect a long vacation has, she went into near hysterical laughter when I suggested the Japanese could say: "By appointment to His Majesty, the Son of Heaven."

The following day, Sunday, November 13th, we (that is, Jane, Bonnie, and I) took the train to Nagasaki. We thought to commence our tour by visiting a restaurant described in the English language guide book as famous for *chanbon*, a Nagasaki specialty based on some Chinese dish. Everyone else begins his tour at the same spot, as we quickly learned when the taxi bringing us from the train station pulled into a parking lot full of tour buses.

So instead we wandered off to a small coffee shop, and discussed our plan of action over coffee and a bowl of curry rice. Jane had no desire to see the Peace Park, the site of the 1945 A-bomb explosion. That left those places connected with Nagasaki's long history as the only port open to foreigners, including a number of Dutch and American merchant houses and an area called the Dutch Slope because it used to be the location of a Dutch settlement. When I asked the coffee shop owner if the Dutch Slope was far (from our map sketch it appeared to be the closest item), she answered with a statement which I was to hear several more times during the course of the day: "*Massugu. Sugu wakarimasu.*" "Straight ahead. You can't miss it." The statement is no truer in Japanese than it is in English.

Notes from Lower Volta

We ultimately saw everything we had come to see, but in a rather roundabout fashion. We were never quite sure we were getting anywhere. The Dutch Slope is of interest only as a matter of history. There is nothing there now related to the Dutch. We did not know whether in fact we had found the Dutch Slope at all, the only indication that we had being the line of Japanese tourists who followed us to the same spot to take a photograph before going back down the hillside.

At Glover Garden the Japanese have reassembled a number of old buildings associated with Nagasaki's role as the door to the West, including a few houses entirely European in their appearance except for the East Asian tiles roofing them. The Japanese have played the Madame Butterfly story for all it's worth, without allowing themselves to be discouraged by the fact the story has no base whatever in history. There's a statue of Butterfly, a plaque of Puccini, and trees planted at various times by various opera figures. A sign with a brief explanation of the Butterfly story includes the information (in English) that an opera of it was written by "an Italian composer named Puccini."

The view of Nagasaki harbor from Glover Garden did not fail to equal all those others which make this country so beautiful.

The only other sight of great interest was the "move lane," the moving sidewalk which the Japanese have installed to carry the tourists to the top of the hill on which stands Glover Garden.

In an attempt to come home with something typically Nagasakian, and to honor the Japanese tradition of always bringing back something from a trip as a small present for friends and family, we all bought cakes called *kasutera*, something apparently borrowed from the Portuguese many years ago and described in our guide book as a common Nagasaki souvenir. What the guide book did *not* tell us, and what we learned, after returning to Fukuoka, is that *kasutera* can be bought anywhere in Japan.

The visit of the U.S.S. *John A. Moore*, a frigate, to the port crowned Jane and Bonnie's visit to Fukuoka. Dick Morley, as part of his official duties, hosted a reception for the ship's officers (fourteen of them) at his house the night of November 14th, to which he invited about forty Japanese.

The reception went smoothly except for one incident. Most of the officers came to the reception in a bus provided by the base at Sasebo, except for the Commander and his Number Two. The local shipping agent provided them with a car and driver. Both car and bus left the ship at the same time. The bus arrived at Dick's; the car did not.

It turned out the car's driver did not know that the Consulate's Principal Officer now lives next door to the Consulate. He thought the Morleys still occupied the old Japanese house which had been the Principal Officer's residence for many years until the spring of last year. It lies some distance away. So the Commander arrived an hour late for his own reception.

After the reception, we all adjourned to Shakey's Pizza Parlor, an all-American institution if there ever was one (along with McDonald's, Kentucky Fried Chicken, Mister Donut, 7-11, and the other American fast food shops here), and gorged ourselves on pizza. I was not keen on the cheese and tuna, but found the shrimp and squid pizza quite interesting.

Jane and Bonnie returned to Tokyo that Wednesday and to the United States that Friday.

December 13, 1983 Tuesday

Sunday Ken called. If I sounded out of sorts it was most definitely not because I was unhappy to hear his voice. I had a hangover which left me feeling somewhat queasy. I had started drinking about 8:00 p.m. Saturday and stopped at 3:00 a.m. Sunday morning, first beer and then *mizuwari*. Mizuwari, the Japanese name for whisky and water, is the only Western drink besides beer which the Japanese are familiar with. Please do not be alarmed and think I spend my weekends on drinking binges. Saturday night was an unusual case.

Notes from Lower Volta

Saturday night I finally made the local gay bar scene. Soon after my arrival in Fukuoka, I discovered the gay bar district based on information in the Spartacus guide. Although I had walked past the places, I had not gone into any of them.

My reluctance to do so came from a combination of reasons: my dislike of going anyplace by myself, a lack of confidence at speaking Japanese, suggestions that Japanese gays do not welcome foreigners (helped, recently, by the discovery of AIDS in Japan and the assumption it came from Americans), and most of all by the uncertainty of what I would do in a Japanese gay bar. Look for a trick? For one thing, the men all smoke! For another, the thrill of sex has largely disappeared except for the thrill of having it with a certain someone not on this side of the Pacific Ocean.

On the other hand, it can be very lonely sitting at home, and very irritating wearing a straight mask and dealing with the constant questions about marriage and girlfriends which afflict me when I go out. I wanted to see if there wasn't some place where I could go for a drink and *relax*, without having "hostesses" pushed at me to offer things I don't want.

So last night I went bar-hopping. It took me four tries before I worked up the courage to enter the first bar. Was it even courage? All of a sudden I found myself walking in, or rather, *up* a very narrow, steep flight of stairs to the second floor of a building.

I soon learned that in addition to those places listed in Spartacus, there appear to be maybe twenty others all located in the same neighborhood of Gion-machi. Such places are each very small, with space at the bar for maybe ten customers and no standing room. At first glance, they are indistinguishable from other Japanese bars, since most customers in any bar are usually men anyway. While it is unusual to have only male bartenders and no "hostesses," it does happen.

I arrived at 8:00 p.m. I thought that was early enough to avoid a crowd, and I was right. There was only one other customer. I still had some doubt whether I was even in a gay bar at all (by name,

Sanbangai, or Third Street) until the bartender asked where I had heard of the place. I mentioned Spartacus, which he knew. The bartender seemed to be in his twenties. An older man in his thirties seemed to be the owner, or "master" (one of those many Japanese words which just coincidentally sounds like an English word with a similar meaning). Both were very pleased to have my business. We ran through the conversation which predictably follows my meeting a Japanese:

"You speak Japanese so well."

"Not at all."

"How many years have you been in Japan?"

"I came this year, at the end of September."

"At the end of September? But where did you learn Japanese?"

"I studied in America."

"How long did you study?"

"Seven months."

"You speak Japanese very well."

"Not at all."

"How long will you be here?"

"Two years."

"For work?"

"Yes."

"Are you married?"

"No, I'm a bachelor."

"Oh, a bachelor."

As I observed through the course of the evening, the bars seem to have a set of regular customers. The master personally greets whoever comes in. Not at all like American bars where you're pretty well ignored except when you order a drink (and sometimes even then).

After I had been at *Sanbangai* a while, a middle-aged man came in and struck up a conversation. He was married and had three teen-aged sons. (Societal pressure makes gay married men an even more common phenomenon in Japan than in the United States.) We had a pleasant conversation, particularly because I did not appear to be his "type," too old, I guess. He seemed to enjoy talking to a foreigner and offered, since it was my first time, to show me around. We went to a second bar, on the way to which he pointed out all the other gay bars in the neighborhood.

The second bar came complete with *karaoke*, but its English numbers were limited to a few selections from "Sound of Music." The master preferred that I sing "My Way," which I was compelled to do without lyrics, making up words as I went along.

As in the United States, the bars fill up later in the evening with a variety of types, some coming with friends, some by themselves. Cruising did not appear to be a regular activity. At least, I could not identify any two guys who wandered off together after showing up separately. When the bars closed at 3:00 a.m., I went home, alone. (My guide had gone home to wife and kiddies.)

1984

January 1, 1984 Sunday

The year which has haunted the world for thirty-five years has arrived. It seems no discussion of this coming year takes place without reference to George Orwell's book. Even this diary is not exempt.

In Japan *Oshogatsu* (New Year's) is the great holiday, but the Japanese do not celebrate it as we do. It is very much a family holiday, a time to go home to one's parents and renew one's ties for another year. Japanese do not go *out* on New Year's Eve. They stay *in*. In many respects, Japanese New Year more closely resembles our Christmas: the family visits, the exchange of presents, decorations for the house, praying at the local shrine.

Oshogatsu does not last only one day. It reaches its greatest intensity from January 1st to 3rd, with ripple effects for several days in either direction. The last three days of December see a huge flood of humanity drawn out of the great cities to the hometowns, with every seat on every train, plane, and bus spoken for. The shops are jammed with people buying *oseibo* presents and Oshogatsu food. On New Year's Eve a great quiet descends on the country as virtually everything shuts down. Tokyo in particular becomes a ghost city, since very few Tokyoites come from Tokyo originally.

The Japanese equivalent of America's New Year's Eves with Guy Lombardo are two television programs featuring the most popular songs of the past year and awards for the best singers, each show now having run more than twenty-five years. The winners, overwhelmed with winning the most prestigious prizes in Japanese pop music, are suitably emotional as they belt out once again the songs which made them famous. One of last night's winners, a singer of sentimental ballads, was so overcome with emotion that he could barely finish his song, tears streaming down his face.

Then at midnight temple and shrine bells throughout Japan

ring in the New Year. People crowd into the shrines to pray for good fortune during the coming year, tie little slips of paper bearing their prayers to the branches of shrine trees, and purchase various articles of good fortune such as winged arrows. The duality of Japanese religious feeling associates Shintoism, the old Japanese religion of emperor- and ancestor-worship, with happy events like birth and marriage, and Buddhism with unpleasant times such as death. So at New Year's, Shinto shrines have capacity crowds and Buddhist temples are virtually empty.

By January 3rd, the great flow of humanity reverse itself. All methods of transportation become as congested as they were days earlier, this time in the other direction.

January 7, 1984 Saturday

Today Virginia Mayberry departed Fukuoka to continue her round-the-world trip back to Barcelona, with stops in Hong Kong, Singapore, and London. And thus ends a very busy week, at least in regard to my position as host. I had four visitors.

I had known that both Virginia and Verity Conger, an English friend from Washington also circling the globe, would pass through Japan about the year end. But neither had forwarded detailed arrival/departure information with dates, times, flight numbers.

On December 26th Virginia called from California. She would arrive in Fukuoka the evening of Friday, December 30th. Fine. On Friday, I decided to double-check the flight information, only to learn that her Singapore Air flight from Los Angeles would arrive at Tokyo Narita ten minutes after her Fukuoka flight left. Not good. Even though the Singapore flight was now expected an hour ahead of schedule, JAL assured me that at least ninety minutes were required to transfer from an international to a domestic flight. Because of the New Year rush, all flights were booked solid. Eventually we got Virginia a reservation the following morning involving a plane change in Osaka.

Even as we worked on Virginia's arrival, Verity called from

Tokyo. She had arrived the night before, found Tokyo deserted, and thought she would like to come to Fukuoka if it would not greatly inconvenience me. I had no objection. She said she would go to inquire about trains (she had one of those marvelous Japan National Rail passes which allows tourists unlimited travel during a set period) and call me back. She didn't.

I went home from work Friday afternoon without knowing when guests would arrive. (Dick Morley, the Principal Officer, had gone home to Indiana for Christmas, leaving me Acting Principal Officer. Under not too subtle prompting from the staff, I allowed them to go home early on the 30th, after we toasted the New Year with two bottles of passable champagne.)

About 7:30 p.m. the phone rang. Verity had arrived at Hakata Station. I rushed down by subway to bring her back by taxi. She arrived at Tokyo Station to find a bullet train about to depart. No seats were available, but Verity was afraid that she would be unable to find even standing room on later trains. So she got on, and stood for the seven-hour ride to Fukuoka.

Within an hour of returning home from the train station with Verity, Virginia called from Fukuoka Airport. She had made her original connection, even though her original reservation had been canceled, and here she was. She had received a somewhat obscure message upon her arrival in Tokyo concerning her changed schedule, but she chose to ignore it.

I don't know what the police who watch the Consulate around the clock thought. Twice in the same evening I rushed out, only to return within an hour accompanied by a Western female with luggage. Their worst ideas could only have been confirmed on January 3rd when two more females showed up, these two Australians, one of whom was the sister of a friend in the Tokyo Embassy.

Although the effects of the New Year holiday were probably not so severe here as in Tokyo, most shops and restaurants did close. On New Year's Eve the three of us (after a bottle of champagne) went out to see what nightlife there was. There was none. Even Nakasu, the island which is Fukuoka's entertainment district, was quiet, no flashing lights, no traffic, no crowds. We soon gave up and went home to watch TV like good Japanese. And drink another bottle of champagne.

On New Year's Day, we went to one of the local Shinto shrines. We each invested in a four-dollar good luck arrow. The ritual would probably be more efficacious if performed at midnight, but I calculated that we arrived at the shrine just about the time the East Coast of the United States, fourteen hours behind us, entered 1984. We also visited a couple of Buddhist temples. They were, as expected, deserted.

We had spaghetti for supper. I thought that would accord well with the custom of eating long noodles for long life, even though one is supposed to do it on New Year's Eve, not Day.

February 12, 1984 Sunday

Life has remained dreary since the departure of my New Year's visitors. The weather plays its part, giving lie to the claim of warm, sunny Kyushu. All the inhabitants insist that this winter has been unusually cold. I have never been much of a winter person, and have become even less so since Africa.

The local weather, in spite of its miserable drizzle and occasional snow flurries, pales in its severity when compared to the incredible weather afflicting the United States. Why is it that every winter there seems to set new records for low temperatures, breaking the old records which have stood for a century?

I recently read that depression in winter time is common. We don't get enough sunlight, more a matter of biology than attitude. Perhaps. It may be too that the start of a new year reminds me that I will be in Japan for a long time to come, when the place I want to be in and the person whom I want to be with are both an ocean and a continent away. I have no desire to socialize. I come home from work, read, eat dinner, watch some TV, go to bed.

This weekend, as on the past several weekends, I have slept until late in the morning, made a pot of coffee, had a late breakfast, and then wasted the rest of the day. Often I don't go out of the Consulate compound for days at a time. My only solid link with the "outside world" (outside of work) is my weekly tennis lesson which I have gone to since November. At least there I can see progress of some kind. (I may never learn how to serve a ball.) Even going to the local barber requires summoning effort.

In mid-January I attended a conference at the Embassy in Tokyo on terrorism and emergency evacuation procedures. Attendees came from most Embassies in East and South Asia, as well as a Washington contingent and a group from Pacific Command headquarters in Honolulu.

The message from Washington came across. Next time there's a disaster like the truck bombing of the Marine headquarters in Beirut last fall, heads are going to roll, if they haven't already been blown off. Reagan accepted responsibility for the Beirut bombing. Next time the people on the spot will be left holding the bag.

The Defense Department's counter-terrorism strike force provided lengthy presentations on their capability to assist an Embassy in an emergency. The presentations probably would have been briefer, if the speakers hadn't kept telling us the U.S. counter-terrorism force is the best in the world, "bar none," specifically including such also-rans as the Israelis, West Germans, and Brits. In response to the request for some examples of the group's prowess, the reply came: "The answer is classified at a level which we cannot address in this meeting."

The highlight of the counter-terrorists' presentations was a demonstration of their portable communications equipment which could instantly put them in touch with anywhere in the world. The effect was somewhat marred by the fact that repeated, increasingly frantic calls to home base went unanswered. Very reassuring.

The visit to Tokyo provided the chance to see a number of friends now stationed there. It also confirmed my feeling that I would not care to live in Tokyo for any great length of time. It is a great city, indeed. Too great. I think that before long I would be overwhelmed by its sheer size, its population, its constant motion.

The idea of an assignment to Tokyo is a moot subject. These past four months have emphasized what I already knew. The Foreign Service is not for me. Three times in my life I have packed up and moved off to exotic locales, leaving behind friends in favor of a place where I knew no one. Korea as an experience stands by itself and will not be duplicated. Ghana was a nightmare which even now ties knots in my stomach. Japan is the assignment I have wanted ever since I left Korea, and now I have it. Now I don't want it.

I have spent a significant part of the past nine years being alone, being rootless. The prospect of a lifetime of frequent uprooting and transfers to places which I might or might not wish to live in troubled me even before last year. Now I have my lover, the lover I can only be with by leaving the Foreign Service. By the time I depart Japan next year, I will have spent ten years with the State Department, nine of them overseas. The thrill of foreign living is gone, the fascination of observing another culture firsthand outweighed by the isolation of always being the outsider. I want to settle down in my own country and be an American, not an American diplomat.

February 29, 1984 Wednesday

I came to Fukuoka for a quiet assignment, a place where I could sit back with my feet on the desk and play the stereotype of the American diplomat. Even here the occasional problem case pops up.

Take, for example, the young American who previously served in the U.S. Army in Korea. In his year there, he came to like the country and, after being discharged in the United States, he returned to Korea on a tourist visa. The fact he showed up in Seoul with a one-way ticket should have suggested to Korean Immigration that something was amiss. But the Inspector let him in. Soon he was living with his Korean girlfriend on the fringes of the official military, where East meets West in a not particularly attractive compromise. With no particular skills and completely ignorant of the local language except for the GI/bargirl lingo, he looked for a job.

Six months later Korean Immigration made it clear he had to leave Korea. The explanation offered was that he had to go to a Korean consulate in Japan to renew his visa. The Koreans neglected to tell him that they had put his name on their blacklist and would not allow him to return.

He took the train to Pusan, got a visa to Japan at the Japanese Consulate there, and boarded the ferry which passes back and forth across the Korea Strait between Pusan and Shimonoseki. As he got off the boat in Japan, the ticket agent for the ferry company let him know the company had instructions not to take him back.

There he was, in Japan for the first time, a country about which he knew even less than Korea. He thought he had come for only an overnight stay and, planning accordingly, had brought no luggage and little money. What to do?

What do you do in such a situation? You call the American Consul. And what does the American Consul do? Not much, actually, other than suggesting he find a cheap place to spend the night and find his way from Shimonoseki to the Consulate the next day. No mean feat for someone speaking no Japanese and not knowing the local geography.

Somehow the next day he did arrive at the Consulate. In sequence we found him a cheap hotel, loaned him money for subsistence, confirmed with the Korean Consulate that he was on their blacklist, made a collect call to his mother to ask that she send him the money for a ticket home ("I told him no good would come from his going back to Asia. How does he look?"), and, after determining that the family could not get the money together, processed a loan for him to fly home at U.S.G. expense with a promise that he would pay the loan back.

It took a week to get through this process, a not uncommon occurrence. There are many Americans who, were they to read the above description of how they were unwittingly deported from Korea and left destitute, would think I had written their story.

April 24, 1984 Tuesday
The late winter depression which had held me in its grip has passed. Now I am almost too busy to find time to write. I still take tennis lessons once a week, with uncertain results. The Consulate staff recently got together to buy a ping pong table, so ping pong has become a daily activity at lunch and after work. I have also begun teaching English on Wednesday nights to a group of about twenty Japanese.

Teaching English in Korea gave me an opening wedge into Korean society, and led to some of my fondest memories. I had made no effort, however, to become a teacher in Japan, until I met several people socially who belonged to a group which had recently lost its American when he returned to the United States. Native speakers of English are a rare commodity in this part of the world, so they descended on me like vultures. I agreed to meet the group on a trial basis, have done so twice so far, and have quite enjoyed it. The group's composition is interesting. It includes college students, businessmen and women, housewives, and one eighty-year-old grandmother, all speaking varying levels of English.

William J. Duffy

1985

February 11, 1985 Monday

More than nine months since last I wrote in these pages. What has caused this silence, unprecedented in the eleven years since I began this diary? Have I been so busy I could not spare the time to write? Have I been so happy? Have I been so sad?

No, none of these reasons. I have not written because I have not wanted to write. The longer I put it off, the more difficult it became to start again. That answer is not entirely honest. The past year has given a fair share of trouble, a bittersweet mixture, neither as bleak as the Ghana years or 1974-75 in Detroit, but also not the joy of Korea.

I have been very happy in Fukuoka, as happy as I expected to be, returning to Asia. Japanese have welcomed me, have made efforts to know me in spite of the weaknesses in our knowledge of each other's language. I will leave this summer with many happy memories which will brighten my heart when I reflect on them in years to come.

When I leave, it will be with the knowledge that my life in Asia is behind me. Five years in Korea, two years in Japan, most of my adult life. But always a foreigner remains the outsider. Always most of the life and speech around me flows past uncomprehended. I will never know Korea or Japan. In making the attempt I risk losing the chance to know my own country.

I will always admire these two peoples, so alike and yet so different; two nations, without natural resources, leveled by war within our lifetimes, now the economic wonders of the world; two ancient civilizations who have made the transition to the twentieth century; two peoples who have shown the world that a nation's most precious resource, its only necessary resource, is a citizenry with the determination that their children shall live better than they, and the will to work to make it happen.

But I am an American, and as much as Korea and Japan command my affection and respect, I am heart, soul, and mind an American. Nine years of travel in Asia, Africa, and Europe have made me look at my native land from a different point of view. It has led me to marvel at the glory of the American idea. Even with all the weaknesses and deficiencies we have, our country provides more freedom to its people than any other. Travel is broadening, they say, but in my case this education about the world has turned me into an ultra-nationalist.

In more personal terms, the last twelve months have been difficult with my relationship with Ken. My first months in Japan, I pined away and was miserable. Then, last March, I made a decision, only partially conscious, that there was no point in moping at home for two years. I was in Japan and might as well make use of the opportunity. In short, I put Ken on the back burner.

While this had an exceptionally salutary effect on my life in Japan (coinciding with a natural increase in my circle of Japanese acquaintances), it had a nearly catastrophic effect on the relationship itself. Ken perceived an increasingly distant tone in my letters and, during his three-week visit in May, he discovered that I had a very nice life in Japan, thank you, with no place for a lover resident in America.

The more Ken's visit recedes into the past, the more disastrous it appears to me. Its purpose was to act as a bridge between our separation in September 1983 and our reunion this summer. It well-nigh became a wall. Before long Ken's letters, which I had so eagerly awaited, became chores to receive and chores to answer. No matter how long it limped along, our relationship seemed finished. I questioned my maturity. Here was the love I thought worth living for, and now writing a polite letter in reply had become too much to ask.

If Ken's May trip to Japan almost ended our relationship, my New Year's trip to Virginia restored it and confirmed it. The idea of a New Year's trip had emerged at some point in the past and became one of those things with a life of its own. To back out would invite certain disaster; to go ahead offered only uncertain prospects of success.

It was a smashing success. Putting us back where we belonged, in the familiar sights of the Washington area, we picked up where we left off. In two weeks we reaffirmed all that the preceding year had cast into doubt, and removed the lingering doubts. I think this favorable result came from the fact that we were both on familiar ground, indeed, the very ground where we had fallen in love. Also, the end of our separation was now only months, not years, away. And Ken has wonderful friends who talk sense to him.

The icing on the visit came when I visited the Department of State and found out that I have been assigned to the Bureau of International Narcotics Matters as program Officer for Southeast Asia (i.e., opium eradication efforts). The assignment should include occasional travel to Southeast Asia.

The year 1985 has begun well. I hope so much it goes on like this.

February 18, 1985 Monday – Fukuoka

Taking advantage of the Washington's Birthday holiday today, I spent the weekend in Seoul. As on my previous visit last May with Ken, the changes in Korea since my 1980 departure overwhelmed me. I left at the peak of the disorders which followed Park Chung-hee's 1979 assassination, with Chun Du-hwan's two coups, the first December 12th, 1979 and the second the very day of my departure, May 17th, 1980. I left at the end of a week of student demonstrations in the streets which closed down Seoul every afternoon, with tanks and soldiers and traffic barriers everywhere, with the Kwangju Rebellion about to erupt. The vaunted stability of the Yushin era was gone, the future was uncertain, and the present seemed like a reenactment of the 1960 Student Revolution.

A far cry from Korea today. The economy is again on track, the country is stable, and the people have regained their self-confidence. The physical transformation of Seoul is startling. Construction everywhere: office buildings, apartment complexes, subways, the 1988 Olympic complex. I could scarce recognize some neighborhoods, and many familiar (and favorite) spots have disappeared.

The single greatest aspect of this transformation is south of the Han River. When I first arrived in Korea in 1975, Seoul was a city on the North Bank of the Han. Three bridges crossed it. In spite of government efforts to disperse businesses and residential areas south of the river, little had changed by 1980, other than an increase in the number of bridges and the construction of a street network which passed through fields empty except for a few housing complexes. The heart of the city remained north of the river.

No more. Twelve bridges now cross the river, linking the old city with what appears to be the new heart of the city. High-rise buildings stretch for miles in all directions across the once-empty fields. Where once I rarely had a reason to go south of the river (because my friends, their homes, their businesses, their social activities were in the historical city), the situation has reversed. This past weekend I did not venture into the North Bank even once. The center of the city's life, and almost everything with it, has crossed south. What is in old Seoul is there because it has always been there, but the growth is in the new Seoul.

March 28, 1985 Thursday – Chiang Mai, Thailand

On the eve of St. Patrick's Day, Saturday, March 16th, I had twenty-five guests for a party. Somehow I put together an entire dinner, including three five-pound hams, five loaves of Irish soda bread (baked by myself), a macaroni salad (donated by Helen Mishima), a lettuce salad, a tub of corned beef and cabbage (made by Barclay Macrae), and five apple pies (baked jointly by Barclay and me).

I did not stop to think beforehand how much work such a party entails. Fortunately, everything turned out, including the five pies. We baked them a week earlier, froze them, and rebaked them, something I never attempted before.

Most of the guests were Japanese, and everyone wore green as required. My intermittent explanations between crises in the kitchen never clarified in their minds who St. Patrick was, why I was having a party for him, or what all this had to do with the color green. The Japanese did enjoy the green crème de menthe which I served after dinner.

I have not done much entertaining at home in Fukuoka. The only other extravaganzas I had were two Christmas tree decorating parties in early December, one on a Friday evening for the Consular Section staff (total of ten guests) and one the following Sunday afternoon for my English class (total of thirty, including a number of people I never saw before in my life).

I arranged the Sunday party first. Most of the work for that was done by the women in the group, although I baked a ham and three pumpkin pies. I thought a Christmas tree decorating party would be an interesting cultural experience. So I arranged to rent (*rent*) a tree (and what a sad excuse for a Christmas tree) from the local nursery for 7,000 yen, about $30.

When I invited my staff for dinner, it occurred to me that it would look strange to them to have an empty tree in the room. So we decorated it Friday night, I took the decorations down Saturday morning, and we decorated it again Sunday afternoon. True cultural sensitivity.

Now I am enjoying the first fruits of my next assignment. Next week the East Asia Narcotics Conference will take place in Kuala Lumpur, so I will go to that. This week is an orientation visit to Thailand, which will be my major area of responsibility. I came to Thailand once before, in December 1979, and hated Bangkok. It was hot, dirty, noisy, crowded. It still is, only more so. This time I enjoyed it rather more than in 1979, perhaps because this time I had no mistaken preconception that it was the Venice of East Asia, perhaps because in the interim I have visited enough other Third World nations not to expect too much, perhaps because this time the purpose was business and I do not feel I must enjoy myself.

This time most certainly is business. Not only am I completely unfamiliar with the subject (narcotics), but also the Deputy Assistant Secretary for International Narcotics Matters is here visiting. He believes that a schedule which allows free time is incomplete. Surely there is always one more meeting which can be arranged, one more lunch or dinner with a local official.

March 30, 1985 Saturday – Songkhla, Thailand

Now I have really returned to the Third World, in a hotel very like those in which I passed so many nights in Korea, with the distinctive features of wild dogs howling outside on the beach and an organist in the hotel bar murdering "Stardust." Songkhla is a beach resort whose time has yet to come, this hotel (the Samila) the only manifestation of an unsuccessful government policy to make southern Thailand a tourist center.

We have come here because it is on the way to Kuala Lumpur, there is a U.S. Consulate here, and there is a narcotics problem.

Aside from a lunch today at the Consul's house, we have been free to relax, sit on the beach, and do nothing. I took a nap after lunch in the hotel room, but abandoned plans to sit on the beach when it occurred to me how hot outside it was.

Tonight we had a delicious seafood dinner on the beach in an outdoor restaurant (any health inspector would blanch at the filth, the flies, and the dogs) after which we returned to the hotel.

A performance of classical Thai dance in the outdoor bar induced us to have another drink before retiring. However, the Thai dancing gave way to an organist who enthusiastically mutilated song after song, the worst entertainment I have ever seen in a public place. Presumably he wished to drive the guests to drink.

Last night we stayed at Hatyar, a town thirty minutes by car from Songkhla, a tourist trap for people escaping from strait-laced Malaysia, but very seedy. Tomorrow we go to Kuala Lumpur, for the narcotics conference. Wednesday afternoon I fly to Singapore to overnight at Raffles Hotel, and Thursday I return to Fukuoka, an all-day affair with stops in Hong Kong and Taipei.

May 28, 1985 Tuesday – Fukuoka

In less than two months I will close the chapter on my life in Japan. In length of time, it approximates my Ghana assignment. But what a difference. It took three hundred hand-written pages to accommodate my thoughts on Africa. Japan has needed only seventy. And yet the difference in the number of pages doesn't indicate life in Ghana was more interesting by a factor of four (in heartaches and headaches, perhaps). There have been so many things which I have wished to record about life in Japan. But somehow I never got around to it. Now I don't know where to begin.

Shall I begin with *karaoke*? Yes, I will. Most foreigners make the mistake of thinking that they will learn about Japan and Japanese by studying the traditional culture, visiting Shinto shrines and Buddhist temples, watching *kabuki* plays, or attending a tea ceremony. They are wrong. These things are no more a part of the everyday life of Japanese than opera, ballet, and the great cathedrals of Europe fit into a normal Westerner's life.

The soul of modern Japan is in the *karaoke* bar. I have mentioned *karaoke* previously. The fact that I return to it again should suggest how central it is to the experience of Japan – or maybe merely how central it is to *my* experience of Japan.

The quintessential *karaoke* music is called *enka*. Although more Western, pop-oriented songs also appear in *karaoke* "menus," *enka* are what it is all about.

Enka have been called "Japanese blues." A more informative analogy is to American country and western music. Both are working class, denigrated by intellectuals, scorned in front of foreigners because a person hesitates to admit he likes the style. Both sing of heartbreaks, lost loves, tears, last partings, betrayal. Both have a whiny quality to the singer's voice and a twangy quality in the instrumentation.

Enka songs have a set formula in their structure which makes them indistinguishable from each other to the untutored ear. An *enka* almost invariably has three verses, with musical interludes between them lasting ten to thirty seconds. These musical interludes are important in allowing listeners to applaud the *enka* singer. And he must be applauded, whether he sings well or badly, perhaps particularly if he can't sing at all, in order to encourage him on.

For those who scoff at my assertion that *enka* is at the center of modern Japanese culture, let me point out that the Number One TV show all the time I have been in Japan has been *NHK Kayo Hall* (NHK Song Hall), a weekly hour-long parade of *enka* singers.

I have had the good fortune to attend three weddings during my time in Japan, fortunately none of them my own.

East Asian weddings (Japanese and Korea are very similar, I don't know about Chinese) offer an interesting contrast to American weddings. In America the wedding ceremony is essentially open to everyone, even someone who wanders in off the street; and receptions are the smaller, more typically controlled affairs.

In Japan no one except the immediate families and the matchmakers attend the actual wedding ceremony, which as like as not is held in a hotel conference room or wedding hall rather than a church or Shinto shrine. Curiously, Christian church weddings have become very popular in this non-Christian country whose only true religion is being Japanese.

Even couples who have found each other must have a matchmaking couple. It would be no more possible to have the wedding without the matchmakers than to have an American wedding without the minister or priest. The wedding ceremony has no legal significance. The marriage is not legal until the couple march down to the ward office where their families' records are kept and submit the proper forms to have the new wife transferred from her father's register to her husband's (or, actually, to her father-in-law's, listing her as wife of Son Number One or Two or whatever).

Since I have not seen a Japanese wedding ceremony myself, that's about all I can say on the subject. I have attended three wedding receptions (they immediately follow the ceremony). I was even one of the speakers when Consulate employee Matsuda-san got married. I worked with a couple of the Japanese staff to turn my speech from English into Japanese, and then to practice practice practice it to get the rhythm right and to minimize my atrocious accent. It came off very well, or so everyone told me. At the other two receptions I did my part and got up to sing one of my favorite *enka* songs. (Trying to find an *enka* that didn't include loss or despair took some effort.)

Notes from Lower Volta

Three Letters
June 27, 1985

Dear Mother,

Everyone asks if you had a good trip to Japan in May and if you returned home safely.

I am leaving Japan July 19th, spending the weekend in Korea, flying to San Francisco on July 22nd, and to Washington on July 24th. I start work on July 26th. The person I am replacing has already moved to her new job, so they want me to start work yesterday. I will be able to take the leave which I would normally take immediately after returning sometime in the fall.

Aside from that, I wanted to clear up something. When you were here, you asked about what Ken would do when I came back to the U.S. I was surprised by the question, since I assumed you already understood. Ken is homosexual and so am I; and we will live together, as we did before I came to Japan. The last two years have not been easy, and I expect the future will have its share of troubles, but we expect to face them together.

So you can expect that if you come to Alexandria you will be visiting Ken's home as well as mine. Perhaps this is a little too direct a way to tell you, but I wanted to be sure you had no doubts about my relationship with Ken.

Love, Bill

July 11, 1985

Dear Bill,

Your letter arrived yesterday and I now know why I hadn't heard from you as I had written twice and a postcard as well about my plans to visit Detroit.

I am sorry for the way the question was asked but at the time we were talking about where you would put your piano as I knew Ken's buffet would probably be in the way, plus I knew he had an apartment.

Call it mother's intuition and I seem to be well endowed with it, but I have thought for a long time that maybe you were homosexual. Since I had no proof who was I to make such an assumption? Even when Ken moved in it didn't really register because at the time he was having such difficulty with purchasing his apartment. I like Ken and hope he will feel at ease when I come to visit. I am sorry that the last two years have been difficult and I am worried about your reference to the future. In what way do you mean? Maybe after you are home we can talk at greater length.

You are my son and I love and admire you very much. Nothing in this world can change that.

You can call me at the Browns as I will be anxious for your return to the States with all terrorism and hijacking going on.

Much love, Mother

My subsequent "coming out" letter to my friends:

Here's a letter from someone you don't hear from very often, good intentions to keep in touch notwithstanding. I have a few things to tell you, none of which is the usual stuff of letters or Christmas cards. They don't really even fit into a single letter, but there's no point in doing two letters when this one will be bad enough. (In case you're wondering, "you" is really "y'all". This is going to many people, since trying to do individual letters would be too time-consuming. So some of what follows may not be "news" to you.)

I'm gay. Well, maybe that's not news to you. I don't know. But I want to make sure people I know are clear on this point.

I'm telling you this for two reasons. First, I'm getting really fed up with the lies and hate and ignorance that pops up when the subject is homosexuality. Most people think they don't know any gays and assume they don't have any experience to judge homophobic claptrap for what it is. In fact, whether you realize it or not, everybody knows gays. You probably know some people you think may be gay, and maybe they are. But what about all the people you assume are straight because they don't fit a stereotype? I'll bet some of them are gay too. I just want to make sure the next time the subject of gays comes up, you have someone other than a stereotype to connect it to.

I think keeping my homosexuality to myself adds to the problem. That's why the homophobes want us to stay in the closet: they're afraid people will find out most gays are pretty normal and run-of-the-mill. The false stereotypes used to judge us have about the same connection to reality as saying that straight men beat their wives and rape their daughters.

Reason two: On a personal level, I'm finding it increasingly hard to deal with people without their knowing as much about me as I do about them. I'm no longer willing to wear a mask and live a lie as the price of keeping my friends. For example, I want to be able to tell people that, like most of my gay friends, I am in a relationship with a man. It's a little hard for me to talk about myself without mentioning that basic fact. I'd call it a marriage except that upsets some people, especially the ones who say gays can't form relationships. We've been a couple for several years, including the two years spent apart when I was in Japan. We expect to be together the rest of our lives.

I won't bore you with, say, a discussion of whether sexual orientation is a choice. I can't help but wonder, though, about people who say it is. Is their grasp on heterosexuality that weak? I always just knew what I was, even when I was too young to comprehend the differences.

Some may decide they can't deal with the truth and our friendship. I hope that is not the case with you. But I've decided I can't deal with relationships based on false assumptions about who I am.

Reading this letter was undoubtedly a lot less fun than you expected when you fished the envelope out of all the junk mail. I expect you've already heard more than you probably wanted to. So here I'll end the letter but not, I hope, our friendship.

Your friend, Bill

William J. Duffy

The Hakata-Gion-Yamagasa Festival

Japanese festivals show an aspect of Japan different from the image provided by *kabuki*, tea houses, and Zen meditation. Vaguely religious in nature, the oldest festivals date back hundreds of years and involve wild displays of emotion bordering on frenzy.

Every July for most of the past seven hundred years, the people of Fukuoka's Hakata district have held the *Hakata-gion-yamagasa*, one of the most famous festivals in all Japan. Several theories explain the festival's origins. The most commonly accepted version traces it to a plague in 1241, when priests carried shrines through the city streets as a rite of purification.

In modern terms, *Yamagasa* strengthens the relationships among Hakata residents (today participants are commonly businessmen with shops in Hakata and residences in other parts of Fukuoka). And *Yamagasa* is great fun, Hakata's Fourth of July, Thanksgiving Day parade, and homecoming weekend all rolled into one.

Coinciding with the traditional end of the rainy season, the two-week festival revolves around the colorful floats which each participating neighborhood constructs. The floats are of two types, the *kazariyama* ("display mountains") and the *oiyama* ("running mountains").

The festival culminates in a race in the dawn hours of July 15th, with each team (called a *nagare*, pronounced nah-gah-ray, meaning "stream") competing to carry its *oiyama* through the streets of Hakata in the shortest time.

A series of practice runs during the preceding days gives a *nagare*'s members experience in carrying their *oiyama*. These elaborate *yama*, decorated with traditional themes from history and mythology, weigh several tons and tower as much as twenty feet high. They have no wheels. Only muscle energy moves these monsters, supplied by the twenty-four-man teams who carry them and the larger number who push from behind.

Each year all the *nagare* carefully build new *yama*, which they display on Hakata streets from July 1st. Large white tents, open at either end, protect the *yama* from the weather (this is, after all, the rainy season) while allowing passers-by an easy view of the colorful decorations. *Nagare* members watch the *yama* in shifts twenty-four hours a day during the festival's two weeks.

My understanding of the festival's underlying significance reaches no deeper than my limited command of Japanese. The festival relates to ritual purification. Two things are clearly taboo: sex and cucumbers. People offer two explanations for the latter prohibition. According to the polite theory, a cut cucumber slice resembles the shape of the chrysanthemum, a flower of great importance in Japan, reflected in its frequent appearance in *Shinto* decoration. The other theory says the problem with the cucumber is its phallic shape and its surfeit of seeds.

Since January, Yamamoto Kenichi had urged me to join *Yamagasa* with him. I remained noncommittal, unsure how serious the invitation was. And, I had not found the 1984 festival, part of which I watched, particularly thrilling. (Perhaps the fact that I had been up drinking all night beforehand limited my enthusiasm.) But since Yamamoto-san continued to urge me on every time we met, I finally agreed to participate the first afternoon and the last morning, thinking that would satisfy my interest.

The first day, July 9th, I report to Yamamoto-san's *kimono* shop to begin my initiation: getting dressed. This is a man's festival, reflected in the unique costume all participants wear: around the head, a blue and white headband (*hachimaki*); on the feet, black leggings; around the middle, a loose-fitting white shirt open in the front (*mizuhappi*), with the neighborhood name written on the back; and around the crotch, the very tight-fitting white *shimekomi*, a cross between loin-cloth and G-string which scarcely covers the front and leaves the buttocks bare. A hemp rope hangs from the waist. Gentlemen with too generous a girth may also wear a tight-fitting *haramaki*, a piece of cloth wrapped around the middle as a girdle.

Modesty is relative. It is difficult to be self-conscious about the outfit while surrounded by a crowd of thousands similarly dressed. In fact, spectators may be the ones more likely to blush. Whatever its mystic origins, the costume is an exceptionally comfortable running outfit for a person who will spend a good part of July jogging through the streets of Hakata. (That assumes the shimekomi has been wound properly.)

Even those who have run in *Yamagasa* since childhood find it difficult to dress by themselves. I depend on Yamamoto-san to wrap the shimekomi around me, not so tight as to risk physical injury, and not so loose as to risk unraveling at an inopportune moment. Although tying the shimekomi is the most difficult aspect of arraying oneself properly, it is only the first step in a series of potential pitfalls. For example, the knots tying the hachimaki headband or the mizuhappi shirt must be done a certain way, so that the loose ends point in the correct directions. The rope must ride on the waist at an appropriate height (too low and it trips the runner up). I feel like, and look like, a helpless child.

Once dressed, we have a photo session in front of the kimono shop, where the sight of a six-foot *gaijin* dressed as an ungainly *Hakatakko* (child of Hakata) occasions some amusement to passers-by. That completed, Yamamoto-san and I, with his two young sons similarly dressed, put on *happi* coats and walk around the corner to the rendezvous of our subteam, called *Kotobuki-doori* ("Felicitations Street"), which runs as part of *Dai-koku-nagare* ("Big Black Stream").

At the *Kotobuki-doori* meeting site, we down a shot of *sake*, doff our happi coats, and with the other thirty team members jog to the *nagare*'s meeting site, the location of our *yama*. Very quickly I learn that, as in so much else, there is a correct way to run. One keeps the arms hanging straight down at the side, resisting the urge to swing them, while jogging along with very short steps and calling out the cadence (*"Osshyoi! osshyoi! osshyoi!"*). My embarrassment at doing it incorrectly lessens when I notice that many of the younger men don't know these traditions any better.

As we approach our *yama*, the *nagare* members who have

already arrived welcome us with rhythmic clapping. Removing our headbands, we stop in front of the *yama* and bow to the *nagare* leaders sitting on it. Following their lead, we stretch out our hands, palms up, to perform a traditional Japanese cheer (*"Oy!"* – clap – clap – *"Mo hitotsu* [Once more]" – clap – clap – *"Oy!"* – clap/clap – clap). Then the group breaks up to drink the proffered cups of sake, making way for the next arrivals.

As the starting time for the first day's run approaches, the scene resembles a marathon's beginning. *Nagare* officials count down the minutes. Each group takes its appointed place in line. Members check their headbands. At last the moment arrives. With the banging of a drum and a great shout from the assembled horde we start, running to the rhythm of the shouted cadence.

This first day, called "Taking the evening tide," is essentially a practice run. For some (including me), this is their first *Yamagasa*. For others, the older ones, this might be their last, the year they decide it is better to leave the running to younger legs. So the pace is slow, the rest stops frequent, the entire distance relatively short. The course winds through the *nagare*'s district. Neighbors line the streets and stand in second floor windows, shouting encouragement and soaking the runners with water from hoses and buckets.

Yamagasa is a wet festival. From the moment the drum announces the start, water flies from all directions. At first I attempt to avoid the water. But once doused (and no runner can long avoid a thorough soaking), I eagerly seek out the next water carrier. Regardless of its ritual importance, the water's bracing freshness comes as a welcome relief in the summer heat.

The men sweep aside everything in their path, bringing rush-hour traffic to a halt as they run down narrow streets and broad avenues. After thirty minutes and a couple of miles, just short of sunset, the *nagare* rounds one last corner to come in sight of our objective: the Bay of Hakata, framed through the *torii* gate of a Shinto shrine. Beyond it across the bay looms, less ethereally, the Fukuoka Expressway. To this place the thousands of members of all the *nagare* converge, seeking ritual purification. Given the condition of the waters, no other is possible.

We remove our headbands as we pass beneath the torii. The men wash their hands in the oily water. Many scoop handfuls of the coarse sand into little charm pouches to carry with them. I prefer physical to spiritual cleanliness, and do neither. That completed, we walk back to the shrine which stands about half a mile from the waterfront, there to toss a hundred yen (forty cents) offering into the donation box, ring the bell, clap our hands for the gods' attention, and receive a blessing from the brightly dressed priests.

Each *nagare* takes a beer and sake break before regrouping and jogging on to Kushida Shrine, *Yamagasa*'s home shrine. The same sequence: donation, ringing of the bell, clapping of the hands, and a blessing from the Shinto priest. Then we jog back to our *yama* and, removing our headbands, close the run with the same cheer with which we opened it. (The headbands, you can see, are off and on all the time, giving me many opportunities to perfect my tying techniques.)

Each group adjourns to its own meeting place for the post-run gathering called *naorai*, held after every day's practice, for which the men's wives set up tables and prepare a dinner. Food, however, runs a distant second in the thirsty runners' affections behind beer and sake. The free flow of alcohol is helped along by the Japanese custom of quickly refilling one's neighbor's empty glass, an offer not easily refused.

After a few short speeches by the group leaders, each of us stands up to introduce himself, a prospect which I face with horror. I dislike speaking in front of groups even in English without prepared remarks. Somehow I pull through, and am not even as tongue-tied as some of the younger men.

Yamagasa being a neighborhood festival, even other Japanese cannot easily join. I had been somewhat concerned that the men might resent me as an interloper. But they never show anything but pleasure that I take part. Several men, asking if I will run every day, are disappointed when I reply that I do not plan to run again until the final race. One says I cannot appreciate the full spirit of *Yamagasa* unless I take part every day. Still flushed with the excitement of the afternoon, I have already begun to think so myself. His comment completes my conversion.

The first day's excitement obscures the central importance of the *yama*. In fact, the first day's run is the only time the *nagare* runs without the *yama*.

When we gather on the second day and repeat the greeting ceremony, the air seems even more charged with excitement. Already the previous run's shared experience has made the *nagare* members begin to feel more like a cohesive team.

The members who will first move the *yama* take up their positions. The leaders who will call cadence and shout directions perch on the front and back. The carriers stand in front and behind along the *yama*'s six heavy wooden carrying poles. The pushers follow, ready to help the *yama*'s forward motion through the incremental addition of each man's strength.

Speed will come on following days. This first run practices technique, so we stop frequently for explanations. How does the *nagare* turn the *yama* around a corner? How does one group relieve another on the *yama* without slowing it down?

Most runners, even those running for the first time, already have a good understanding of the process. They have studied the *Yamagasa* pamphlet which describes all aspects of the festival, including such things as the proper height and build for the carriers in each pole position. Shorter and lighter runners occupy the inner positions, and taller and stockier runners the outer. The ideal average height of 163 centimeters, ranging from a short 160 on the inside to 173 on the rim, assures that they will never call upon me with my 183 centimeters to bear the burden.

Again the banging of the drum announces the run's start. With a great shout from all the *nagare* members, the massive *yama* shudders and rises slightly on the men's shoulders. It moves forward, hesitantly at first, then with greater speed. *Nagare* members and spectators run to escape it. A car parked to the side nearly loses its windshield before the lumbering mountain skids to a halt.

The *nagare* regroups, and the *yama* resumes its travel. Pushers form a tapering tail behind the *yama*, each man with his head down and his hands grasping the waistbands of two comrades in front of him. Runners sprint ahead, some to stop traffic, some to check water supplies, and some to wait their turn to carry or push.

The *yama* turns briefly onto a wide boulevard before plunging back into the neighborhood's narrow side streets. The *nagare*'s uncertain control causes it to weave from side to side, threatening to crush this car or to collide with that wall.

For an hour the barely controlled chaos goes on. Twice the low-riding bottom hits speed bumps, which jolts the *yama* to a stop. *Nagare* members struggle desperately to regain control as the *yama* tilts precariously forward, hesitates, and crashes back, threatening to brain the ducking carriers. With grunts from the carriers and deprecations from the leaders, the *yama* gets underway again.

The *nagare* moves from the open streets into the covered shopping arcade which forms the heart of *Kotobuki-doori*. The arcade roof, looking perilously low, turns the shouting into a deafening roar. Shopkeepers appear oblivious to the threat which the crowd and the water pose to their open-front stores. The tile pavement, slick from the water, brings more than one runner crashing down, where he frantically scrambles to get back to his feet before his comrades get him under theirs.

The *nagare* returns to the open streets, and brings the *yama* back to its home. Exhausted, wet, exhilarated, the men pull off their headbands, and perform the closing ceremony. The small groups wander off to their meeting places for another *naorai* of food and drink.

With each succeeding day, the turnout of runners and spectators grows. Television stations carry daily progress reports. On July 12th, they move to live coverage, a trial heat involving all the *nagare*. To avoid comparisons between this race and the main race on July 15th, the *nagare* do not run the complete course, but stop at an earlier finish line. Even so, nobody can avoid forming opinions of each *nagare*'s relative strength on the basis of this run.

The afternoon of July 13th brings a ceremonial parade of the *yama*. Next to the final race itself, this draws the greatest number of runners and spectators. The *yama* move at a slower pace, and many children and infants join in for the luck which "coming out" in *Yamagasa* will bring them.

Even I am dragooned into carrying a friend's year-old infant, dressed in a baby's *Yamagasa* costume. The distance of only a few blocks is apparently sufficient to ensure the festival's spiritual benefits. The child, however, fails to appreciate the luck the jog will bring him, not to mention his doing it in the arms of a foreigner. He bawls the whole time. The bucket of water thrown in his face does not help. His mother is no more relieved to have him back than I am to hand him over.

The parade portion of the afternoon concludes with each *nagare* carrying its *yama* to City Hall. Here the members pay their respects to the dignitaries assembled on a dais in front of the building.

With the niceties out of the way, each *nagare* returns to the business at hand: getting ready for the Big One. Only two practice runs remain, the afternoons of the 13th and the 14th. But past efforts begin to pay off. The *nagare*, flowing faster, sweeps the *yama* down the middle of streets rather than weaving back and forth, and slows only slightly when rounding a corner.

On the 14th, Yamamoto-san and I have an even busier time than most other participants. We play tennis in the morning as part of our regular bi-weekly tennis club, run with the *nagare* in the afternoon, and then attend the tennis club's farewell party for me in the evening. What a sight we must be: Yamamoto-san and I dressed for *Yamagasa* in white cotton shorts, blue-and-white checked happi coats, and *geta* wooden sandals (he scolds me for forgetting to bring my headband with me); the other ten Japanese all dressed in Western clothes. The party includes dinner at a restaurant followed by drinks at a *karaoke* bar, where we all take turns singing doleful *enka* ballads.

About midnight we return to *Kotobuki-doori*, where the small display *yama* are being destroyed, the more elaborate sections disappearing into storerooms for use next year.

About 3:00 a.m., we walk to Kushida Shrine to observe the different *nagare* bring their *yama* from the neighborhood bases. I think we have avoided any further running until the dawn race. But no, as our *yama* pulls abreast of where we stand, I watch in alarm as Yamamoto-san with a thundering "*osshyoi!*" disappears into the mob sweeping down the street and over the sidewalk. With no other choice, I follow, painfully learning that *geta* do not make comfortable running shoes.

In the darkness lit only by the flickering light of hundreds of paper lanterns, the *yama* truly look like mountains rising out of the sea, out of the waves of the scarcely visible runners.

With the *nagare* positioned for the race, we return to the apartment above Yamamoto-san's nearby kimono shop for a two-hour rest. I hesitate to nap, fearing that once asleep I will never awaken for the race. Lying on my back on the hard *tatami* floor, I doze on and off, resisting my body's craving for sleep. All too soon the alarm tells us to get up.

As we make our way through the dark streets leading to Kushida Shrine, the crowds slow our passage, leading me to wonder if we will arrive in time.

All the *nagare* line the street outside Kushida Shrine in their running order, waiting, the starting times set at intervals long enough to avoid the confusion which would result if a faster *nagare* overtook a slower one.

This is the day. This is the race. Nothing which has preceded this morning matters, except insofar as it has prepared the *nagare* for this event. Today's race is the one which Hakata will talk about and replay in conversations for the next year, today's winners the ones who will be remembered for years to come.

The first hint of dawn begins to dispel the darkness. Even at this early hour the July heat warms the nearly naked runners.

Officials count down the minutes: "Five minutes to go!" The number passes back through the *nagare* in a shouted wave.

"Four minutes!" Two schoolboys lean forward too far and jump for safety as the tin shed on which they perch collapses under them.

"Three minutes!" *Nagare* members take up their positions.

"Two!" Family and friends retreat to the sidewalk.

"One!" Men test their shoulders against the *yama*'s poles.

"Thirty seconds!" *Nagare* leaders shout last minute instructions.

"Ten seconds... five... one!"

The drums boom and the *nagare* surges forward with a shout. The *yama* sweeps into the shrine's courtyard, careens in a circle around a column standing there, and rushes back onto the street and off toward the distant finish line. Drumbeats time the courtyard circuit.

As the shrine recedes behind it, the *nagare* hears its speed announced. A fast time lifts the runners' spirits. A slow time makes them redouble their efforts. Speed is essential, stops fatal. The next *nagare* moves its *yama* to the starting line and waits with anxious anticipation.

Dai-koku-nagare starts third. With many others, I choose to avoid the crush of bodies in the shrine courtyard and sprint ahead. The roar behind us becomes muted as the *nagare* disappears into the shrine. Something approaching silence falls on the crowd waiting outside, undercut only by the drum tolling the passing seconds. Then, the front wave of the *nagare* erupts noisily back onto the street, immediately followed by the *yama*.

It has taken 30.5 seconds, two-tenths of a second slower than the fastest *nagare* already running, and one-tenth slower than our performance July 13th. Not a bad start, not promising either.

The undisciplined groups of men with whom I first ran less than six days earlier are gone. They have become a *nagare*, a stream, rushing single-mindedly toward the finish line like a river towards the sea. The rhythm of "*Osshyoi! osshyoi! osshyoi!*" rises and falls from a thousand throats.

The *yama* rumbles along, scraping over the street pavement, while steady streams of water from hoses and buckets refresh the men who struggle to move it forward. On the major streets, the *nagare* pours out across the traffic lanes like a river overflowing its banks. It backs up into swirling eddies as the stream funnels into narrow alleys, where the running cadence thunders off the walls like the roar of rapids through a gorge.

Relief carriers slip into line, loop their hemp ropes over the carrying poles, and with taps on the shoulder signal the men being relieved to stand clear. The *yama* tail grows longer and wider as more runners join in, until the accumulated pressure from behind overwhelms those in front and the tail buckles. The *yama* slows dangerously. *Nagare* leaders running alongside scream for pushers, grabbing laggards by their waistbands and throwing them into line.

The *yama* turns into the final stretch, a straight street whose slight downslope helps speed the *nagare*. Hearts pounding, legs aching, eyes blinded by water, the runners fly forward with new energy. The rolling cadence booms louder, drowning out the waiting crowd's cheers. "*Osshyoi! osshyoi! osshyoi!*" The men pack close together, wanting to be near the *yama* at the finish.

And then the race is over. Thirty minutes and twenty-nine seconds after the Kushida Shrine drum sent us on our way, another drum announces that *Dai-koku-nagare* has carried its *yama* across the finish line. The *nagare* stops, all our energy suddenly spent. Its efforts have made it the fastest of the first three *nagare*, one second ahead of second-place *Higashi-nagare* ("East Stream"). The exhausted men congratulate each other, but any one of the ten *nagare* still to come might unseat us and claim the final victory. We can only hope, and wait.

It is now 6:00 a.m. Back at the *yama*'s resting place, the *nagare* members rock the *yama* back and forth in rhythm with the *Yamagasa* song, the oldest member riding it and holding on for dear life. We close with a final cheer, and the *nagare* dissolves, not to meet again for another year. Men begin to dismantle the *yama*, ripping it apart with crowbars and bare hands.

Yamagasa is not quite over. Our *Kotobuki-doori* subteam moves on for our final meal together, a breakfast heavy on fish and rice, beer and sake. With only two hours of restless sleep during the past twenty-four, I am barely able to face the prospect of either food or drink. But having come this far, I am determined to see it all out. This time the wives have set up long tables in one of the *Kotobuki-doori* arcades where many of the men have their shops. My Japanese language ability, at the best of time an uncertain variable, is close to failing me completely. Only with great difficulty can I maintain any degree of comprehension. I can keep my usual morning surliness under control only by reminding myself that a foreigner represents not himself alone but all his fellow citizens, a frightening proposition even when I feel social.

I cannot get enough liquid to quench my thirst. But while the beer and sake (whose odor by this point is enough to set my stomach churning) are as usual available in abundance, tea and water are as rare as precious jewels. Do we truly appreciate the glorious taste of water until we can't have it?

Almost anti-climactically, word arrives that the last of the *nagare* has completed the race, and none has bested our time. *Daikoku-nagare* has won *Hakata-gion-yamagasa*. Even that news can scarcely arouse our subdued group. Soon the morning papers arrive, the front pages dominated by a color photo of our *yama* and a full story of our victory, with complete listings for all the *nagare* on page two. Surely there is no news in the world this July 15th morning more important.

When breakfast is finished, the subteam which has been

responsible for organizing this year's *Dai-koku-nagare* arrives, making the traditional visit to each subteam's meeting place to thank everyone for their efforts. With an exchange of compliments and cheers, we end *Yamagasa*.

Yamamoto-san and I walk to his kimono shop, where I unravel out of my outfit for the last time. I bid farewell to the Yamamotos, with many promises to return for next year's *Yamagasa*. I go home to sleep until the Second Coming.

***

I participated in the Hakata-gion-yamagasa festival four times, from 1985 through 1988. Ken refers to it as "The Running of the Butts."

Notes from Lower Volta

November 22, 1985 Friday - Washington, D.C.

Already four months have passed since I departed Japan. Predictably, in some ways it seems like yesterday; in others, Japan has already become a fading memory. All the thoughts I wanted to put down on paper remain unwritten, and now probably will never get written.

I left Fukuoka on July 19th, taking a flight to Seoul for one last weekend at Soraksan with Choi Gun-ho and Lee Yong-gun and their families. In true Japanese style about thirty people came to Fukuoka Airport to see me off: several of the Consulate employees, Sohei and Helen Mishima, half my English-language students, a number of the members of the Monthly Second and Fourth Sunday Tennis Club, Arai Miyuki, Inakazu-san, and Nagasawa Yuji.

The last-minute going-away presents were fewer and smaller than I feared, the most unwieldy being Miyuki's flower bouquet. It wilted by the time the plane landed in Seoul two hours later. The Inakazus, who had already been more than generous, gave me a traditional "parting money" gift, 20,000 yen, about $80. It of course came discretely in an attractive envelope, so I didn't know the amount of money until I reached Korea.

Modern-day security checks have taken much of the romance out of departures. We all had to bid farewell before I went through the metal detector. Everyone watched as I set off alarms and was subjected to a body search, my hands upraised, clutching Miyuki's flower bouquet, Helen Mishima shouting in the background: "Get the camera!" My carry-on luggage was packed so tightly that the x-ray machine couldn't make any sense out of it, and the guard had to examine both bags by hand.

1986

March 1, 1986 Saturday – Alexandria

What has happened? What has brought this remarkable silence? Nothing at all for nine months, little in the past two years. Since 1974 I have been surprisingly diligent in filling these pages. Whether the results justify the effort I don't know.

Somehow, once Ghana was out of the way, once I resumed a more normal life in 1982, the drive to keep this record of my life left me. Just compare how many pages I covered with the two years in Ghana, with how few I have filled in the four years since. Am I at thirty-three already so old and the end of my life so close that there is no reason to write some of it down, even for myself? How is it that my previous diary covers only two years, and this diary four and a half?

It is with regret that I recall memories which now will live only in my head, and die when I die.

And so I close this volume.

Made in the USA
Middletown, DE
10 September 2016